P9-AOF-229

Property of
No.
Wood River Elementary School

McGRAW • HILL

HEALTH

SENIOR AUTHORS

Susan C. Giarratano-Russell

Donna Lloyd-Kolkin

PROGRAM AUTHORS

Danny J. Ballard

Alisa Evans Debnam

Anthony Sancho

New York Farmington

PROGRAM AUTHORS

Susan C. Giarratano-Russell, MSPH, Ed.D, CHES
Health Education Specialist
University Professor and Media Consultant
Glendale, California

Donna Lloyd-Kolkin, Ph.D.
Partner
Health & Education Communication Consultants
New Hope, Pennsylvania

Danny J. Ballard, Ed.D
Associate Professor, Health
Texas A & M University
College of Education
College Station, Texas

Alisa Evans Debnam, MPH
Health Education Supervisor
Cumberland County Schools
Fayetteville, North Carolina

Anthony Sancho, Ph.D.
Project Director
West Ed
Equity Center
Los Alamitos, California

PROGRAM REVIEWERS

Personal Health
Josey H. Templeton, Ed.D
Associate Professor
The Citadel, Military College of South Carolina
Charleston, South Carolina

Growth and Development
Jacqueline Ellis, M Ed, CHES
Health Education Consultant
Brunswick, Maine

Emotional and Intellectual Health
Donna Breitenstein, Ed.D
Professor of Health Education
Appalachian State University
Boone, North Carolina

Family and Social Health
Betty M. Hubbard, Ed.D, CHES
Professor, Department of Health Sciences
University of Central Arkansas
Conway, Arkansas

Nutrition
Celia J. Mir, Ed.D, RD, LD, CFCS
Associate Professor, Nutrition
University of Puerto Rico
Rio Piedras, Puerto Rico

Physical Fitness
James Robinson III, Ed.D
Visiting Professor of Health
Department of Health and Kinesiology
Texas A & M University
College Station, Texas

Disease Prevention and Control
Linda Stewart Campbell, MPH
Executive Director
Minority Task Force on AIDS
New York, New York

Alcohol, Tobacco, and Drugs
Kathleen Middleton, MS, CHES
Administrator for Health and Prevention
Monterey County Office of Education
Monterey County, California

Safety, Injury, and Violence Prevention
Philip R. Fine, Ph.D, MSPH
Director
Wendy S. Horn, MPH
Project Coordinator
Matthew D. Rousculp, MPH
Assistant to the Director
University of Alabama at Birmingham
Birmingham, Alabama

Andrea D. Tomasek, MPH
Epidemiologist, Injury Prevention Division
Alabama Department of Public Health
Montgomery, Alabama

Community and Environmental Health
Martin Ayong Ayim, Ph.D, MPH, BSPH, CHES
Assistant Professor of Health Education
Grambling State University
Grambling, Louisiana

Teacher Reviewers
Miriam Kaeser, OSF
Assistant Superintendent
Archdiocese of Cincinnati
Cincinnati, Ohio

Christine Wilson
3th Grade Classroom Teacher
Stout Field Elementary School
M.S.D. of Wayne Township
Indianapolis, Indiana

Multicultural Reviewer
Sylvia Peña, Ed.D
Dean, Graduate Studies
University of Texas at Brownsville
Brownsville, Texas

HEALTH ADVISORY BOARD MEMBERS

Lucinda Adams
State Advisor, Health Education
Former Director of Health
Dayton City Schools District
Dayton, Ohio

Clara Arch-Webster
Vice Principal
Duval County Schools
Jacksonville, Florida

Linda Carlton
Coordinator, Elementary Science & Health
Wichita, Kansas Public Schools USD 259
Wichita, Kansas

John Clayton
6th Grade Health Teacher
Orangewood Elementary School
Phoenix, Arizona

Pam Connolly
Subject Area Coordinator/HS Teacher
Diocese of Pittsburgh
Pittsburgh, Pennsylvania

Larry Herrold
Supervisor of Health Education, K–12
Baltimore County Public Schools
Baltimore, Maryland

Hollie Hinz
District Health Coordinator and Health Teacher
Menomonee Falls School District
Menomonee Falls, Wisconsin

Karen Mathews
5th Grade Teacher
Guilford County School
Greensboro, North Carolina

Patty O'Rourke
Health Coordinator
Cypress-Fairbanks I.S.D.
Houston, Texas

Sarah Roberts
6th Grade Health Teacher
McKinley Magnet School
Baton Rouge, Louisiana

Lindsay Shepheard
Health & Physical Education Program Coordinator
Virginia Beach City Public Schools
Virginia Beach, Virginia

Bob Wandberg
Health Education Curriculum & Instruction
Bloomington Public Schools
Bloomington, Minnesota

McGraw-Hill School Division
A Division of The McGraw-Hill Companies

McGraw-Hill School Division
1221 Avenue of the Americas
New York, New York 10020

Printed in the United States of America
ISBN 0-02-276417-8 / 3
4 5 6 7 8 9 071 03 02 01 00 99

CONTENTS

YOUR TEXTBOOK AT A GLANCE viii

MCGRAW-HILL HEALTH AND THE HEALTH PYRAMID x

WHAT ARE LIFE SKILLS? xi

AM I HEALTH WISE? xii

PERSONAL HEALTH 1

CHAPTER 1

1 WHAT IS HEALTH? 2

2 PERSONAL CARE 6

3 CARING FOR YOUR TEETH AND GUMS 10

4 CARING FOR YOUR EYES AND EARS 16

5 CARING FOR YOUR SKIN AND HAIR 20

YOU CAN MAKE A DIFFERENCE MILES FOR SMILES 25

CHAPTER REVIEW 26

CHAPTER TEST 28

GROWTH AND DEVELOPMENT 29

CHAPTER 2

1 GROWTH AND CHANGE 30

2 YOUR BONES AND MUSCLES 36

3 YOUR HEART AND LUNGS 42

4 YOUR DIGESTIVE SYSTEM 48

5 YOUR NERVOUS SYSTEM AND SENSES 52

YOU CAN MAKE A DIFFERENCE X-RAY TECHNICIAN 57

CHAPTER REVIEW 58

CHAPTER TEST 60

CHAPTER 3 EMOTIONAL AND INTELLECTUAL HEALTH 61

1 LEARNING ABOUT YOURSELF 62
2 GETTING ALONG WITH OTHERS 66
3 EMOTIONS AND CONFLICT 70
4 MANAGING STRESS 74
YOU CAN MAKE A DIFFERENCE SHOWER YOUR STRESS AWAY 79
CHAPTER REVIEW 80
CHAPTER TEST 82

CHAPTER 4 FAMILY AND SOCIAL HEALTH 83

1 A HEALTHY FAMILY 84
2 A HEALTHY CLASSROOM 88
3 HEALTHY FRIENDSHIPS 92
YOU CAN MAKE A DIFFERENCE SCHOOL COUNSELOR 97
CHAPTER REVIEW 98
CHAPTER TEST 100

CHAPTER 5 NUTRITION 101

1 WHY YOU NEED FOOD 102
2 THE FOOD GUIDE PYRAMID 108
3 CHOOSING HEALTHFUL FOODS 114
4 SHOPPING FOR HEALTHFUL FOODS 118
5 FOOD SAFETY 122
YOU CAN MAKE A DIFFERENCE SPACE FOOD 125
CHAPTER REVIEW 126
CHAPTER TEST 128

Chapter 6 Physical Activity and Fitness 129

1 Physical Fitness Is Important 130
2 Fitness Skills 134
3 Physical Fitness and You 138
4 Safety and Fairness 144
You Can Make a Difference Helping the Community 149
Chapter Review 150
Chapter Test 152

Chapter 7 Disease Prevention and Control ... 153

1 Learning About Diseases 154
2 Communicable Diseases 160
3 Fighting Diseases 164
4 HIV and AIDS 170
5 Staying Healthy 176
You Can Make a Difference Robots Help Out 179
Chapter Review 180
Chapter Test 182

Chapter 8 Alcohol, Tobacco, and Drugs 183

1 Medicines and Safety 184
2 Tobacco and Health 190
3 Alcohol and Health 196
4 Other Drugs 202
You Can Make a Difference Changing People's Lives 207
Chapter Review 208
Chapter Test 210

CHAPTER 9 SAFETY, INJURY, AND VIOLENCE PREVENTION 211

1 INJURY PREVENTION 212

2 VIOLENCE PREVENTION 218

3 INDOOR SAFETY 222

4 OUTDOOR SAFETY 228

5 EMERGENCIES 234

6 FIRST AID 238

YOU CAN MAKE A DIFFERENCE A NEW USE FOR BALLOONS 243

CHAPTER REVIEW 244

CHAPTER TEST 246

CHAPTER 10 COMMUNITY AND ENVIRONMENTAL HEALTH 247

1 COMMUNITY HEALTH CARE 248

2 A CLEAN ENVIRONMENT 252

3 PROTECTING PLANET EARTH 258

YOU CAN MAKE A DIFFERENCE BEARABLE TIMES 263

CHAPTER REVIEW 264

CHAPTER TEST 266

Contents	267
Life Skill 1: Make Decisions	268
Life Skill 2: Set Goals	270
Life Skill 3: Obtain Help	272
Life Skill 4: Manage Stress	274
Life Skill 5: Practice Refusal Skills	276
Life Skill 6: Resolve Conflicts	278
Nutrition	280
Physical Activity	284
Safety	288
First Aid	290
Resources	292
Glossary	294
INDEX	300

YOUR TEXTBOOK at a glance

McGraw-Hill Health has ten chapters, each one focusing on a special area of health. Every chapter has three or more lessons, plus special features for you to study and enjoy.

Each lesson begins by highlighting **What You Will Learn** and the key lesson **Vocabulary**.

The **QUICK START** gives you a real-life problem to think about as you begin each lesson.

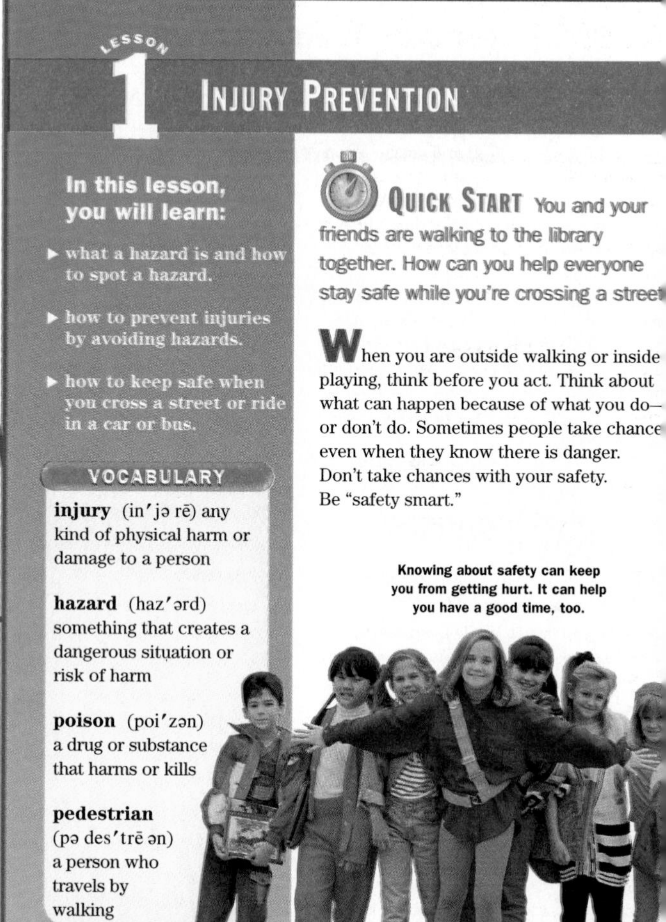

LESSON 1 INJURY PREVENTION

In this lesson, you will learn:

- what a hazard is and how to spot a hazard.
- how to prevent injuries by avoiding hazards.
- how to keep safe when you cross a street or ride in a car or bus.

VOCABULARY

injury (in′jə rē) any kind of physical harm or damage to a person

hazard (haz′ərd) something that creates a dangerous situation or risk of harm

poison (poi′zən) a drug or substance that harms or kills

pedestrian (pə des′trē ən) a person who travels by walking

QUICK START You and your friends are walking to the library together. How can you help everyone stay safe while you're crossing a street

When you are outside walking or inside playing, think before you act. Think about what can happen because of what you do—or don't do. Sometimes people take chance even when they know there is danger. Don't take chances with your safety. Be "safety smart."

Knowing about safety can keep you from getting hurt. It can help you have a good time, too.

212 CHAPTER 9

HEALTH ACTIVITY

Being "Safety Smart"

LIFE SKILL SET GOALS

1. With your partner, talk about the hazards listed on pages 213–214. Think of five ways that you can plan to act more safely at home or at school. Set goals for how to do so.
2. Make a "Playing It Safe Handbook." List the five ways you can improve your safety.
3. Exchange handbooks with classmates. Share ideas for being "safety smart."

LESSON WRAP UP

Show What You Know

1. What is a hazard? Name two examples of hazards.
2. How can you be "safety smart" to avoid hazards at home?
3. THINK CRITICALLY How could a passenger talking to a driver of a car or bus be a hazard?

Show What You Can Do

4. PORTFOLIO APPLY HEALTH ACTIVITY Set Goals Think of ways that you can be even safer as a pedestrian or passenger. Make a "safety first" checklist. List five ways you can be safer.
5. LIFE SKILL PRACTICE LIFE SKILLS Obtain Help Make a list of hazards that you find in and around school, on the bus, and at the crosswalk near school. Ask a teacher to review your list and help you correct the hazards.

HANDBOOK LIFE SKILLS pp. 268–279

LESSON 1 · INJURY PREVENTION 217

▲

Every lesson has a **Health Activity** to get you and your classmates actively involved in health issues. Every lesson also ends with a **Lesson Wrap-Up**.

HEALTH FALLACY

"Personal

HEALTH FACT

"Buckle up—it's the law."

This is true. All 50 st now have child passe safety laws. The reas these laws is that bu up saves lives. Sevel percent of all car cra happen close to hom more than half of th crashes involve drivi

CULTURAL PERSPECTIVES

"A man kicks a stone in

nes he story kicks points when with- the the

HEALTHWISE CONSUMER

It's a Life Saver

Never borrow the batteries from a smoke detector, no matter what. Smoke detectors can save lives—if they have power.

Most smoke detectors need fresh batteries every few months. Most make a beeping noise when the power is low. As a rule, try

◀ A variety of features can be found within the lessons. **Health Fact** and **Health Fallacy** help you sort out the facts in health issues.

Do you wonder about health issues around the world? Check out **Cultural Perspectives** in each chapter.

Learn to be a **HealthWise Consumer** with tips on product safety and informed purchasing.

At the end of each chapter is a special page called **You Can Make a Difference**. Here you'll learn about health heroes who promote health and save lives, advances in health-related technology, or careers in health that might help you plan your future.

YOU CAN MAKE A DIFFERENCE

TECHNOLOGY

Infographics bring you information with pictures, diagrams, charts, and other visual clues.

INFOGRAPHIC

BEING SAFETY SMART

Here are some other hazards you can avoid. Just think "play it safe."

FALLS

Falls hurt! Here's how to prevent them.

- Keep rooms, hallways, and stairs clear. Don't leave things lying around that could make you trip.
- Don't try to find your way around in the dark. Turn on a light or use a flashlight.
- Use nonslip mats in tubs and showers.
- Do not run on wet or waxed floors.
- Never use a chair as a ladder.

HEAT HAZARDS

Be "safety smart" about what's hot!

- After using an appliance that produces heat, turn it off. Then unplug it.
- Take special care with heaters. Heaters can keep you warm in the winter. But they can also burn you or start a fire. Keep heaters away from anything that might catch fire.
- Hot water can burn. Test the water before you get into a shower or tub.

ELECTRICAL HAZARDS

Electricity can cause fires. It can give a harmful shock. Here's how to prevent burns and shocks.

- Never use a cord that is cracked or frayed.
- Don't put too many plugs into the same outlet.
- Pull the plug, not the cord, to unplug an appliance.
- Don't use electrical appliances around water.

SAFETY, INJURY, AND VIOLENCE PREVENTION

243

263

What Is a Hazard?

A burned finger is an injury. An **injury** is ...y kind of physical harm or damage to you ... another person. To prevent injuries, think ...efore you act—avoid hazards. A **hazard** is ...mething that creates a dangerous situation ... risk of harm. For example, a hot iron is a ...zard—it can burn your finger.

Many household products can be hazards. ...oducts such as bleach, insect spray, and ...ue contain poisons. A **poison** is a drug or ...bstance that harms or kills. Some products ...ch as bleach or glue give off a gas that has ...smell. Inhaling this gas or *fume* can make ...u dizzy or sick.

Keep these rules in mind when using ...ousehold products.

- Do not use household products by yourself. An adult should help you.
- Household products should be stored properly—in sealed containers.
- Avoid any fumes. While the products are in use, open a window and turn on a fan. Never breathe in the fumes on purpose!
- Never swallow these products. Don't let them get into your eyes or on your skin.

Even very common household products need to be used carefully.

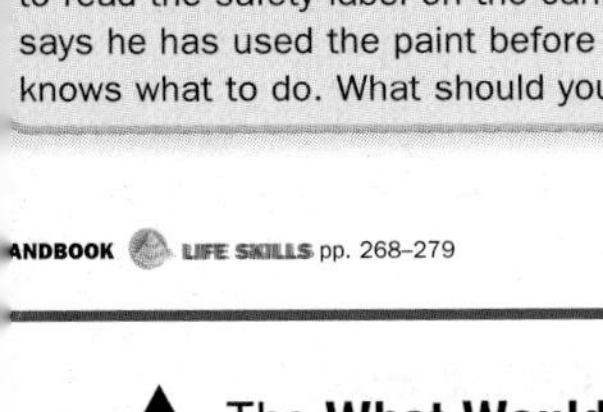
MAKE DECISIONS

What Would You Do?

You are helping your older brother paint a bookcase. He teases you for wanting to read the safety label on the can. He says he has used the paint before and knows what to do. What should you do?

...ANDBOOK LIFE SKILLS pp. 268–279 LESSON 1 • INJURY PREVENTION 213

▲ The **What Would You Do?** features help you apply life skills and what you've just learned.

The **Handbook** is a convenient reference tool with information on everything from setting health goals to performing first aid. It also lists health-related books, videos, and Web sites.

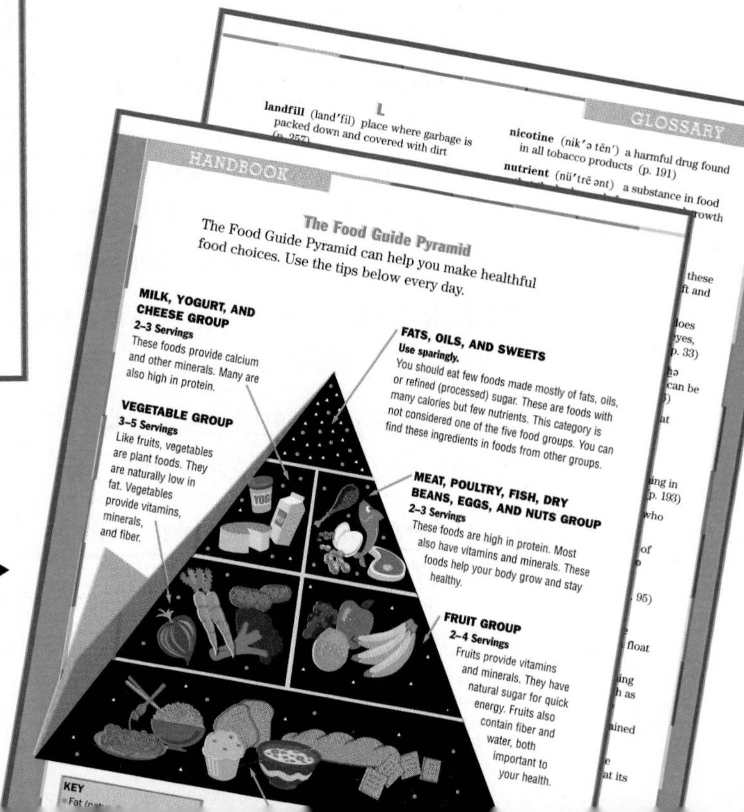
GLOSSARY

landfill (land′fil) place where garbage is packed down and covered with dirt

nicotine (nik′ə tēn′) a harmful drug found in all tobacco products (p. 191)

nutrient (nü′trē ənt) a substance in food

HANDBOOK

The Food Guide Pyramid

The Food Guide Pyramid can help you make healthful food choices. Use the tips below every day.

MILK, YOGURT, AND CHEESE GROUP
2–3 Servings
These foods provide calcium and other minerals. Many are also high in protein.

FATS, OILS, AND SWEETS
Use sparingly.
You should eat few foods made mostly of fats, oils, or refined (processed) sugar. These are foods with many calories but few nutrients. This category is not considered one of the five food groups. You can find these ingredients in foods from other groups.

VEGETABLE GROUP
3–5 Servings
Like fruits, vegetables are plant foods. They are naturally low in fat. Vegetables provide vitamins, minerals, and fiber.

MEAT, POULTRY, FISH, DRY BEANS, EGGS, AND NUTS GROUP
2–3 Servings
These foods are high in protein. Most also have vitamins and minerals. These foods help your body grow and stay healthy.

FRUIT GROUP
2–4 Servings
Fruits provide vitamins and minerals. They have natural sugar for quick energy. Fruits also contain fiber and water, both important to your health.

KEY

McGraw-Hill Health and the Health Pyramid

McGraw-Hill Health was created to help you explore all aspects of your health. The lessons, features, questions, and activities are designed to help you be as healthy as you can be.

We've created the McGraw-Hill Health Pyramid to help you take charge of your health. It shows the skills and abilities that will help you attain the goal of health.

Five Abilities That Really Help

Communicate Effectively Talk and listen to people to share information, ideas, and feelings.

Think Critically Use your brain power to solve problems and make wise choices.

Take Responsibility Take charge of your life by protecting your rights and sticking to your responsibilities.

Develop Self-Esteem Build a positive and realistic picture of yourself.

Respect Others Consider how your decisions and actions affect other people.

What Are Life Skills?

The base of the pyramid shows six life skills that are the foundation of health. As you develop these skills, the abilities shown in the middle of the pyramid will also develop.

You will have many opportunities to practice the six life skills as you work with *McGraw-Hill Health.* The Handbook that begins on page 267 gives you more information about each skill.

Make Decisions Can't make up your mind? You need to practice decision making. You face decisions every day. What kind of after-school activities will you get involved in? How can you help your friend deal with a bully? What will you do Monday night?

Set Goals The best way to get something done is to set a goal and then figure out how to reach it. You might have individual goals, like learning how to swim, or group goals, like discovering a great place to explore with your family.

Obtain Help Getting help when you need it is a key part of health. Help might be first aid, advice, or factual information about an important topic. You can get help from many different people, including your family, teacher, and doctor.

Manage Stress Your teacher announces a surprise quiz. Does your hair stand on end because you're tense or nervous? That's stress, a feeling of tension you get when something bothers you. It's a normal part of life, but with practice, you can learn how to manage your stress wisely.

Practice Refusal Skills Being responsible for your health means saying "no" to unhealthy offers. If someone suggests something that you know isn't healthy, you can use your refusal skills to say "no."

Resolve Conflicts Conflicts between people create stress and tension. To stay healthy, you can learn how to resolve conflicts. These ideas can help you find solutions to even the hardest problems.

Am I Health Wise?

Your **physical health** relates to your body. Your **emotional and intellectual health** relates to your thoughts and feelings. Your **social health** has to do with your relationships with other people. On a separate piece of paper, try this quiz to see whether the three parts of your health are in balance.

PHYSICAL HEALTH

1. I eat well-balanced meals.	ALWAYS	SOMETIMES	NEVER
2. I eat healthful snacks.	ALWAYS	SOMETIMES	NEVER
3. I get enough sleep.	ALWAYS	SOMETIMES	NEVER
4. I am physically active.	ALWAYS	SOMETIMES	NEVER
5. I avoid alcohol, tobacco, and drugs.	ALWAYS	SOMETIMES	NEVER
6. I get regular checkups.	ALWAYS	SOMETIMES	NEVER

EMOTIONAL AND INTELLECTUAL HEALTH

1. I feel good about myself.	ALWAYS	SOMETIMES	NEVER
2. I do many things well.	ALWAYS	SOMETIMES	NEVER
3. I have people I can talk to.	ALWAYS	SOMETIMES	NEVER
4. I apologize when I'm wrong.	ALWAYS	SOMETIMES	NEVER
5. I can be angry without being violent.	ALWAYS	SOMETIMES	NEVER
6. I love learning new skills.	ALWAYS	SOMETIMES	NEVER

SOCIAL HEALTH

1. I make friends easily.	ALWAYS	SOMETIMES	NEVER
2. I can say "no" if necessary.	ALWAYS	SOMETIMES	NEVER
3. I get along with classmates.	ALWAYS	SOMETIMES	NEVER
4. I cooperate with others.	ALWAYS	SOMETIMES	NEVER
5. People seem to like me.	ALWAYS	SOMETIMES	NEVER
6. I can resolve conflicts without fighting.	ALWAYS	SOMETIMES	NEVER

Score 2 points for each ALWAYS, 1 point for each SOMETIMES, and 0 points for each NEVER. Add up your score for each category.

8–12 points:	4–7 points:	0–6 points:
HealthWise	Needs Improvement	Must Do Better

In which area do you score highest? Are your three scores balanced? Where could you use improvement?

CHAPTER

PERSONAL HEALTH 1

THE BIG IDEA

You can:

- choose to be healthy.
- do many things to keep yourself healthy.

CHAPTER CONTENTS

1 WHAT IS HEALTH? 2

2 PERSONAL CARE 6

3 CARING FOR YOUR TEETH AND GUMS 10

4 CARING FOR YOUR EYES AND EARS 16

5 CARING FOR YOUR SKIN AND HAIR 20

YOU CAN MAKE A DIFFERENCE MILES FOR SMILES 25

CHAPTER REVIEW 26

CHAPTER TEST 28

LESSON 1

What Is Health?

In this lesson, you will learn:

- the three parts of health.
- how to plan to be healthy.

VOCABULARY

physical health (fiz′i kəl helth) health of the body; being able to work and play well

emotional and intellectual health (i mō′shən nəl ənd in′tə lek′chü əl helth) health of the mind, having to do with thinking and feelings

social health (sō′shəl helth) health having to do with relationships with other people

QUICK START "How are you?" people often ask each other. What do you think this question really means?

"How are you?" "What's up?" "How's it going?" When you answer questions like these, you are talking about your personal health. "My cold is gone, thanks," is one way to answer. But your personal health means more than just getting over a cold.

Personal health includes your physical, emotional and intellectual, and social health.

The Three Parts of Health

Health means more than being free from illness. Your personal health is made up of three parts.

One part is **physical health**, the health of the body. When you have good physical health, you have energy. You can work and play hard. You feel well most of the time.

Your feelings and thoughts are part of your **emotional and intellectual health**. Feeling good about yourself is an important part of being healthy. Your thoughts are important too. When you think clearly, you can use your mind to make decisions. You can solve problems.

Your relationships with other people are part of your **social health**. When you have good social health, you get along well with others. You enjoy being with your family, friends, neighbors, and classmates.

These students are performing in a class play. Working together with others helps improve social health.

HEALTH FALLACY

"Only sick people need to see a doctor."

This is false. Even people who are well need to see doctors for checkups. During a checkup, your height and weight are recorded. The doctor examines your nose, mouth, and throat. The doctor also checks your eyes and ears and listens to your heart and lungs. Your doctor uses this information to help plan for your health.

Plan to Be Healthy

Your parents, doctors, and teachers care about your health. When it comes to your own good health, however, you play the biggest part. You can:

- set goals for your own health.
- choose to build good health habits (the things you do often to be healthy).
- keep records about your health.

For example, getting enough sleep is important to your health. Someone your age may need about 10 to 12 hours of sleep. If you think you're not getting enough sleep, you might keep a record for a while to find out. You might set a goal to get more sleep by changing your bedtime.

Trusted adults, such as a parent or guardian, can help you plan to be healthy. For example, they can help you figure out the best sleeping and eating habits. They can also make sure that you see a doctor and a dentist for regular checkups.

LIFE SKILL

PRACTICE REFUSAL SKILLS

What Would You Do?

You and your older brother both have tests at school tomorrow. He wants you to stay up late to watch TV with him. Why might you say "no"? What else might you say to him?

Some people like to read before sleeping. Others find it helpful to listen to music. How do you relax before going to bed?

HEALTH ACTIVITY

What You Can Do

LIFE SKILL
SET GOALS

You will need: poster paper, markers

1 As a class, make a list of good health habits.

2 Talk about the list. Which habits do you already have? Which ones would be new to you? How could the new habits improve your health? What unhealthful habits would they replace?

3 Choose one new habit from the list. Make it a goal for your own good health plan. Write it down and ask someone at home to help you remember your goal.

LESSON WRAP UP

Show What You Know

1. What are the three parts of health?
2. Name two activities that you can do to keep yourself healthy.
3. **THINK CRITICALLY** How does not getting enough sleep affect your health?

Show What You Can Do

4. PORTFOLIO **APPLY HEALTH ACTIVITY** **Set Goals** Draw a picture of yourself practicing a good health habit. Write two sentences telling why this action can help you stay healthy.

5. LIFE SKILL **PRACTICE LIFE SKILLS** **Obtain Help** Think of two questions you would like to have answered about your own health. Write your questions down. Then talk them over with a trusted adult.

LESSON

2 PERSONAL CARE

In this lesson, you will learn:

- about good grooming habits and how they help you to be healthy.
- about grooming and health care products.

VOCABULARY

grooming (grüm′ing) keeping neat and clean

health care product (helth kâr prod′əkt) something you can buy that can help you stay healthy

QUICK START Suppose you are staying overnight at a friend's house. You want to look your best in the morning. What things would you pack?

Before you go on an overnight trip, you make decisions. In fact, every day you make a lot of decisions. Some decisions affect your health. For example, you may decide what snacks to eat. You may decide where to play and when to wash up.

Your job is to make the best decisions—the ones that will keep you healthy. This lesson will help you make healthy decisions about your personal care.

Taking good care of your hair is part of good grooming.

Neat and Clean—and Healthy!

Grooming means keeping neat and clean. By washing with soap and water, you remove dirt and germs from your skin. Germs are tiny living things, too small to see. They can cause odors. Germs can also get inside the body and cause illness.

Grooming is also taking care of the way you look. You wash your hair, for example, to look and feel clean. You also brush or comb it to make it neater.

When you look neat and clean, you feel good about yourself. When you feel good about yourself, it is easier to get along with others, too.

Practicing good grooming habits in the morning is a great way to start out the day. Practicing them at night, before you go to bed, is just as important. What personal health habits do you practice at bedtime?

CULTURAL PERSPECTIVES

Culture and Grooming

Culture is the way of life of a group of people. Culture includes customs and beliefs. It may also include special grooming practices. For example, people from various cultures have different ideas about hair or clothing styles and other personal health habits. A culture's hair styles, clothing, and grooming practices are usually the result of long traditions. Find out about any special health customs that you may practice.

RESOLVE

What Would You Do?

Your family is sitting down to dinner. Your younger brother has dirty hands. He doesn't want to wash them. What can you tell your brother to get him to wash his hands?

Good grooming habits help you stay healthy—and feel good about yourself.

Grooming and Health Care Products

When you brush your teeth or comb your hair, you are using **health care products**. These and other products can help you keep your skin, hair, nails, and teeth healthy.

Brushing and flossing will help keep your teeth and gums healthy.

Shampoo cleans your hair. Use a comb and brush to keep your hair neat.

Soap can help remove dirt and germs from your skin.

One part of good grooming is having clean, trimmed nails.

Clean a small cut with soap and water. Then cover it with a bandage. A bandage will help keep germs from getting into the cut.

Help keep germs from spreading. Cough or sneeze into a tissue. Then throw the tissue away.

HEALTH ACTIVITY

Picture the Product

You will need: used magazines, scissors, poster or chart paper, paste, markers

1 As a group, decide on four health care products you want to use. Cut out magazine pictures of them.

2 Make a chart with three columns. Paste the pictures in the first column. In the second, write how you would use the product and how often. In the third, write how this would help your health.

3 Share your chart with other groups. Which products seem to be the most popular? Why?

LESSON WRAP UP

Show What You Know

1. Give two examples of good grooming habits.

2. Name one health care product. Why is that product useful?

3. **THINK CRITICALLY** Why is good grooming important to staying healthy?

Show What You Can Do

4. PORTFOLIO **APPLY HEALTH ACTIVITY** **Make Decisions** Make up an ad for a health care product. Decide on a slogan that tells why it is good to use. For example, "Sparkle toothpaste makes your smile bright."

5. LIFE SKILL **PRACTICE LIFE SKILLS** **Set Goals** Set a goal to pay more attention to one part of your personal grooming. Write down your goal. What can you do to reach it?

HANDBOOK LIFE SKILLS pp. 268–279

LESSON 3

Caring for Your Teeth and Gums

In this lesson, you will learn:

- the parts of the tooth.
- the importance of brushing and flossing teeth.
- the importance of dental checkups.

VOCABULARY

enamel (i nam′əl) the hard, shiny outer covering of a tooth

root (rüt) the part of the tooth that is attached to the jawbone

plaque (plak) a sticky film of food particles and germs that can weaken tooth enamel

cavity (kav′i tē) a hole in a tooth caused by decay

QUICK START Make the sounds of these letters: *f*, *th*, and *s*. What do the sounds have in common?

Healthy teeth can give you a nice smile. They also help you bite and chew your food. They help you speak clearly. Healthy teeth and gums help you stay healthy. You were probably less than a year old when your first teeth appeared. By the third birthday, a child has about 20 primary teeth, the first teeth to grow.

Permanent teeth probably began to appear when you were about six. Now, you have some primary teeth and some permanent teeth. In time, a person can have 32 permanent teeth.

If you take care of your permanent teeth, they should last all your life.

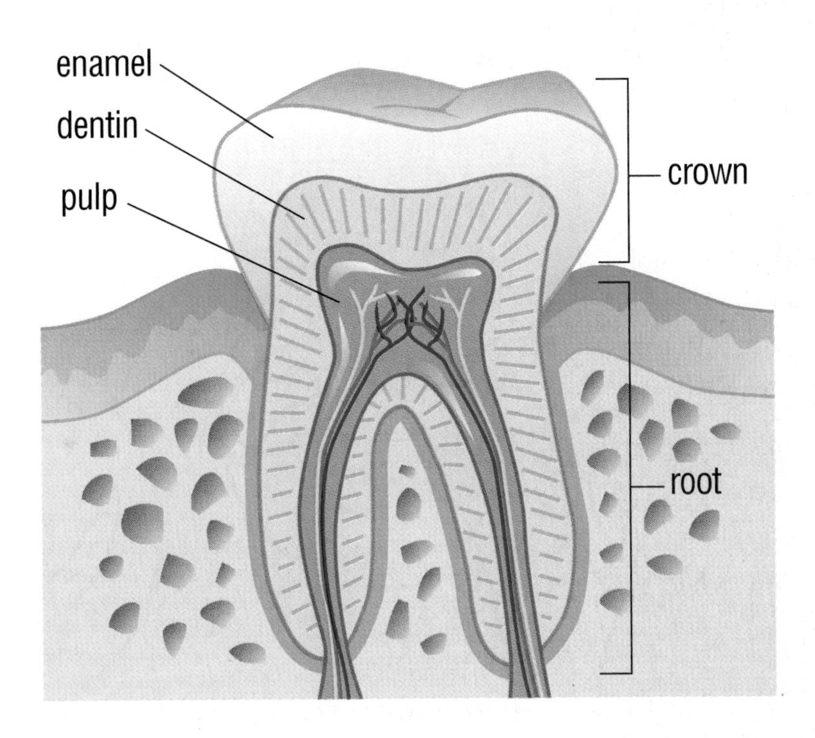

Parts of a Tooth

When you look at your teeth, you see enamel. **Enamel** is shiny and hard. It covers the *crown*, the part of the tooth above the gums. Beneath the enamel is *dentin*, a bony layer. The *pulp* is the center of the tooth. It contains blood vessels and nerves. A tooth's **root** attaches it to the jawbone.

Plaque and Cavities

Food particles and germs in your mouth can form a sticky film on your teeth called **plaque**. When you eat foods that have sugar in them, the germs form acids. The plaque holds these acids on the teeth. If plaque is not brushed away, the gums and teeth can begin to rot, or *decay*.

These acids can weaken the enamel. A hole could form. A hole in a tooth is called a **cavity**. Some cavities hurt, especially if they reach the nerves in the tooth's pulp. The best way to avoid cavities is to take care of your teeth every day.

HEALTH FACT

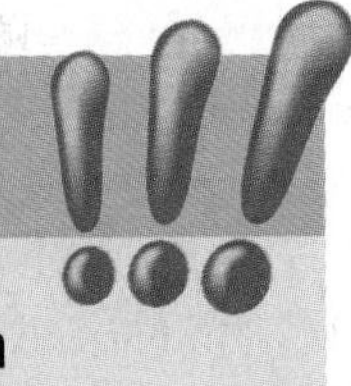

“Healthy teeth don't have to be white.”

That's true! Tooth enamel is usually not bright white in color. Sometimes it is yellowish, brownish, or grayish. Teeth can be any of these colors and still be healthy. Your dentist is the person to check with about the color of your teeth.

INFOGRAPHIC

A Routine for Your

You can practice good dental health by following a simple daily routine. To start, brush your teeth every day—after breakfast and before bedtime. If you can, brush after every meal. You can use these pictures as a guide.

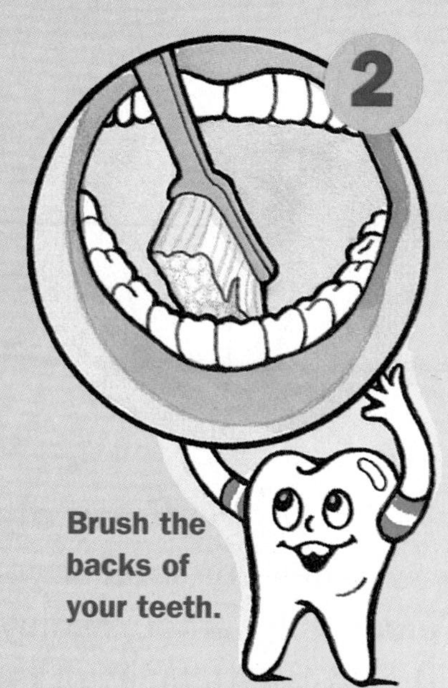

Place the toothbrush against the outside of the teeth. Tilt the bristles against the gums. Gently move the brush back and forth with short strokes.

Brush the backs of your teeth.

Another part of good dental health is flossing every day. Dental floss is thin thread used to clean between teeth. Flossing removes plaque and food from places that a toothbrush can't reach. These pictures show you how to floss.

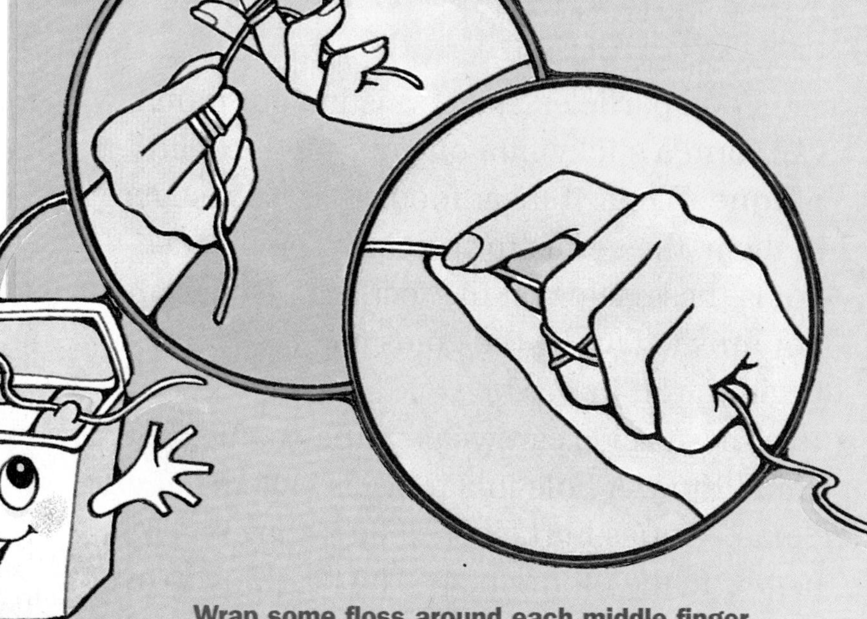

Wrap some floss around each middle finger. Leave several inches of floss between. Hold the floss in place between your thumbs and forefingers.

Teeth and Gums

Here are some other good health habits for your teeth.

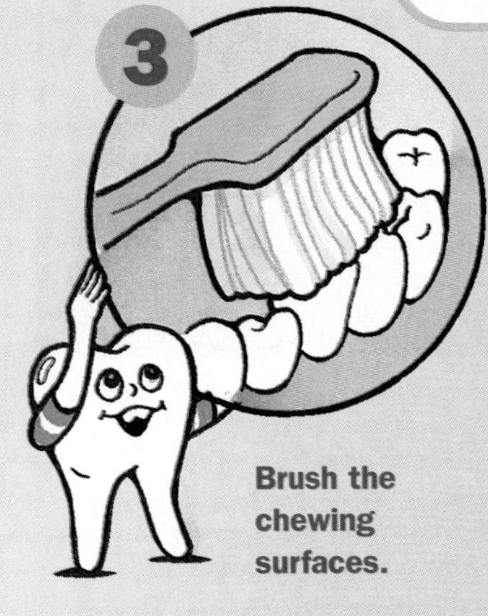

Brush the chewing surfaces.

- Use a toothpaste with fluoride. Fluoride helps to make tooth enamel strong and protects against cavities.
- Eat foods with less sugar. For example, try a snack of carrot sticks or an apple instead of a cupcake or a candy bar.
- Don't bite into hard objects. These can damage and injure your mouth.
- Wear a helmet or mouth guard to protect your teeth when playing a sport.

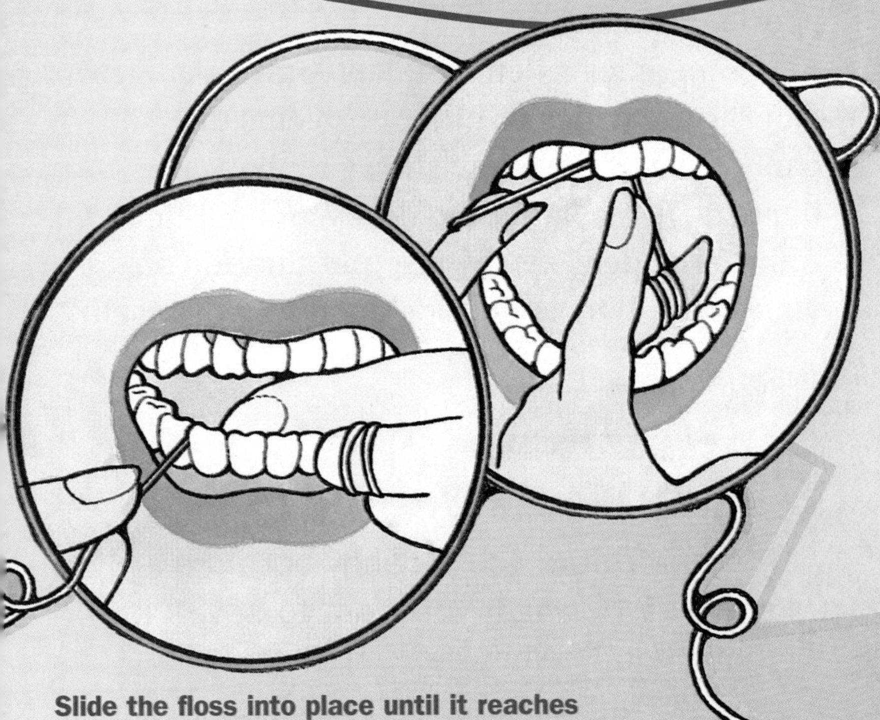
Slide the floss into place until it reaches the gums. Gently slide the floss up and down between your teeth.

Remember this advice too.

- Floss your teeth before you brush. Bedtime is a good time to floss.
- Be sure to floss between all your teeth, including the ones in back.

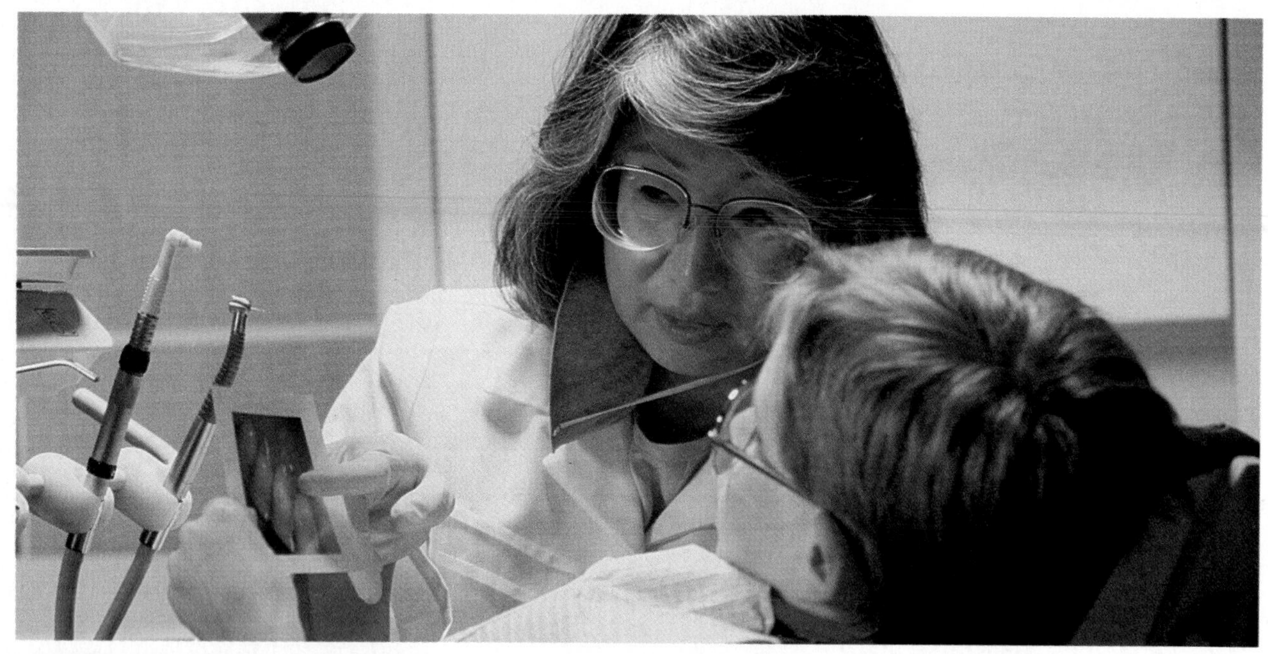

Regular visits to the dentist will help keep your teeth as healthy as possible.

Visiting the Dentist

You can do a lot on your own to keep your teeth and gums healthy. But, your dentist is the person to see to know how your teeth are doing.

Visit a dentist every six months. The dentist will check to see that your permanent teeth are growing properly. He or she will look for cavities. During the visit, your teeth will get a special cleaning.

Sometimes a dentist takes X-rays. An X-ray can show cavities or other problems that you cannot see. If the X-ray shows a cavity, the dentist can clean out the decay and put in a filling. The dentist may also put fluoride on your teeth. Why is fluoride good for your teeth?

HEALTH FALLACY

"One kind of toothbrush is good for everyone."

This is not true. Toothbrushes come in different sizes. Their bristles can be soft, medium, or hard. When picking out a toothbrush find one that you can hold easily. The bristles should be soft. Make sure that its head (the place where the bristles are) is not too big. Check with your dentist to be sure you are using the right toothbrush.

PRACTICE REFUSAL SKILLS

What Would You Do?

A friend offers you a candy bar as a snack. Why might you want to say, "No, thank you"? What else might you want to add?

HEALTH ACTIVITY

Tooth Time

LIFE SKILL
SET GOALS

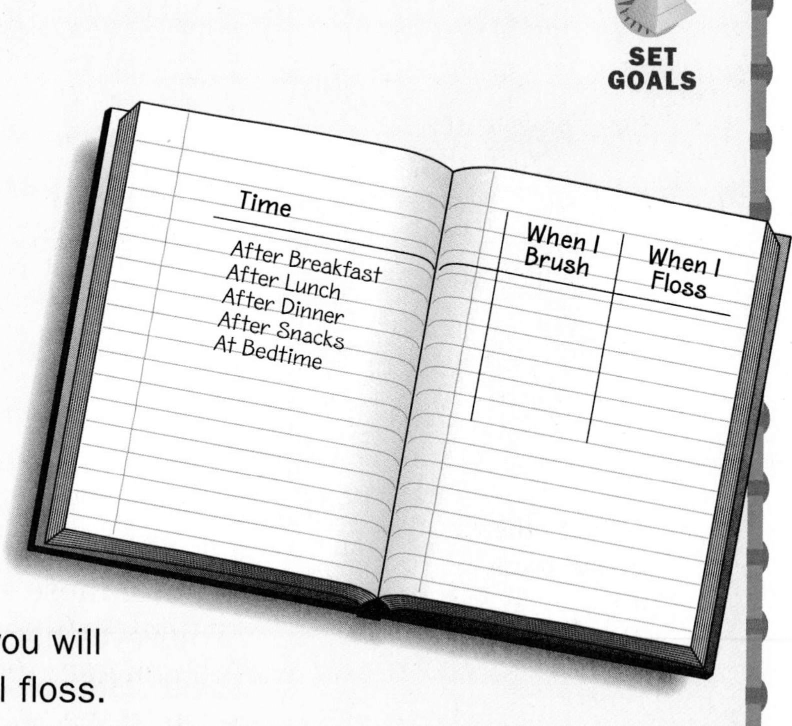

1. Plan on a daily routine for brushing and flossing your teeth.
2. Make a chart like the one shown. Make one column for brushing and another for flossing. Along the side, write different times of the day.
3. Put an X next to the times you will brush and the times you will floss.
4. Record the number of times each day that you stick to your plan.

LESSON WRAP UP

Show What You Know

1. Name and describe three parts of the tooth.
2. How do brushing and flossing help keep plaque and cavities from forming?
3. **THINK CRITICALLY** What might happen if you didn't have regular dental checkups?

Show What You Can Do

4. PORTFOLIO **APPLY HEALTH ACTIVITY** **Set Goals** Plan to brush your teeth to show all the steps on pages 12–13. Make a list of the steps. Do you follow each step each time you brush? Explain.
5. LIFE SKILL **PRACTICE LIFE SKILLS** **Resolve Conflicts** Your classmates tease Josh for carrying a toothbrush to school and using it. How might you help Josh and your classmates?

HANDBOOK LIFE SKILLS pp. 268–279

LESSON

4 CARING FOR YOUR EYES AND EARS

In this lesson, you will learn:

- the importance of healthy vision and hearing.
- about some eye and ear problems.
- how to care for your eyes and ears.

VOCABULARY

vision (vizh′ən) seeing; your sense of sight

eardrum (îr′drum) a thin layer of skin inside the ear that passes sound waves to the hearing nerves

QUICK START As a "joke," a classmate wants to sneak up on your friend and shout in her ear. What should you do—and fast? Why?

Your senses help you get information from other people and from the world around you. Two of these senses are seeing and hearing. Your eyes help you see. Your ears help you hear. They also help you communicate. They keep you safe, too! For example, you need eyes and ears to see and hear cars when you cross a street.

Take care of your eyes and ears. They are very important! In this lesson, you will learn how.

People who cannot see must use other senses—like hearing and touch—to learn about the world around them.

Your Eyes

People use their **vision**, or sense of sight, all day long. Not everyone has perfect vision. Some people have problems seeing things close up or far away. Many of these eye problems can be corrected with eyeglasses or contact lenses.

Do your eyes ever itch or burn? These are other types of eye problems. Be sure to tell a parent, your teacher, or the school nurse if you think you have any eye problem. Many eye problems can be treated and kept from getting worse. Here's how to care for your eyes.

- Use proper lighting for reading, writing, and watching television. The light should be strong but not glaring.

Having your eyes checked regularly is one way to protect your vision.

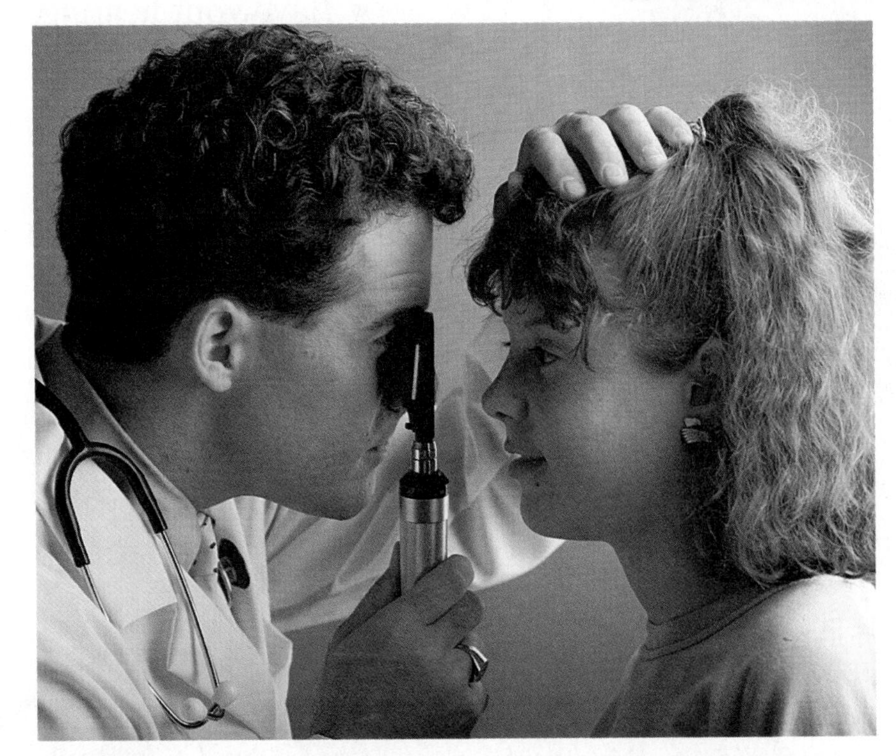

- On bright days, wear sunglasses. Never look directly into the sun.
- Wear safety glasses or goggles when playing certain sports.
- If something gets into your eye, don't rub it. Ask an adult to help you wash it out.
- Never throw, point with, or run with sharp objects.
- Have your vision checked regularly.

One way to care for your ears is to have your hearing checked regularly.

Your Ears

If you think you have an ear problem, such as an earache or "itchiness," get help from a trusted adult. Here are some ways to take care of your ears to protect your hearing.

- Never stick any object into your ear. It can damage your eardrum. The **eardrum** is a thin layer of skin inside the ear that passes the sound waves to the hearing nerves.
- Don't try to clean inside your ears. Clean only the outside part with a damp cloth.
- Avoid loud sounds. Loud music, machines, and fireworks can all cause hearing loss.
- Have your hearing checked regularly.

LIFE SKILL

MANAGE STRESS

What Would You Do?

Your sister listens to very loud music when you are doing homework. You are worried that she may hurt her ears and you want to get your work done. How can you deal with this stress and help your sister?

HEALTHWISE CONSUMER

What Are Eardrops?

Consumers make choices about what they need. Sometimes too much wax builds up in a person's ear. It can harden and become uncomfortable. If so, eardrops might help. Used for a few days, this liquid softens the wax. Then the wax can be removed. Also, a doctor can remove hardened wax. If you think you have this problem, talk to a trusted adult first.

HEALTH ACTIVITY

Sight and Sound Savers

1 Work with a group of classmates. Plan a skit about an eye and ear clinic. Show how doctors and nurses can help people keep their ears and eyes healthy.

2 Assign a role to each person in the group. Practice the skit.

3 Perform your skit for the class. Then talk about all the skits. What did you learn from your own skit? What did you learn from the skits by other groups?

LESSON WRAP UP

Show What You Know

1. Name one health habit that protects your eyes and one that protects your ears.

2. Are earaches and itchy eyes health problems? Explain your answer.

3. **THINK CRITICALLY** Why are healthy eyes and ears important to learning?

Show What You Can Do

4. PORTFOLIO **APPLY HEALTH ACTIVITY** **Obtain Help** Make a helpful hints booklet about proper eye and ear care. In the booklet, tell how to get help if you have eye or ear problems.

5. LIFE SKILL **PRACTICE LIFE SKILLS** **Make Decisions** Where do you read and write at home? Is the lighting good? Is it quiet? Talk to your family. Do you need to change the lighting or noise level?

LESSON 5

Caring for Your Skin and Hair

In this lesson, you will learn:

- about the different layers of your skin.
- the proper ways to care for your skin and hair.

VOCABULARY

epidermis (ep′i dûr′mis) the outer layer of skin

dermis (dûr′mis) the layer of skin just below the epidermis

glands (glandz) parts of the body that make substances needed by the body, such as oil and sweat

scalp (skalp) the skin on the top of your head

head lice (hed līs) small insects that can live on people's scalps

QUICK START David took his sunglasses to the beach. He forgot his beach ball, sunscreen, and comb. Of the things he forgot, which one did he need the most? Why?

Your skin is an organ. That is, it's a body part—like the brain, heart, and lungs. In fact, skin is larger than any of these other organs. Clean skin helps you look good. And it's important for your health.

Clean hair also helps improve your health and appearance. In this lesson, you will learn about how to take care of your skin and hair.

Healthy skin and hair help you look good—and are very important to your health!

The Parts of the Skin

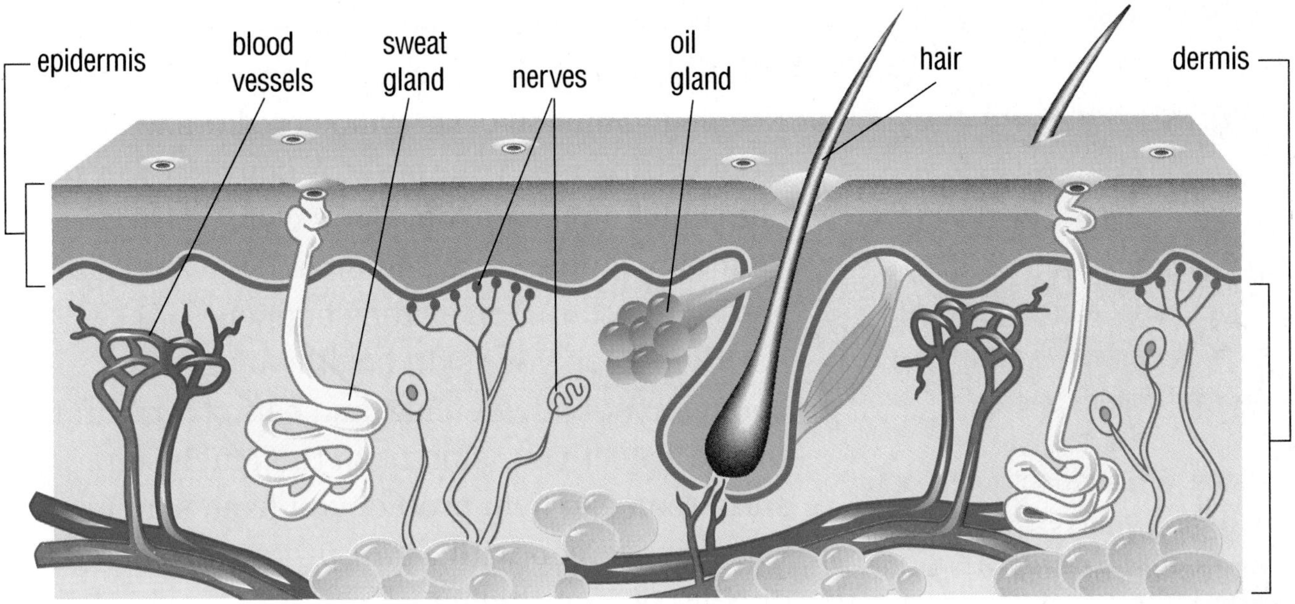

epidermis
blood vessels
sweat gland
nerves
oil gland
hair
dermis

Your Skin

Your skin has many jobs. One job is to cover your body. It keeps germs out and protects your body from harm. Your skin also controls your body temperature. And your skin is the sense organ for touch. It helps you feel whether something is hot or cold, rough or smooth.

Your skin is made up of two layers. The outer layer of skin is the **epidermis**. That's the part that you can see. Your fingernails and toenails grow out of the epidermis. The **dermis** is the layer just below the epidermis. It's the thickest layer of your skin. The dermis includes blood vessels, nerves, and two main kinds of glands.

Glands make substances needed by the body, such as oil and sweat. There are *oil glands* in the dermis. They make oil, which keeps your skin soft and waterproof. The dermis also has *sweat glands*. When your body gets hot, these glands make sweat. As air dries the sweat on your skin, you feel cooler.

Caring for Your Skin

It's important to keep your skin healthy. Dirt, oil, sweat, and germs collect on your skin. Keeping your skin clean will keep dirt and germs from getting into your body. A daily shower or bath can help keep your body clean. Also, wash your hands often. Wash and bandage any cuts and scrapes as soon as they happen.

Help keep your skin healthy by getting enough rest and exercise, and eating healthful food. Protect your skin from too much sun. A sunscreen can help protect you from sunburn. Use a sunscreen with a *sun protection factor*, or *SPF*, of 15 or higher.

HEALTHWISE CONSUMER

Antibacterial Soap

There are many kinds of soaps. Some are called *antibacterial*. These soaps have a special ingredient. It kills certain types of germs called *bacteria*.

Using an antibacterial soap will give your skin added protection against germs. So when you shop with your family, look at the labels on soap products. Your parents may want to try an antibacterial soap.

MAKE DECISIONS

What Would You Do?

You've been playing basketball outdoors during the afternoon. It's time for a snack—a fresh apple. What should you do before you eat the snack?

Be sure to read the label on a sunscreen. It will tell you how often to use it.

Caring for Your Hair and Scalp

Hair grows on most of the skin on your body. Usually people notice the hair that grows from the **scalp**, the skin on the top of the head.

The care that you give your hair and scalp is important. For example, hair that is oily and dirty collects germs. The germs can cause itchy rashes on the scalp. Sometimes white specks of dead skin fall from the scalp. These specks, called *dandruff*, can also collect in hair.

Head lice can be a problem, too. These small insects can live on people's scalps. Shared combs, brushes, and hats can spread head lice from person to person.

How can you keep your hair and scalp healthy? Here are some tips.

- Use a shampoo that is right for your kind of hair. Wash your hair as often as necessary. Remember to scrub your scalp when you wash your hair.

Why is brushing your hair important?

- Brush your hair every day. Brushing helps take away dandruff and loose hair. It also spreads oil from your scalp throughout your hair.
- Keep your comb and brush clean.
- Don't use other people's combs, brushes, or hats. Don't lend out your own, either.

HEALTH ACTIVITY

Personal Advice

1 Make a list of good health habits for today. List all the things you did this morning and what you will do by bedtime. Include all the ways you care for your teeth, gums, eyes, ears, skin, and hair.

2 How is this list like the list you made in Lesson 1, page 5? How is it different?

3 Change your list for today to make an improved list for tomorrow. Plan to follow everything on your list for tomorrow.

LESSON WRAP UP

Show What You Know

1. Name the layers of the skin. Describe each.

2. What are two things that you can do to keep your skin and hair healthy?

3. **THINK CRITICALLY** Think about the jobs that the skin does. Which job do you think is the most important? Why?

Show What You Can Do

4. PORTFOLIO **APPLY HEALTH ACTIVITY** **Set Goals** Write a story about a bar of soap named "Fresh Face." Tell how Fresh Face teaches children to keep clean from head to toe.

5. LIFE SKILL **PRACTICE LIFE SKILLS** **Obtain Help** Invite the school nurse to your class to explain the effects of the sun on your skin. Discuss what changes you might make to protect your skin.

HANDBOOK LIFE SKILLS pp. 268–279

YOU CAN MAKE A DIFFERENCE

HEALTH HEROES

Miles for Smiles

Participants in the "Miles for Smiles" Run/Walk

Children in San Antonio, Texas, have a lot of tooth problems. That's partly because the water in San Antonio does not have fluoride, a chemical that prevents tooth decay.

When dental school students at the University of Texas Health Science Center at San Antonio Dental School learned this, they decided to do something about it. The students started a yearly money-raising run/walk they called "Miles for Smiles."

The first run was held in 1993. Nearly 300 runners and walkers took part. The dental school students signed up runners, set up water stations, gave out awards, and cleaned up afterwards. They raised almost $30,000.

The students used the money to start a fluoride mouth-rinse program in elementary schools in San Antonio. Soon, thousands of school children were rinsing with fluoride at school. The students hope that Miles for Smiles will help educate people about the role of fluoride in fighting tooth decay.

OBTAIN HELP

FIND OUT ABOUT FLUORIDE

Does your drinking water have fluoride? How can you find out? Work with a group to make a list of people who might help you learn about fluoride in your area. (The phone book might help you.) As a class, write a letter to find out about fluoride in your local water.

CHAPTER

1 REVIEW

VOCABULARY

Write the word from the box that best completes each sentence. Use each word only once.

cavity
eardrum
enamel
epidermis
grooming
physical health
social health

1. Getting along well with others is part of your __?__. (Lesson 1)
2. Keeping neat and clean is the meaning of __?__. (Lesson 2)
3. The hard, shiny outer part of a tooth is the __?__. (Lesson 3)
4. The __?__ is a thin layer of skin inside the ear that passes sound waves to the hearing nerves. (Lesson 4)
5. The __?__ is the outer layer of the skin. (Lesson 5)

REVIEW HEALTH IDEAS

Use your knowledge of personal health from Chapter 1 to answer these questions.

1. How is your physical health different from other parts of your health? (Lesson 1)
2. Name three things that you can do to keep healthy. (Lesson 1)
3. Name two daily grooming habits. (Lesson 2)
4. Name two health care products. Tell how each helps your health. (Lesson 2)
5. Why is it important to have healthy teeth? (Lesson 3)
6. How does fluoride help your teeth? (Lesson 3)
7. Name two ways to care for your eyes. (Lesson 4)
8. How can you protect your ears from harm? (Lesson 4)
9. How do sweat glands help keep the body cool? (Lesson 5)
10. How can the sun harm your skin? (Lesson 5)

APPLY HEALTH IDEAS

1. Why is it important to plan for your own health? (Lesson 1)
2. How can good grooming affect other parts of your health? (Lesson 2)
3. How is recognizing eye and ear problems important to good health? (Lesson 4)
4. PORTFOLIO **MAKE DECISIONS** Decide on a skin care habit to add to your daily routine. Make a chart that shows each day of the week. Each time you practice this habit, make a check on the chart. (Lesson 5)
5. LIFE SKILL **RESOLVE CONFLICTS** You and a friend are planning a party. Your friend wants to serve mostly sweets. You want to serve less sugary foods. What could you say to resolve this conflict? (Lesson 3)

With your family, make a list of things a doctor might do during a checkup. Title your list "Checkup Time with the Doctor."

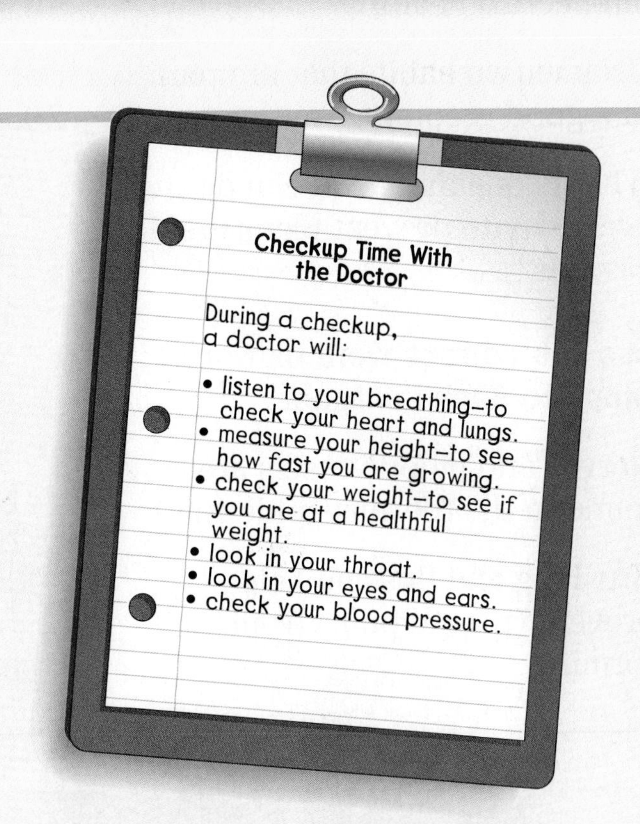

CHAPTER

1 TEST

Write a sentence to answer each question.

1. Name one important job of the skin.
2. Why is it important to have regular dental checkups?
3. Good grooming makes you healthier. In what way is that true?

4–5. Name one common eye problem and one common ear problem.

6. Why shouldn't you use someone else's comb, brush, or hat?
7. What is emotional and intellectual health?

8–9. Name two habits that are part of a good grooming routine.

10. What is one thing you can do every day to prevent plaque and cavities?

Choose the correct word or words to complete each sentence.

11. Nerves and blood vessels are found in the (dermis/epidermis).
12. Brushing and flossing help prevent (plaque/pulp) from forming.
13. The parts of health are physical health, emotional and intellectual health, and (active/social) health.
14. Have an adult (rub out/wash out) dust from your eye.
15. Toothpaste and washcloths are just two of many (health care/safety) products.
16. The (gum/root) attaches a tooth to the jawbone.
17. Sweat glands help keep your skin (smooth/cool).
18. The center of a tooth is called (pulp/dentin).
19. To stay in good health, be sure to (get regular checkups/see a doctor only when you are sick).
20. Healthy vision and hearing help you learn about the world around you. They also help you to (stay safe/look your best).

Performance Assessment

PORTFOLIO

You have been asked to make a Good Health Habits bulletin board. Draw a picture of each thing that you want to include. Write a caption for each picture to tell why that habit is important.

GROWTH AND DEVELOPMENT

CHAPTER 2

THE BIG IDEA

You can stay healthy by knowing:

- how you grow and change.
- how your body works.

CHAPTER CONTENTS

1 GROWTH AND CHANGE 30

2 YOUR BONES AND MUSCLES 36

3 YOUR HEART AND LUNGS 42

4 YOUR DIGESTIVE SYSTEM 48

5 YOUR NERVOUS SYSTEM AND SENSES 52

X-RAY TECHNICIAN 57

CHAPTER REVIEW 58

CHAPTER TEST 60

LESSON

1 GROWTH AND CHANGE

In this lesson, you will learn:

- how people change as they grow from babies to adults.
- how cells are a part of growth and change.
- what affects your growth.

VOCABULARY

adolescence (ad′ə les′əns) the period of time between childhood and adulthood; when a person begins to look more like an adult

cell (sel) the smallest living part of the body

heredity (hə red′i tē) passing of traits from parents to children

environment (en vī′rən mənt) everything around a person

QUICK START You haven't seen your favorite uncle in over a year. When you meet, he says, "My, you're so grown up!" What do you think he means?

How have you changed since your last birthday? Are you taller? Are you stronger? You can see and feel these changes in your body.

You have changed in other ways, too. Maybe you have learned new ways to solve problems. Maybe you have become more kind and helpful. Growing up means changing in many ways.

As you grow, you learn how to do new things.

The Life Cycle

People grow and change differently. They change in how they look, what they can do, and what they know. But, all people go through the same stages, or steps, as they grow.

The first year after birth is called *infancy.* In its first year, a baby is called an infant. Infants grow quickly. At 1 year of age, most infants weigh three times more than when they were born. Infants begin to crawl and stand. Many infants begin to understand and say a few words.

From the end of infancy to about age 11 or 12 is known as *childhood.* This is a time of many changes. Children grow teeth. Their bones and muscles grow stronger. There are other changes, too. They learn to get along with others. They also learn new skills and become better at ones they know.

The period after childhood is called **adolescence**. During this time, people begin to look more like adults. But not all changes are physical. People also learn to tackle harder subjects at school. They develop and share new interests.

After adolescence comes *adulthood.* Adulthood begins around the age of 18 and lasts through old age. Most adults reach their full height at about the age of 20. As adults, people focus on careers. Many adults get married. Some have children—who will, in turn, grow and change.

HEALTH ACTIVITY

Me in Three

You will need: construction paper, marker, photos of yourself (optional)

1. Make a time line like the one shown. Begin with your first birthday. End with your birthday three years from now. Think of a few things you have done. Draw pictures and write about them.
2. Set some goals for what you would like to do in the next three years. Write your goals on the time line.
3. Discuss with someone how you might reach your goals.

How Your Body Grows

Growing begins with cells. **Cells** are the smallest living parts of your body. Your body is made of different kinds of cells. Each kind has a special job. Every day cells divide, or split, to make new cells. You grow when new cells outnumber older cells that die.

In your body, cells that are alike work together in groups called *tissues*. For example, many muscle cells work together as muscle tissue. These tissues make up the muscles that help you bend and move.

Different Kinds of Cells

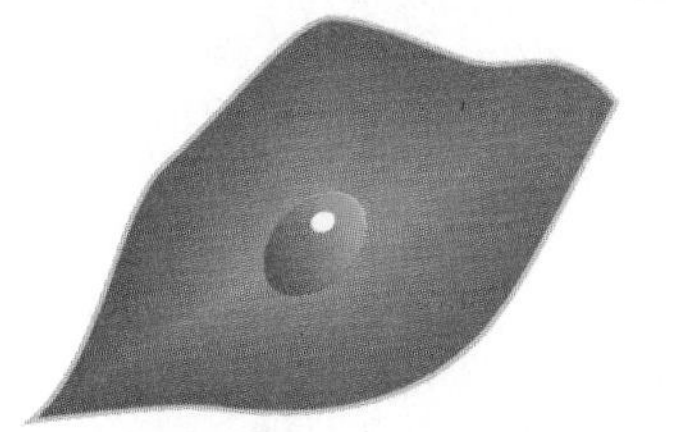

Skin cells cover your body.

Blood cells carry oxygen to all parts of your body.

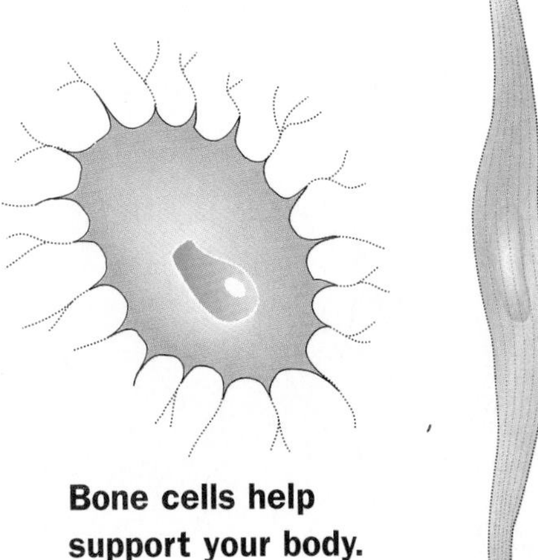

Bone cells help support your body.

Muscle cells help your body move.

Different kinds of tissues also work together. They form *organs* to do special jobs. Your heart, brain, lungs, eyes, and ears are just a few of your organs.

Organs work together in groups, too. These groups make up your *body systems*. Each body system plays an important part in keeping you alive and healthy. In the next few lessons, you will learn about six body systems.

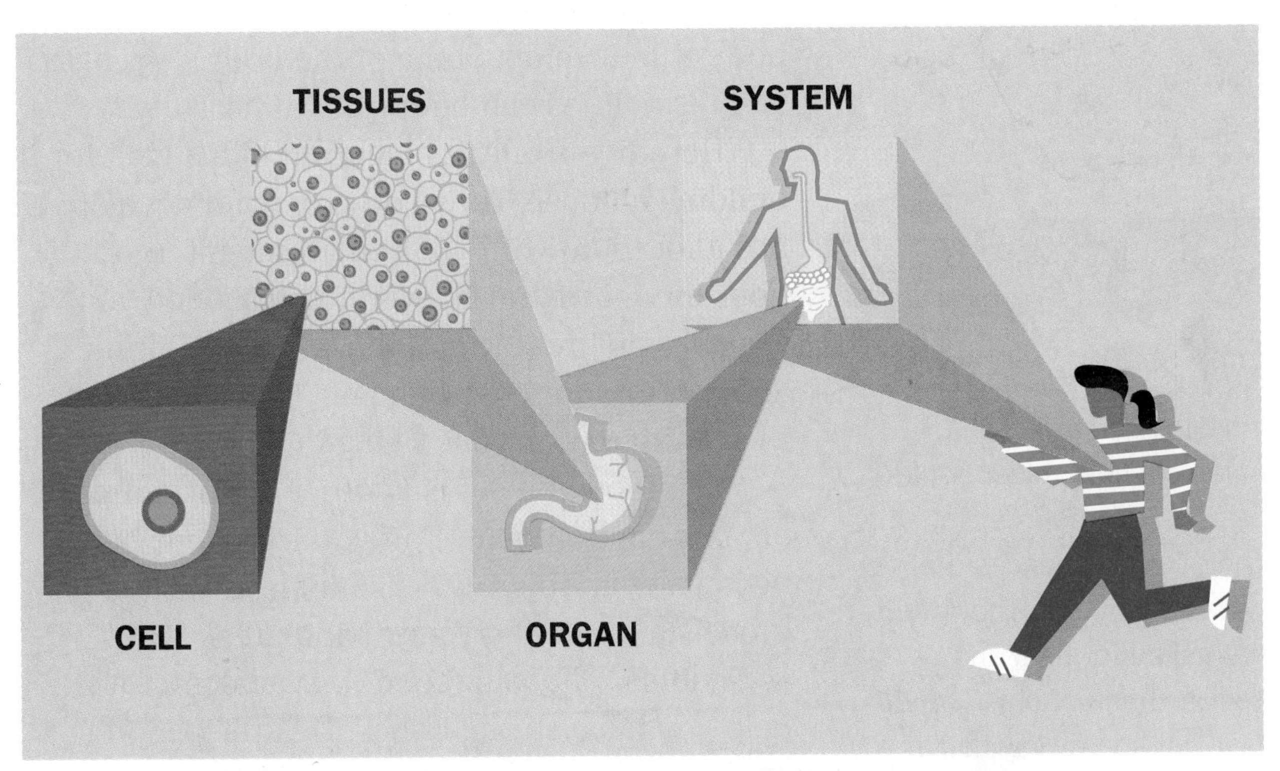

Body systems start with cells. Groups of cells form tissues. Tissues form organs. Organs work with other body parts to form body systems.

HANDBOOK **LIFE SKILLS** pp. 268–279

Eye color and the shape of your face are some of the traits influenced by heredity.

What Affects Growth?

The people in each picture look a lot alike, don't they? If you and some of your relatives look a lot alike, it's because of heredity.

Heredity is the passing of traits from parents to children. A *trait* is something that helps describe you. Your eye color is one of your traits. Other traits include your hair color and the shape of your face. Heredity may affect how tall you will grow. It may affect how your body will develop. Some of the body's strengths and disabilities can be results of heredity.

Heredity is only a blueprint, like a plan for building a house. How you grow and develop has a lot to do with your environment, too. Your **environment** is everything around you. The air you breathe and the water you drink are part of your environment. They can affect the health of everyone living in an area.

The food you eat is another important part of your environment. For example, your bones need calcium to grow. Calcium is in various foods such as milk, yogurt, and green leafy vegetables. Choosing foods with calcium will help you have strong bones. Healthful food choices can help you grow, have enough energy for each day, and think clearly.

Cultural Perspectives

Older Adults

In Native American and Asian cultures, older adults are shown great respect. Their life experiences are valued by others. They often are asked for help and advice. Think of older adults that you know. How could they help you?

People and Your Environment

Your environment includes people, too. Family members, friends, and teachers all play parts in how you grow. For example, you learn about love from a parent. A friend or teacher might teach you about sharing. With their help, your thoughts and feelings can grow. And you affect your growth. Your choices play a big part in how you grow.

Love and support from other people can help you do your best.

MANAGE STRESS

What Would You Do?

Your friend is upset. He's not as tall as some of his classmates. They are teasing him. What could you say to help him?

LESSON WRAP UP

Show What You Know

1. Describe changes that take place as a person grows from an infant to an adult.
2. What is the difference between cells and tissues? Between an organ and a body system?
3. **THINK CRITICALLY** Two third-grade girls were born on the same day to different families. One girl is two inches taller than the other. How could this happen?

Show What You Can Do

4. PORTFOLIO **APPLY HEALTH ACTIVITY** **Set Goals** Write a paragraph about some of the ways you've changed since your last birthday. Then name one goal you would like to reach in the coming year. Describe how you might reach that goal.
5. LIFE SKILL **PRACTICE LIFE SKILLS** **Obtain Help** Decide on a skill you want to become better at. How could you find out what you need to do to improve?

HANDBOOK **LIFE SKILLS** pp. 268–279

LESSON 2

YOUR BONES AND MUSCLES

In this lesson, you will learn:

- why your skeleton is important.
- how bones and muscles work together to move your body.
- why joints are important to movement.

VOCABULARY

skeleton (skel′i tən) the framework of bones that supports the body

joint (joint) a place where two bones meet

QUICK START Cover one hand with the palm of your other hand. Then wiggle the fingers of the hand that is underneath. What does your top hand feel?

Try to picture yourself without any bones. You wouldn't have a backbone or leg bones to hold you up. No skull or ribs would cover your soft insides. You would look very strange—as shapeless as a rag doll!

Your bones work together with muscles. Together they allow you to sit, stand, walk, run, and move in every way. To do this your bones and muscles work together as a "team."

Bones and muscles support the body and allow it to move.

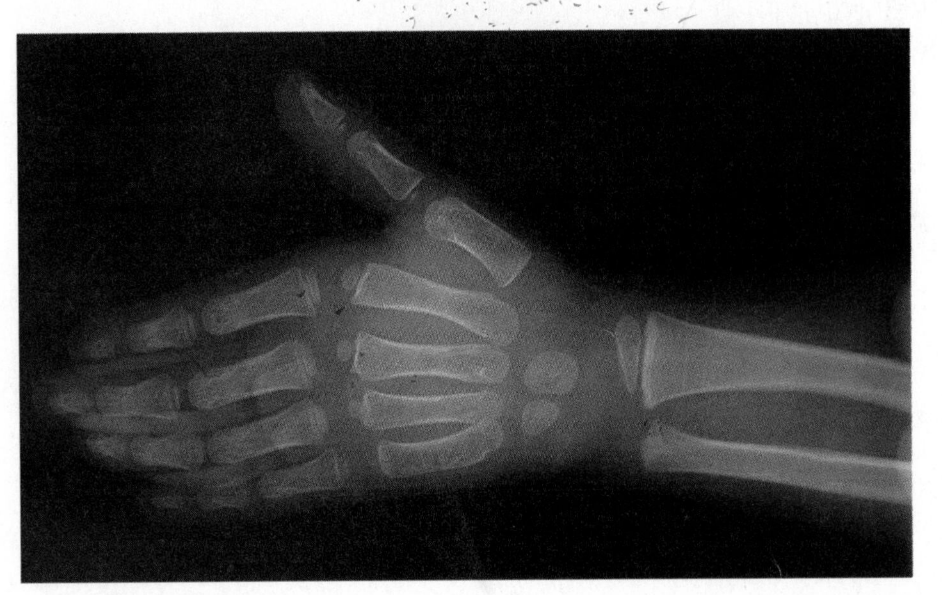

Special machines can take photographs of your bones. Can you feel these or other bones in your own body?

Two Body Systems

The bones of your body make up a framework, your **skeleton**. Your skeleton is a body system, *the skeletal system*, that supports your body. It helps give your body its shape. Bones also protect parts of your body. For example, the bones of the skull protect your brain. The bones that make up your ribs protect your heart and lungs.

Bones work with muscles to help you move. *Muscles* are strong fibers made of muscle tissue. All the muscles in your body make up another body system—your *muscular system*. The muscular and skeletal systems work together so that you can move.

LIFE SKILL

RESOLVE CONFLICTS

What Would You Do?

Your friends are practicing headstands they learned at school. They want you to join in the fun by standing on your head. You've never tried this before. You feel afraid. Why might this be dangerous? How could you resolve this conflict safely?

HANDBOOK LIFE SKILLS pp. 268–279

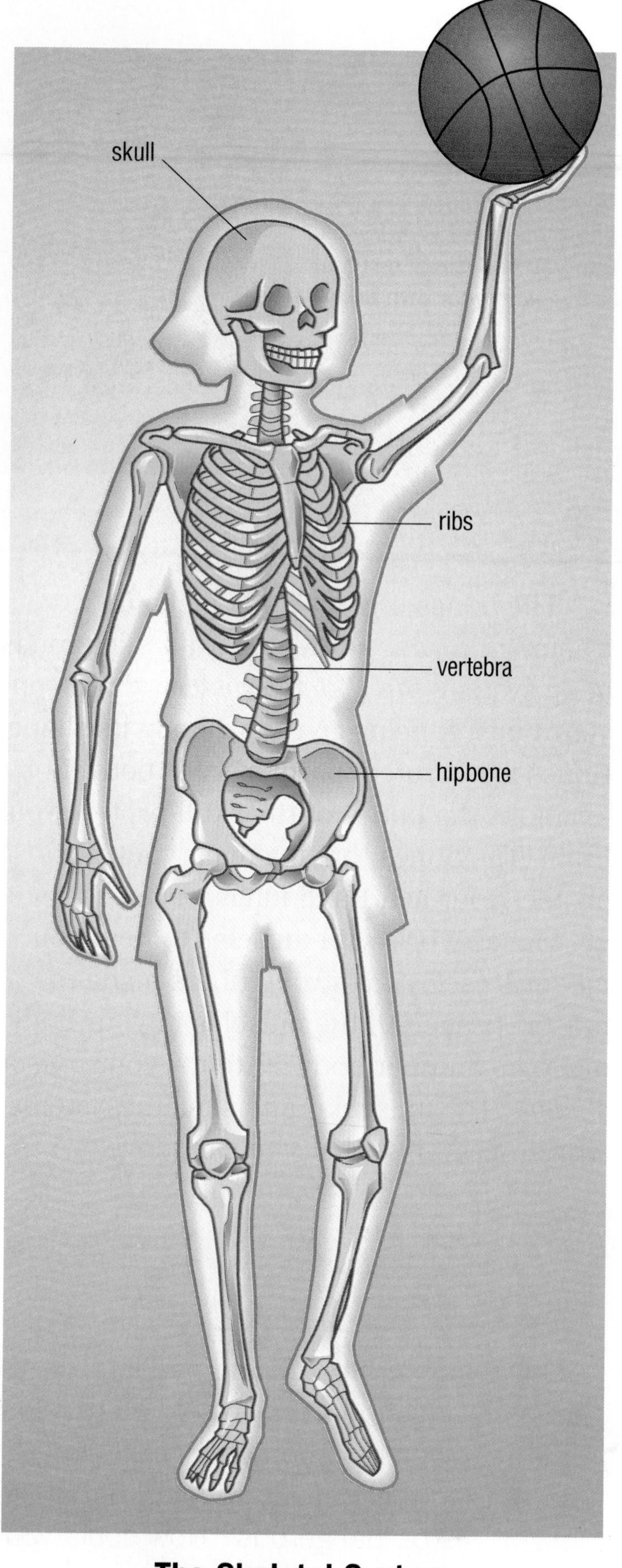

The Skeletal System

Health Fallacy

"An adult and a baby have the same number of bones."

Not true! Most babies are born with 350 bones. As people grow from infants to adults, many of these bones join together. When people stop growing, they usually have 206 bones. Those bones are bigger than a baby's—but a baby still starts out with more.

Working Together for Movement

Not all muscles work with bones. For example, muscles in the walls of the heart work without bones to keep the heart beating.

The muscles that do work with bones are connected to bones. Muscles can pull bones but not push them. So muscles work in pairs to move body parts. As one muscle tightens, the other relaxes. These pictures show that the muscles on the front and back of your upper arm work this way.

HEALTHWISE CONSUMER

Growth Helpers

Some products promise to increase muscle size and strength fast. Be careful! Such drinks and pills can be dangerous. They can cause serious damage to many organs. To grow big and strong safely, exercise every day. Get rest and eat foods low in fat, salt, and sugar.

As you bend your arm, the muscle shown in red shortens to pull up your forearm. The muscle underneath, shown in blue, stays relaxed.

As you straighten your arm, the muscle underneath shortens to pull down your forearm. The muscle on top relaxes.

These are two kinds of joints that help you move.

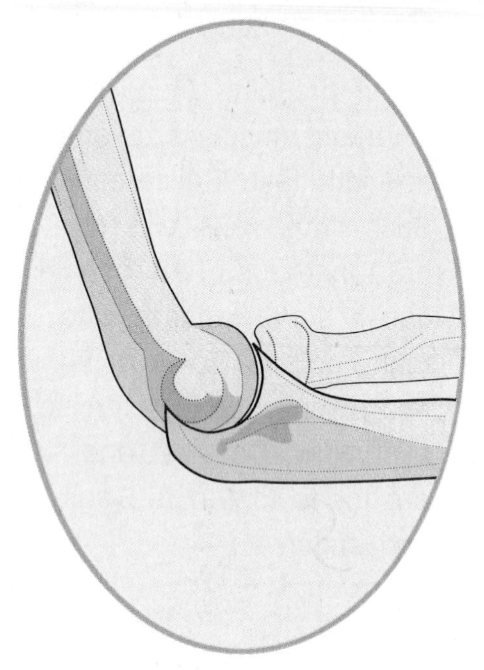

Elbow Joint

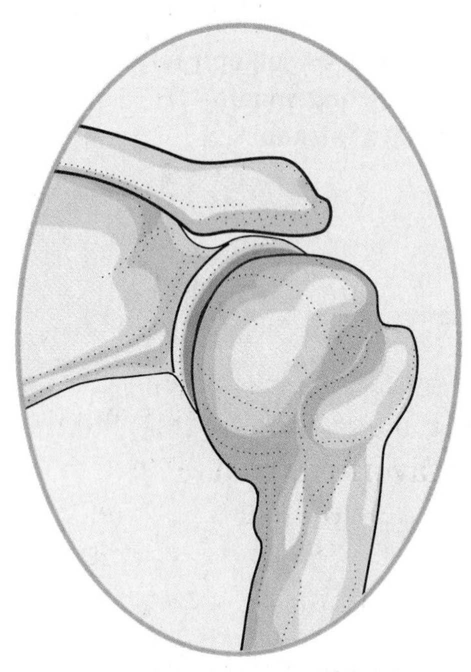

Shoulder Joint

Your Joints

Think about the different ways you can move your body—such as bending and swinging. How is this possible? Bones are hard and solid. They can't bend.

Your body can bend in different ways because it has joints. A **joint** is a place where two bones meet. For example, your elbow is the joint that allows your arm to bend. Your shoulder joint lets you swing your arm. You have joints at your knees, wrists, and jaw, too. Where else do you have joints?

Caring for Your Bones and Muscles

Here's what you can do to help your bones and muscles work their best.

- **Eat healthful foods.** Foods with calcium such as dairy products and leafy green vegetables help keep bones strong. Foods with protein, like meats, beans, and eggs, help keep muscles healthy.

- **Do physical activity safely.** Physical activity keeps your body strong. But bones can break. Muscles can tear. So it's important to know how to work and play safely. It's also important to wear safety equipment to help avoid injury.

- **Keep good posture.** *Posture* is the way you hold your body. Good posture means standing and sitting straight, with your head up and shoulders back. Good posture helps blood flow to all parts of your body—including muscles. Good posture helps your bones and joints stay in place.

HEALTH ACTIVITY

SCIENCE CONNECTION

Joint Study

You will need: large roll of brown paper, paper fasteners, scissors, crayons or markers

1 As a group, trace the body outline of one group member. Cut it out.

2 Cut the outline apart at the large joints. For example, cut the arm apart where it bends at the elbow. Attach the parts together with fasteners to make joints.

3 Take turns posing and then making the body outline match the pose. How are real joints alike and yet different from these?

LESSON WRAP UP

Show What You Know

1. What does the skeletal system do?
2. How do muscles and bones work together to move the body?
3. **THINK CRITICALLY** Pick one of your body's joints. Pretend that you can't use that joint. How would this affect the things you do?

Show What You Can Do

4. PORTFOLIO **APPLY HEALTH ACTIVITY** **Science Connection** Think of your favorite activity. Decide which joints you use to do the activity. Use words or pictures to show the joints you use.
5. LIFE SKILL **PRACTICE LIFE SKILLS** **Set Goals** Set a goal to protect the health of your bones and joints. Describe what you need to do (perhaps each day) to meet your goal.

LESSON 3

YOUR HEART AND LUNGS

In this lesson, you will learn:

- why your heart and lungs are important.
- how blood moves through your body.
- how oxygen gets to and helps different parts of your body.

VOCABULARY

blood vessel (blud ves′əl) a tube that carries blood

oxygen (ok′sə jən) a gas in the air that cells need to stay alive

artery (är′tə rē) a blood vessel that carries blood away from the heart

vein (vān) a blood vessel that carries blood from the body back to the heart

QUICK START You're running so hard that you must stop to catch your breath. Why do you think you breathe harder when you're active?

In Lesson 1, you learned that organs are parts of the body made up of different tissues. Your heart, brain, and lungs are some of your organs. They work all the time, whether you are playing hard or sleeping. They work to keep you alive and healthy.

Each organ has its own job. Organs work together in body systems to carry out large jobs for your body. In this lesson, you will learn about two important body systems.

Your heart and lungs work harder when you exercise.

Your Heart

The heart is made up mostly of muscle tissue. It's a very strong muscle that beats all the time to pump blood throughout the body.

Blood enters and leaves the heart through tubes called **blood vessels**. Blood vessels form a pathway for blood to reach all the cells of your body.

Your heart, blood vessels, and blood are all part of your *circulatory system*. This body system carries blood through the body. Blood carries supplies to all body cells. These supplies include food and oxygen. **Oxygen** is a gas that comes from the air you breathe. Cells need oxygen to live. Blood also carries away wastes made by the body cells.

The picture shows how blood moves through the circulatory system. **Arteries** are blood vessels that carry blood away from the heart. Arteries carry blood that is rich in oxygen. The picture shows arteries in red. **Veins** are blood vessels that carry blood from the body back to the heart. Veins carry blood that is low in oxygen. The picture shows veins in blue.

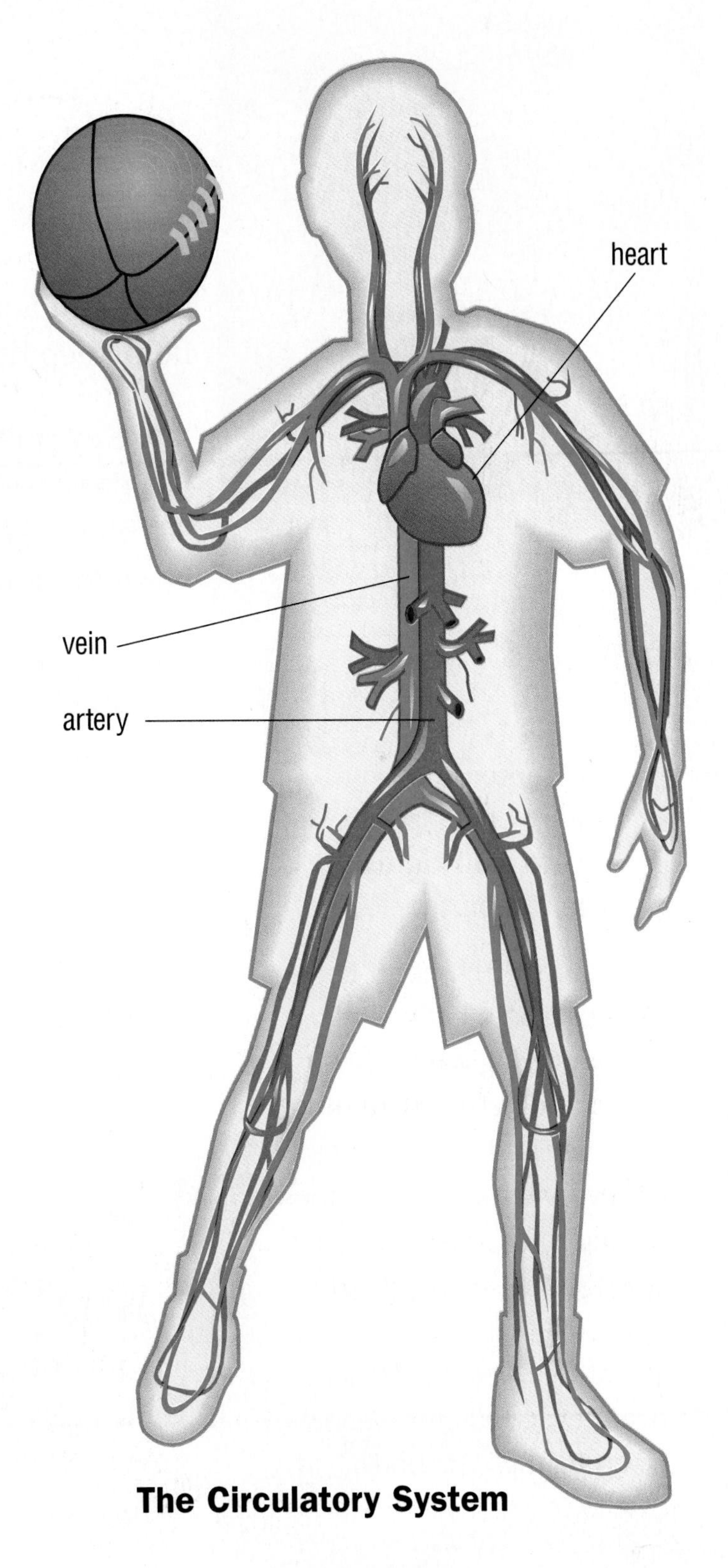

The Circulatory System

Whole grain foods are good for your heart—in fact, for all of your body!

Caring for Your Circulatory System

You need your circulatory system to stay alive and healthy. Here's what you can do to help keep this body system going strong.

- **Get moving.** Walk, run, bike, skate, swim, dance—whatever you like. Just be active. Being physically active makes your heart and blood vessels stronger.
- **Eat healthful foods.** A variety of foods like fruits, vegetables, bread, pasta, rice, milk, and meats will help your heart. Avoid salty and fatty foods. Foods low in fat and salt help keep blood flowing smoothly through the blood vessels.
- **Don't smoke.** Avoid places with smoke-filled air, too. The smoke from tobacco can cause heart disease. A diseased heart can't pump blood as well as a healthy heart.

HEALTH FACT

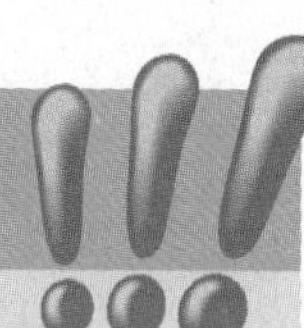

"A person's heart beats about 70 to 100 times each minute."

That's right! The heart beats for a person's entire life without taking a rest. But it beats at different speeds for all of us, at different times of our lives. If it beats 90 times a minute for a person, that's 5,400 beats an hour and 129,600 beats a day! While you are active, your heart beats even faster to send blood through the body quickly.

LIFE SKILL

RESOLVE CONFLICTS

What Would You Do?

Your friend insists on watching sports on television all afternoon each Saturday. You would rather play sports. How could you resolve this conflict?

Your Lungs

Your lungs are two large organs, one on each side of your chest. They take in air when you breathe in. The lungs are soft and feel something like a sponge. They are protected by your ribs. Many blood vessels run through each lung.

The picture below shows the *respiratory system*—the organs that help you breathe and use the air you take in. When you take a breath, air travels through your nose or mouth. It goes down your *windpipe* and into your lungs. The air contains oxygen, the gas your cells need.

When the air gets into the lungs, oxygen passes into very tiny blood vessels. As your heart beats, this oxygen-rich blood is carried to cells throughout your body.

After oxygen is used by body cells, a waste gas called *carbon dioxide* is produced. The blood carries this waste gas to your lungs. When you breathe out, carbon dioxide leaves your lungs.

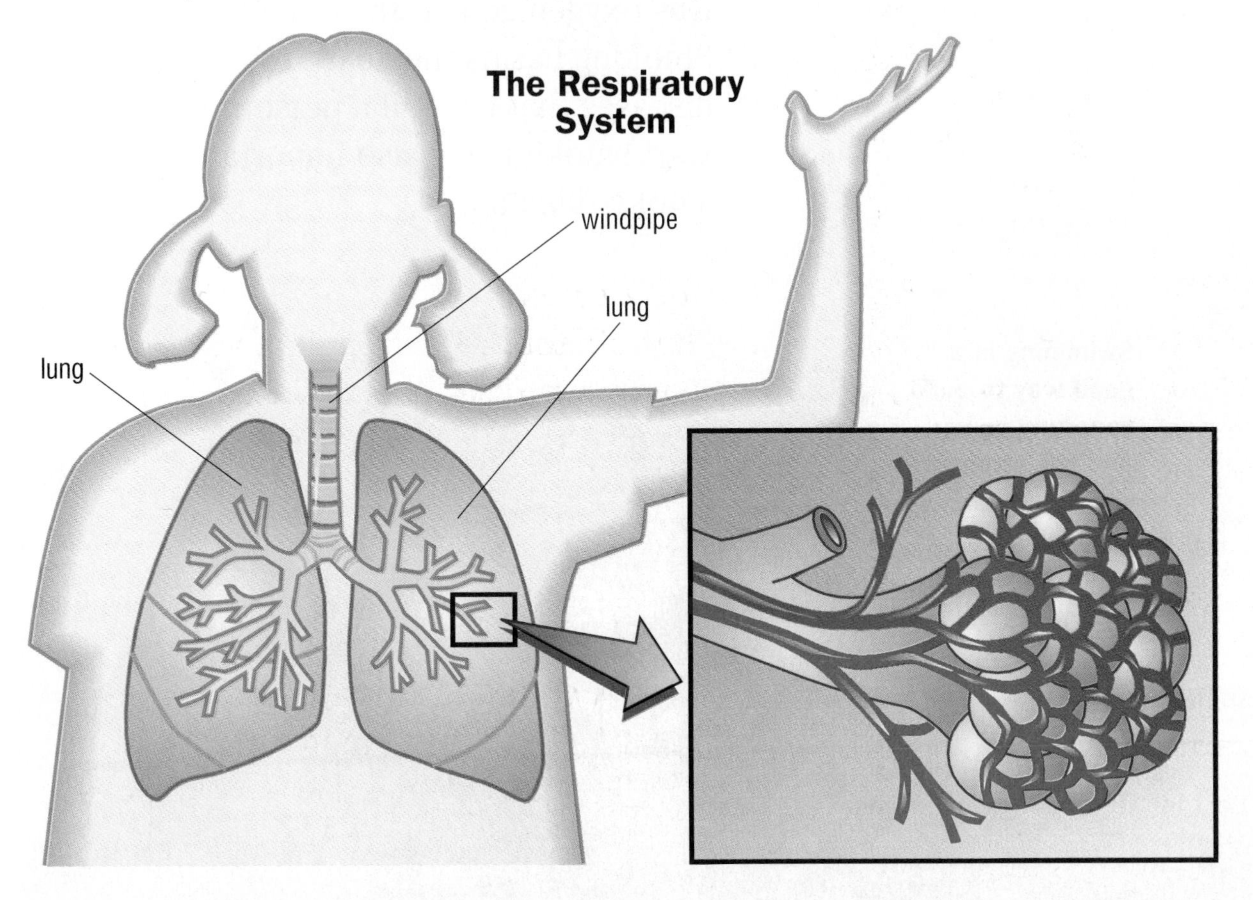

Caring for Your Respiratory System

You need to keep your respiratory system healthy so that your body gets the oxygen it needs.

- **Keep active.** You know that being active can help keep your heart in shape. Physical activity can keep your lungs in top condition, too. So try to spend some time each day doing a physical activity that you enjoy.
- **Get enough rest and sleep.** Being active is important, but so are sleep and rest. So rest after physical activity. Get enough sleep, too. It will help your respiratory system. In fact, it will help your entire body.
- **Don't smoke.** Smoking damages the lungs and makes breathing harder. That means that less oxygen gets to the lungs. And less oxygen gets to the rest of the body. Smoking harms the heart, too. It causes diseases that can kill a person. So don't start smoking. It's also important to avoid smoke-filled air.

Swimming is a good way to build your lung power. And the stronger your lungs are, the longer you can swim!

HEALTH ACTIVITY

Saying "No" to Smoking

PRACTICE REFUSAL SKILLS

You will need: construction paper, colored pens, scissors, paste

1 Smoking often starts by trying "just one cigarette." Think of ways to persuade young people to refuse the offer of a cigarette.

2 Create a poster that shows how to say "no" to smoking. Be sure to state the health of your heart and lungs. State how smoking can affect your growth.

3 Share your finished work with your classmates.

LESSON WRAP UP

Show What You Know

1. What do the heart and lungs do?
2. How does blood move through the body?
3. **THINK CRITICALLY** Why does it take both the circulatory and respiratory systems working together to get oxygen to all parts of the body?

Show What You Can Do

4. PORTFOLIO **APPLY HEALTH ACTIVITY** **Practice Refusal Skills** Write a letter persuading someone not to smoke. In your letter let that person know about the harmful effects of smoking on the heart and lungs.

5. LIFE SKILL **PRACTICE LIFE SKILLS** **Obtain Help** A friend wants to become physically fit. How can she find out what physical activities to do?

HANDBOOK **LIFE SKILLS** pp. 268–279

LESSON 4

YOUR DIGESTIVE SYSTEM

In this lesson, you will learn:

- why digestion is important.
- about the parts of your body that digest food.
- what happens to food as it is digested.

VOCABULARY

digestion (di jes′chən) the process that breaks down food into a form that the body can use

stomach (stum′ək) an organ whose walls are made of strong muscles that churn and mash food

small intestine (smôl in tes′tin) tubelike organ where most digestion happens and is completed

large intestine (lärj in tes′tin) the organ that removes water from undigested food

QUICK START Think about a juicy red apple. Suppose that you are about to bite into it. What happens in your mouth just by thinking of an apple? Why is this important?

Your body needs energy to stay alive, grow, and develop. You get this energy from the foods you eat. But first, food needs to be broken down into a form the body can use. This process is called **digestion**. In this lesson, you will find out what happens to food as it is digested.

Your body uses food for energy, growth, and development.

Digestion Begins

Your body needs food for energy and growth. Many body parts and organs work together to help your body use food. Together they make up your *digestive system.*

Digestion begins in your mouth when you bite food. Your teeth grind food into small pieces. As you chew, food mixes with saliva. *Saliva* is a liquid in your mouth. It helps soften and break down food. You may feel saliva fill in your mouth when you think of a tasty food—when your mouth "waters."

When you swallow, food moves down a muscular tube to the stomach. The **stomach** is an organ whose walls are made of strong muscles. Stomach muscles churn and mash the food. At the same time, juices in the stomach break down some of the food. By the time food leaves the stomach, it is a soupy mixture.

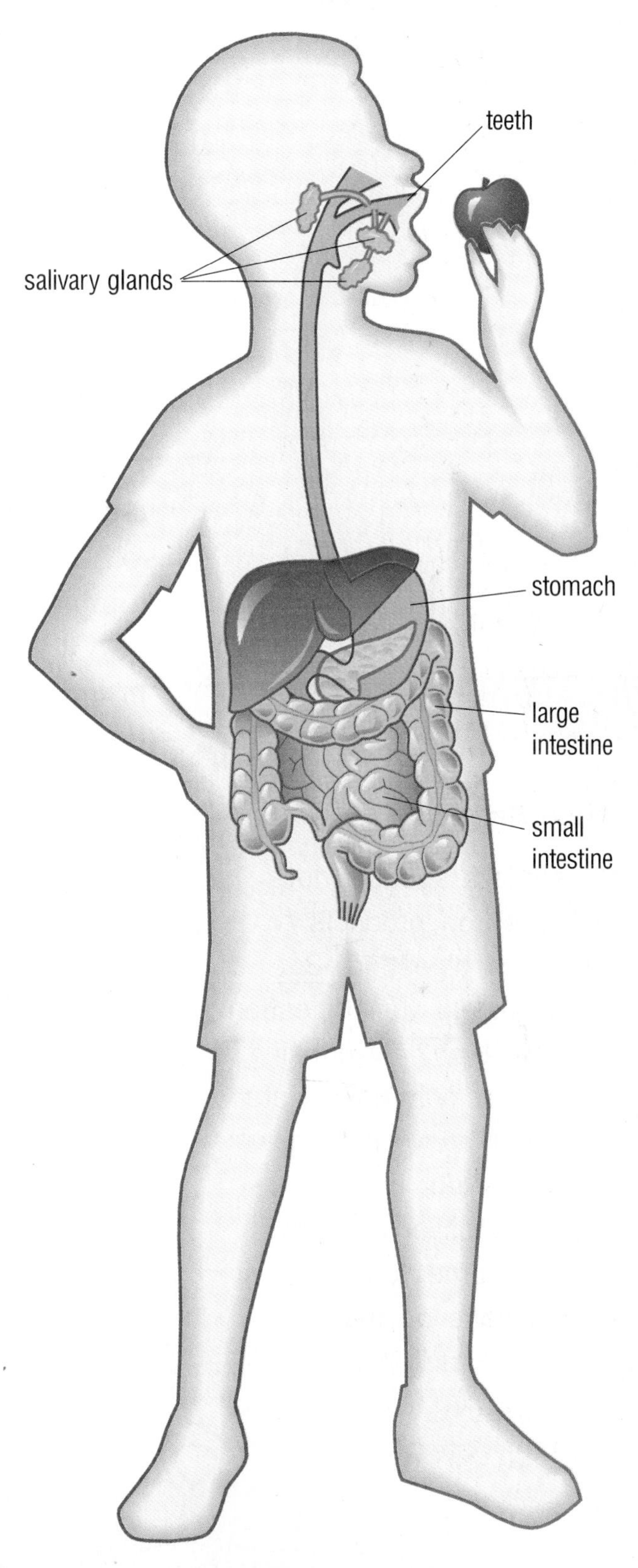

The Digestive System

LIFE SKILL

MAKE DECISIONS

What Would You Do?

Some of your classmates "goof off" at the lunch table. They have food races to be the first to finish lunch. They seem to have a great time. Should you join them? Explain.

Digestion Continues

After food leaves the stomach, it moves to the **small intestine**. This tubelike organ fits into the body in loops. Most digestion takes place in the small intestine.

The small intestine's job is to finish breaking down food. Digested food moves through the walls of the small intestine. It passes into tiny blood vessels in the walls. Blood then carries it to every cell.

Not all the food in the small intestine is used by the body. For example, stringy parts of some fruits and vegetables cannot be digested completely. The undigested food passes, along with water, into the **large intestine**. In the large intestine, the water is removed from the undigested food. What's left is solid waste. It is pushed along by muscles in the walls of the intestine until it leaves the body.

HealthWise Consumer

It's a Bargain!

Consumers spend a lot of money on products to help their digestion. But you can help your digestion for free. How? By drinking water! Not only does water help your body break down food, but your body needs it to stay alive and grow. So, next time you're thirsty, pass on the soda. Pick up the best bargain around—water.

Caring for Your Digestive System

Here are some tips for keeping your digestive system healthy.

- Eat fresh fruits and vegetables every day. They help move waste through the digestive system.
- Chew carefully and thoroughly. Careful chewing and swallowing keeps food from going down the windpipe. If food gets into the windpipe, a person can choke.
- Have regular mealtimes each day. That way, you help your digestion work on schedule.
- Drink eight glasses of water a day.

HEALTH ACTIVITY

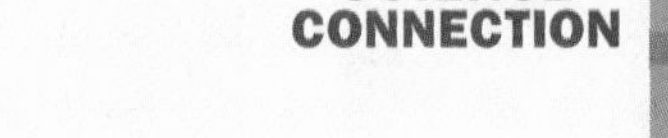

SCIENCE CONNECTION

Dinner Tour

You will need: any props that your group chooses

1. Form four groups. Choose one part of the digestive system that your group would like to represent.
2. Together, create a skit. Show how food passes through your part of the digestive system. Think of it as a "Dinner Tour." One person acts as the Tour Guide. Others act out what happens to food at that point.
3. Groups present their skits in the order that food passes through the digestive system.

LESSON WRAP UP

Show What You Know

1. Why do we need a digestive system?
2. Name the main parts of the digestive system. What does each do?
3. **THINK CRITICALLY** How do the digestive system and circulatory system work together?

Show What You Can Do

4. PORTFOLIO **APPLY HEALTH ACTIVITY** **Science Connection** Make a booklet about digestion. On separate pages list parts of the digestive system. Briefly explain what each part does.
5. LIFE SKILL **PRACTICE LIFE SKILLS** **Manage Stress** Everyone is rushing to do something after dinner. The family is too busy to relax. How might this stress affect digestion? What might everyone do to relax?

HANDBOOK LIFE SKILLS pp. 268–279

LESSON

5 YOUR NERVOUS SYSTEM AND SENSES

In this lesson, you will learn:

- why your brain, nerves, and senses are important.
- how your brain receives and sends messages.

VOCABULARY

brain (brān) the main organ of the nervous system; the command center of your thoughts and actions

nerve cell (nûrv sel) a cell that carries messages between the brain and all parts of the body

spinal cord (spī′nəl kôrd) a long bundle of nerves that stretch down your back from your brain

QUICK START Close your eyes. Can you still tell what is going on around you? How? Now open them and cup your hands over your ears. Can you still tell what is going on around you? How?

Your sight and hearing are only two of your senses. The other three are touch, taste, and smell. These five senses give you information about the world around you. That information is received by one main organ—an organ that puts it all together for you. That main organ, which receives information from your senses, is your brain. Your **brain** is the command center of your thoughts and actions.

Your brain receives information about the world from each of your five senses.

Parts of Your Nervous System

The brain is the main organ of your *nervous system*. The nervous system allows your thoughts, actions, and emotions to work together. Your brain controls things you think about doing, such as speaking and moving. Your brain also controls things that you do automatically. For example, it controls your breathing and heartbeat.

To do all this, the brain receives and sends out messages. It works with nerves. *Nerves* are long, thin bundles of nerve cells. **Nerve cells** carry messages between the brain and all parts of the body.

Your nervous system works with your *sense organs*—your eyes, ears, nose, skin, and tongue. They help you see, hear, smell, touch, and taste things. *Sensory nerve cells* carry messages from your sense organs to the brain. The brain quickly figures out these messages and tells your body how to respond.

Your sense organs also help you stay safe. Suppose you're crossing the street. You hear a car horn. Nerve cells in your ear send a message to the brain. The brain realizes danger. It sends back a message—look out!

Messages travel to and from the brain along the spinal cord. The **spinal cord** is a long bundle of nerves that stretch down your back from your brain. Your spinal cord is protected by your backbone or spine.

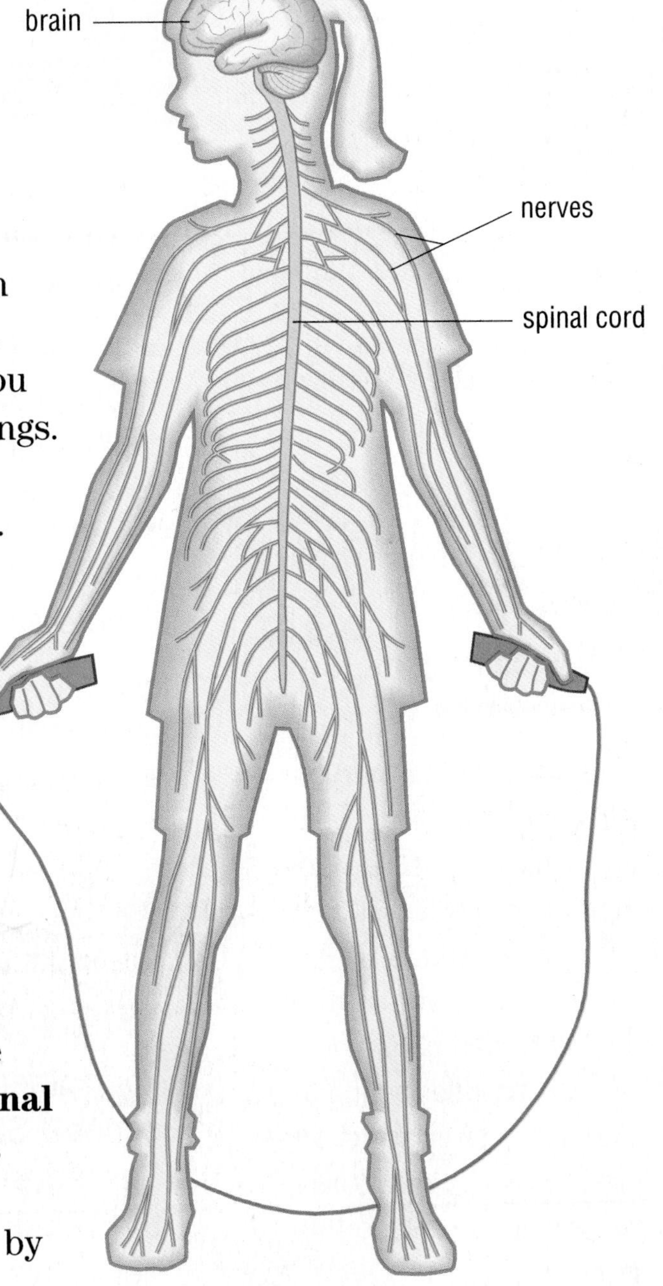

The Nervous System

Your brain and your nervous system process a lot of information, every minute of the day.

Caring for Your Nervous System

Your nervous system performs hundreds of functions. Keep it healthy.

- Protect your head and spinal cord. If you do an activity that uses a helmet, wear one. When you ride in a car, wear a safety belt.
- Never look directly at the sun or bright light. It can damage your eyes. Avoid loud noises to protect your ears.
- Get enough physical activity, rest, and sleep.
- Do not use alcohol. Never touch illegal drugs. They can harm your nervous system.

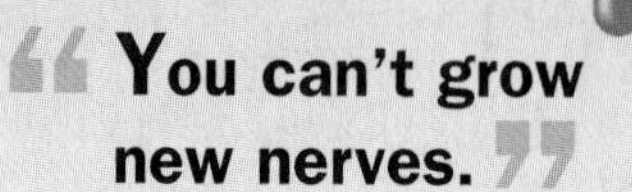

HEALTH FACT

"You can't grow new nerves."

This is true. All the nerves you'll ever have are in your body at birth. When a nerve is damaged or dies, it's gone forever. That's why an injury to the nerves in the spinal cord can cause someone to lose feeling in his or her legs or arms. The injured person can't grow new nerves to replace the damaged ones.

MAKE DECISIONS

What Would You Do?

Your older sister is driving you to school. She doesn't wear a safety belt. She says she doesn't need to because the ride is short. How can you convince her to wear one?

INFOGRAPHIC

The Nervous System at Work

The brain, spinal cord, and nerves work like a telephone system. Nerves run through your entire body. They receive and send messages. Here's how the nervous system helps you cross the street.

You are out walking, and you are coming close to a corner. Suddenly the traffic light blinks DON'T WALK. Nerves in your eyes receive the information. The nerves, in turn, send this information to the brain.

DON'T WALK

DON'T WALK

The brain receives the information. It understands that the information is a warning. It sends a message to your muscles to react to what you see.

You react. Your muscles work so that you stop quickly at the curb. You wait for the next WALK light to blink.

HEALTH ACTIVITY

Plan Ahead for Safety

SET GOALS

1 Work with a partner. List some situations in which your senses help you learn of danger.

2 For each situation, think about what you could do ahead of time to keep safe. For example, your senses can let you know if there is a fire. You could plan ahead to know how to exit your home, school, and other buildings safely.

3 Together, set a "plan ahead" goal for safety. Share your goal with the class.

LESSON WRAP UP

Show What You Know

1. Why are the brain, nerves, and spinal cord important?

2. Your pet dog greets you at your door. What do you do? How do your brain and nerves work together when you react?

3. **THINK CRITICALLY** How could damage to the spinal cord change the way the body works?

Show What You Can Do

4. PORTFOLIO **APPLY HEALTH ACTIVITY** **Set Goals** Make a poster. Label it "I'll Keep My Senses Safe." Use your poster to help classmates pay attention to ways they can protect eyes, ears, and skin from harm.

5. LIFE SKILL **PRACTICE LIFE SKILLS** **Make Decisions** Your best friend lends you her in-line skates. You've never tried them before. Decide what you should do to protect your nervous system.

HANDBOOK LIFE SKILLS pp. 268–279

YOU CAN MAKE A DIFFERENCE

CAREERS

X-ray Technician

Jackie West, X-ray Technician

Q: When do people need X-rays?

Ms. West: People who have an illness or injury sometimes need X-rays. For example, they might have a lung or stomach illness or an injury caused by a bicycle or car crash. Also, some people have X-rays as part of a checkup, to check for cancer or other diseases.

Q: What can an X-ray tell you about bones?

Ms. West: An X-ray can tell me whether a bone is broken or not. It can also show whether a bone has separated from another bone at a joint. For example, an X-ray image will show if an elbow has popped out of its joint.

Q: What did you study to become an X-ray technician?

Ms. West: I studied anatomy and physics as well as basics such as English and math. I also studied radiology, which is the science of how X-rays work.

SCIENCE CONNECTION

WHAT'S INSIDE?

X-rays aren't the only way to look inside the body. Find out about some new methods such as CAT scans or MRI scans. Prepare a brief report to present to other students in your class.

CHAPTER

2 REVIEW

VOCABULARY

Write the word or words from the list that best complete each sentence.

artery
cell
large intestine
skeleton
small intestine
spinal cord
stomach
vein

1. The smallest living part of the body is a(n) __?__. (Lesson 1)
2. The framework of bones that supports your body is your __?__. (Lesson 2)
3. The blood vessel that carries blood away from the heart is known as a(n) __?__. (Lesson 3)
4. Most digestion happens and is completed in the __?__. (Lesson 4)
5. The __?__ is a long bundle of nerves that travels inside the spine to the brain. (Lesson 5)

REVIEW HEALTH IDEAS

Use your knowledge of growth and development from Chapter 2 to answer the following questions.

1. What stages of growth and development do people go through after being born? (Lesson 1)
2. Explain how a body system is made out of cells. (Lesson 1)
3. How is a skeleton necessary to your body? (Lesson 2)
4. How do the muscles and bones work together when you move? (Lesson 2)
5. What does the circulatory system do? (Lesson 3)
6. Why are lungs necessary for you to live? (Lesson 3)
7. What are the main parts of the digestive system? (Lesson 4)
8. What part of the digestion process takes place in the large intestine? (Lesson 4)
9. What is the job of sense organs? (Lesson 5)
10. How do messages travel from the hand to the brain when you stroke your pet cat? (Lesson 5)

APPLY HEALTH IDEAS

1. Describe a scene in which you would use all five of your senses. (Lesson 5)
2. How do your lungs and heart get oxygen to the rest of your body? (Lesson 3)
3. What happens to your breakfast after you chew and swallow it? (Lesson 4)
4. PORTFOLIO **MAKE DECISIONS** Work with a small group to plan a skit about wearing a helmet when biking or skating. Include in your skit someone who says, "Helmets are for babies." (Lesson 2)
5. LIFE SKILL **SET GOALS** Write a story about yourself as you grow and change from infancy through adulthood. Include goals about what you would like to reach at each stage. (Lesson 1)

What can you do at home to keep your body systems healthy?

Make a list like the one shown. Compare the list to what you do now. What can you and your family do to improve the health of your body systems?

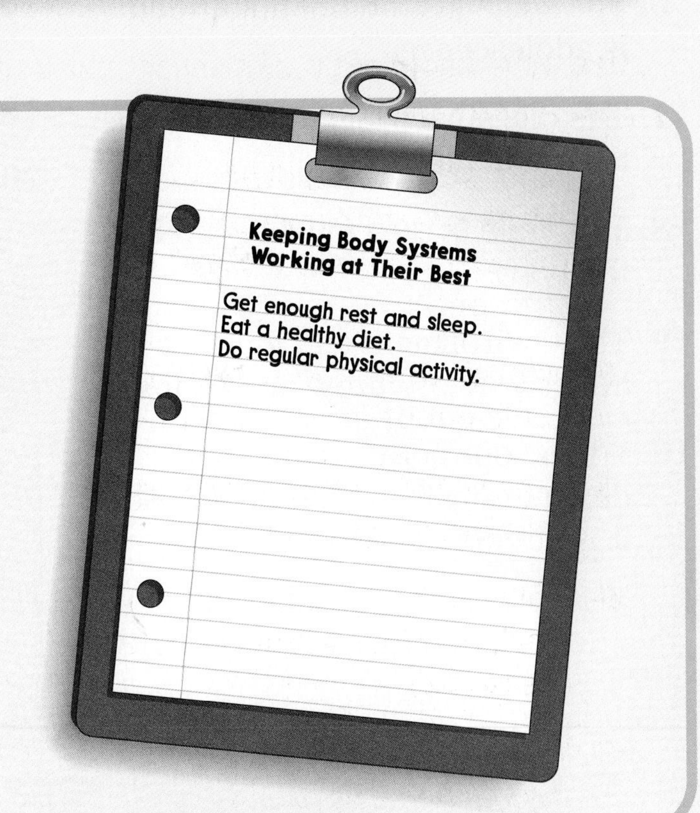
Keeping Body Systems Working at Their Best

Get enough rest and sleep.
Eat a healthy diet.
Do regular physical activity.

CHAPTER

2 TEST

Write True or False for each statement. If false, change the underlined word or phrase to make it true.

1. The heart and lungs work together to bring food to all parts of the body.
2. Your body needs a skeleton for shape or support.
3. Your heart, brain, and lungs, are some of your organs.
4. Messages travel to and from the brain along the sense organs.
5. The main job of the heart is to make blood for the body.
6. The stage just before adulthood is adolescence.
7. The digestive process begins in the small intestine.
8. The brain is the control center of the body.
9. The environment and muscles affect how you grow and change.
10. When your body breaks food down into a form that it can use, it is circulating that food.

Write a sentence to answer each question.

11. How does the brain receive and respond to information from the senses?
12. Name three ways you change from infancy to adolescence.
13. How do your bones and muscles work when you bend your arm?
14. Why should you chew food well?
15. Why do you need a clean, safe environment?

16–17. What is a joint? Name two places in your body where you have joints.

18. Name two ways to protect your nervous system.
19. What do veins and arteries do?
20. What happens to food after it leaves the stomach?

Performance Assessment

Suppose that you throw a ball. How are your brain, nerves, muscles, and bones all at work? Why can you throw a ball farther now than you could when you were one year old?

CHAPTER 3

Emotional and Intellectual Health

THE BIG IDEA

Healthy people:

- feel good about themselves.
- get along with others.
- manage stress.

Chapter Contents

1 Learning About Yourself 62

2 Getting Along With Others 66

3 Emotions and Conflict 70

4 Managing Stress 74

You Can Make a Difference: Shower Your Stress Away 79

Chapter Review 80

Chapter Test 82

LESSON 1

LEARNING ABOUT YOURSELF

In this lesson, you will learn:

- healthy ways to think about yourself.
- what it means to feel good about who you are.
- ways to improve your self-esteem.

VOCABULARY

self-concept (self′ kon′sept) the picture that comes to mind when you think about yourself

personality (pûr′sə nal′i tē) everything that makes you a special person, such as things you do, think, and feel

emotion (i mō′shən) strong feeling that affects the things you do

self-esteem (self′e stēm′) how good you feel about who you are

QUICK START What would you say if someone asked you to describe yourself? What are the first three words that come to mind?

How did you answer the Quick Start? A word such as "student" tells who you are to other people. "Singer" or "catcher" tell about things you do. "Happy" and "kind" show how you feel about yourself.

Knowing and liking yourself are important parts of being healthy. You can find out how well you know yourself. You can also decide how you feel about yourself. Both are important.

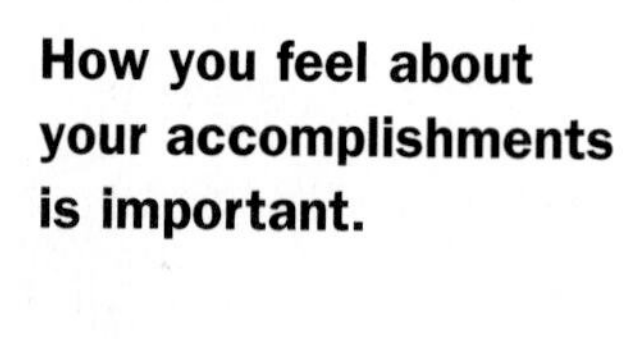

How you feel about your accomplishments is important.

Your Self-Concept

You probably look at yourself in a mirror every day. But you can also look at yourself without a mirror. Think about who you are. A picture of yourself comes to mind. That picture is your **self-concept**.

Your self-concept is made up of many parts. A large part comes from your personality. Your **personality** is everything that makes you a special person. It includes how and what you think, do, and feel. Here are some ways you might describe your personality.

"I have a good sense of humor."

"I'm a hard worker."

"I like being with my friends."

Part of your self-concept is knowing your strengths and weaknesses. A *strength* is something you do well. A *weakness* is something you do not do well. Maybe math and drawing are some of your strengths. Maybe spelling and ice skating are two of your weaknesses. You don't have to be the best at everything. What is important is doing the very best you can.

Your emotions are also part of your self-concept. An **emotion** is a strong feeling that affects the things you do. Love, fear, anger, pride, sadness, and joy are emotions. Look at the picture on page 62. What emotions do you think this girl is feeling? How can you tell?

CULTURAL PERSPECTIVES

"A smiling face dispels unhappiness."

This saying comes from the Hausa people of West Africa. To *dispel* something means to make it go away. Has someone's smile ever driven away your sadness and made you feel better? Around the world, a smile shows emotion. What are the Hausa saying about the power of a smile?

What words might this boy use about himself?

Your Self-Esteem

How you feel about yourself is what **self-esteem** is all about. If you feel good about who you are, your self-esteem is high. You feel that you matter. You feel that people like you for who you are. You feel healthy.

If you don't like yourself very much, your self-esteem is low. You may feel unhappy. What can you do if your self-esteem is low? Here are some ways to improve your self-esteem.

- Think about what your friends like about you. This makes it easier to like yourself.
- Don't be too hard on yourself. Concentrate on what you do well.
- Be nice to other people. Help out at home and at school.
- Most important, care about yourself!

Having high self-esteem is important for your health. If you like yourself, you will take good care of yourself. You will probably eat food that is good for you. You will avoid doing dangerous things. If your self-esteem is high, you will do things the best way you can.

MAKE DECISIONS

What Would You Do?

You're entering a contest. The entry form says, "Write one sentence about who you are." What things might you want to write? Which one thing would you choose?

HEALTH ACTIVITY

A Self-Esteem Contract

LIFE SKILL **SET GOALS**

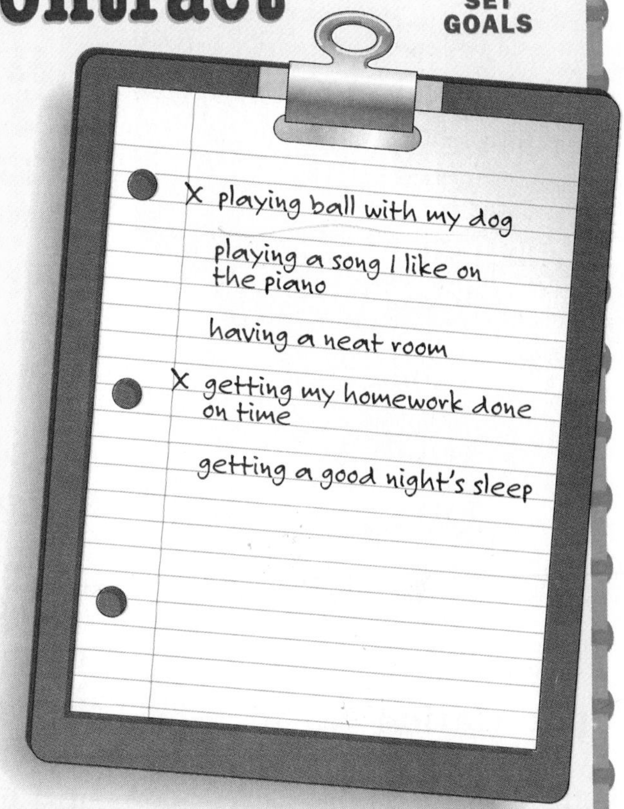

1. On your paper, list several activities that give you a good feeling about yourself. For example, "I like playing the piano."
2. Read your list. Choose two activities that you could do better or more often. Put an "X" next to them.
3. Set a goal by making a contract with yourself. Write this statement: "This week, I will feel good about myself. I will _____ and _____." Fill in the blanks with your two activities. Then keep that promise!

LESSON WRAP UP

Show What You Know

1. Name two parts of a person's self-concept. Explain what each part means.
2. Why is it important to have high self-esteem?
3. **THINK CRITICALLY** Your friend says, "I'm bad at sports. I'm bad at everything." How can you help him think differently about himself?

Show What You Can Do

4. PORTFOLIO **APPLY HEALTH ACTIVITY** **Set Goals** Keep a health notebook. Each week set a goal to do an activity that improves your self-esteem.
5. LIFE SKILL **PRACTICE LIFE SKILLS** **Obtain Help** Sometimes you don't feel good about yourself. Sharing your feelings with someone you trust can help. List two people you could talk to about such feelings. Why would each be a good choice?

HANDBOOK LIFE SKILLS pp. 268–279

LESSON 2

Getting Along With Others

In this lesson, you will learn:

- how to show appreciation and consideration toward other people.
- how to cooperate with family, friends, and classmates.

VOCABULARY

appreciation (ə prē′shē ā′shən) feeling that everyone is special and important

consideration (kən sid′ə rā′shən) thinking about other people and their feelings

cooperation (kō op′ə rā′shən) working together

QUICK START "You promised to wash the dog," your mother reminds you. How could working with a friend or a family member make this job easier and more fun?

It's great to play with friends, or go on a family outing, or work on a group project. Doing things with other people can be a lot of fun! Working together can make jobs easier or faster to do.

Working and playing together well don't just happen, though. People who get along well have the best times. They have good feelings about each other. They listen to each other. They share. They are glad to be together.

Working together can make chores more fun!

Appreciation and Consideration

Life would be pretty boring if everyone were just the same. But no two people are exactly alike. People come in different ages, sizes, shapes, and colors.

An important part of getting along with other people is valuing their differences. This is called **appreciation**—the feeling that someone or something is special or important. Appreciation is important at home, at school, and at play.

You can show appreciation by treating people with **consideration**. That is, you make it clear that their feelings are important to you. A great way to show consideration is to tell people that you appreciate them. Listening to parents is another good example of consideration. So is being interested in new classmates and sharing things you like with friends.

Wherever you go, try to appreciate others. Show people consideration. If you treat others well, they will probably treat you well. And if you treat others well, you'll feel good about yourself.

LIFE SKILL

RESOLVE CONFLICTS

What Would You Do?

You are trying to finish your homework. Your little sister asks you to help her with a puzzle. Your first thought is "No! Go away, I'm busy." What considerate thing might you say instead?

HEALTHWISE CONSUMER

Winning the Game—Together

Many games we play are competitive. *Competitive* means "me" against "you." For someone to win, someone else has to lose. These games can be fun. But other kinds of activities can be fun, too. In some activities, players work together. You can put on a skit, work on a puzzle, or play a word game together. With these activities, everybody wins.

HANDBOOK LIFE SKILLS pp. 268–279

Cooperation

Cooperation, or working together, is part of many activities. Family members cooperate when they share household chores. Teammates cooperate to play softball or soccer. When else do people cooperate?

Here are some cooperation skills. Use them the next time you work with others.

- **Make a plan together.** Decide with others what you need to do. Agree on the steps you should follow.
- **Listen to the other person or people.** Be fair by giving everyone a chance to talk. Pay attention when others are speaking.
- **Be careful about what you say.** Appreciation and consideration are important to cooperation. If you don't like other people's ideas, don't make fun of them. Instead, explain what you think the problem is. Offer a solution. And if you like an idea, say so!
- **Share the work.** Some people can do certain jobs better than others. Everyone can do something to help.

An old saying, "Many hands make light work," has to do with cooperation.

HEALTH ACTIVITY

Cooperation Checkup

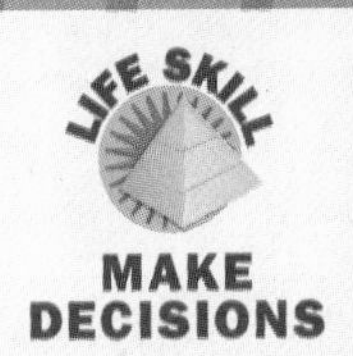

You will need: poster board, markers

1 Work in small groups. Use your cooperation skills. Decide whether to create a poster or prepare a news program about something you think is important.

2 Decide how you will get your project done. What do you need to do? Who will do it?

3 When your project is finished, talk about it. Which cooperation skills did you use the most?

LESSON WRAP UP

Show What You Know

1. How might you show consideration and appreciation for a classmate who has broken her leg? Give three examples.

2. Name two cooperation skills.

3. **THINK CRITICALLY** Suppose a student said, "I won't work in a group. I don't want anyone telling me what to do." What might you say to change the student's mind?

Show What You Can Do

4. PORTFOLIO **APPLY HEALTH ACTIVITY** **Make Decisions** Write a short paragraph. Tell about a time you and a group of friends cooperated to make a decision together.

5. LIFE SKILL **PRACTICE LIFE SKILLS** **Set Goals** Set a goal to show appreciation to someone who is important to you. For example, you could write a letter or draw a greeting card. How do you think the person will feel?

HANDBOOK **LIFE SKILLS** pp. 268–279

LESSON 3

EMOTIONS AND CONFLICT

In this lesson, you will learn:

- healthful ways to show emotions.
- about conflicts and how they make people feel.
- healthful ways to resolve conflicts.

VOCABULARY

conflict (kon′flikt) a struggle or disagreement between people or ideas

resolve (ri zolv′) to settle a problem or conflict

apologize (ə pol′ə jīz′) to admit that you were wrong; to be sorry

compromise (kom′prə mīz′) to settle an argument or reach an agreement by give and take

QUICK START You and your brother want to play with a football at the same time. You are both angry. Your father says, "Stop arguing. Try to work it out." What can you do?

How might you feel if you and a classmate argued? What if you were about to perform at a recital? Or suppose you earned an "A" on a difficult math test.

All these scenes might give you strong feelings, or emotions. It is normal to feel all different kinds of emotions. It's nice to feel good about things. But sometimes you might feel bad. That's okay too. What is important is how you deal with your emotions.

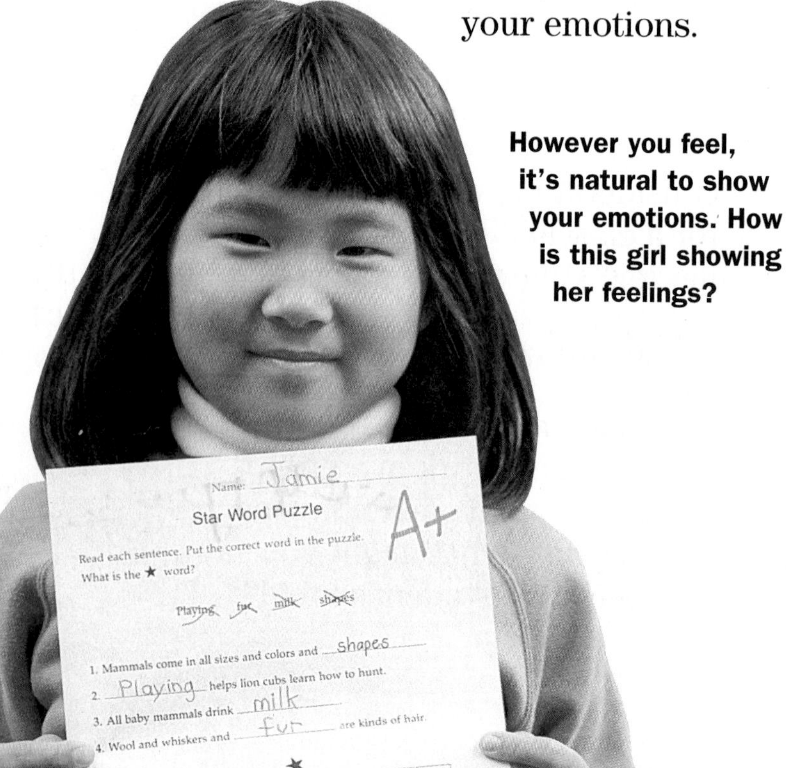

However you feel, it's natural to show your emotions. How is this girl showing her feelings?

Your Emotions

Emotions are a normal part of your life. Showing joy and love in a healthful way may be easy. It may be harder to show anger or fear in a healthful way.

Here are some healthful ways to deal with emotions such as anger or fear.

- Talk to someone. This can help you understand your feelings.
- Be physically active. This can calm you.
- Sometimes just being alone until the emotion passes helps you feel better.

Your Emotions and Conflict

Sometimes emotions like jealousy or anger can cause a conflict. A **conflict** is a struggle or disagreement between people or ideas. For example, what if your brother takes one of your toys without permission? What if he breaks it? This can cause a conflict between you and your brother. Conflicts can make you feel helpless, upset, or angry.

LIFE SKILL

OBTAIN HELP

What Would You Do?

You are upset about a conflict at school. Whom might you go to for help? What would you say?

HEALTH FALLACY

"If you have conflicts, you must have a bad temper."

This is not true. Not all conflicts are caused by a bad temper—yours or anyone else's. Sometimes, it's just that people have different ideas about how to do things. Emotions might make a conflict worse. Many times, though, they don't have to be part of the conflict at all!

How would you feel if someone broke one of your things?

HANDBOOK LIFE SKILLS pp. 268–279

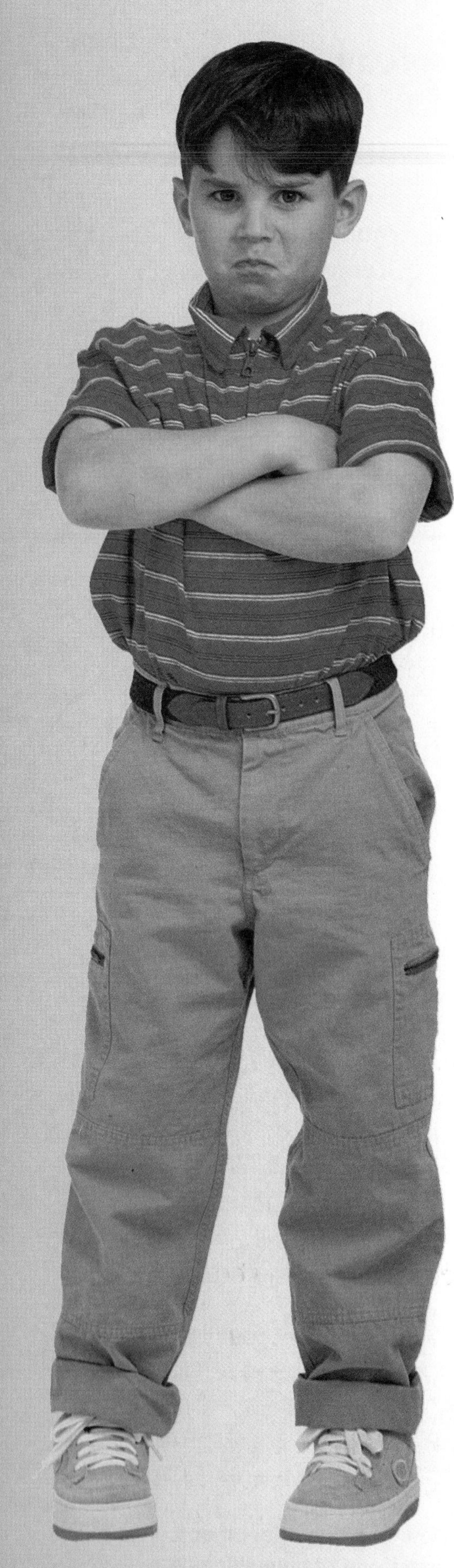

Resolving Conflicts

Conflicts are a part of life. Sometimes a simple problem can quickly become a conflict. Part of growing up is learning how to resolve, or settle, conflicts.

Here are some things that can help you resolve a conflict.

- Calm down. Try counting to ten while you take deep breaths.
- You may be at least partly at fault. If so, **apologize**—admit that you were wrong.
- Use "I" statements. Try saying "I am sad because you forgot my birthday" instead of "You're so forgetful!"
- Work together to settle things. Talk about possible answers. Choose the one that works best for everyone.

In a **compromise**, people settle an argument or reach an agreement by give and take. Each person agrees to give up part of what he or she wants. But each person keeps part, too. That way, everybody wins!

Some reactions to conflict don't do any good. They might even make things worse. Here are some things to avoid during a conflict.

- Don't just do nothing. Hoping that the problem will go away won't help.
- Don't say something you will be sorry about later. Think about what you say first.
- Don't get rough. Pushing and hitting are never good ways to show emotions.

Do you think this boy is ready to settle a conflict? What is this boy saying with his body?

HEALTH ACTIVITY

Freeze Frame

RESOLVE CONFLICTS

1 With your partner, think of a scene in which people might have a conflict. Jot down your ideas.

2 Describe the scene to your teacher. Tell your teacher when you want him or her to stop the action by saying "Freeze frame!"

3 Perform your scene for the class. Stop when your teacher says "Freeze frame!" Ask your classmates for ideas of what to do next. Act out at least one idea for resolving the conflict.

LESSON WRAP UP

Show What You Know

1. What are two healthful ways to deal with emotions such as sadness or anger?

2. What is a conflict?

3. **THINK CRITICALLY** Suppose a classmate pushes you. Write a "you" statement. Then rewrite it with an "I" statement. Which statement works better? Why?

Show What You Can Do

4. PORTFOLIO **APPLY HEALTH ACTIVITY** **Resolve Conflicts** Write a story about a conflict. Show some of the emotions that might come from this conflict. Show how the conflict can be resolved.

5. LIFE SKILL **PRACTICE LIFE SKILLS** **Practice Refusal Skills** With a friend, act out a scene in which it would be hard to say "no." Try different ways of saying "no." Which ways seem to work best?

HANDBOOK LIFE SKILLS pp. 268–279

LESSON 4

Managing Stress

In this lesson, you will learn:

- about different kinds of stress and how they can affect people.
- ways to manage stress.

VOCABULARY

stress (stres) the way the body and mind respond to changes around you

stressor (stres′ər) things, events, people, or places that cause stress

QUICK START As you wait to take the test, you feel nervous. Why do you think you feel that way? What might you do to change that feeling?

Have you ever felt nervous or upset? You probably had these feelings when something unpleasant happened. Even happy events can make you feel nervous, because you want to do your best.

These feelings are a normal part of life. You shouldn't be afraid of them. You can learn to understand and control them.

Even something positive, like wanting to play your best, can cause stress.

What Is Stress?

Feeling nervous and upset is a sign of stress. **Stress** is the way the body and mind respond to changes around you. Stress can be caused by things, events, people, or places. Anything that causes stress is called a **stressor**.

Some stressors are minor. They touch only a small part of your life. Other stressors are big. They may touch almost every part of your life.

For example, you would feel stress if your pencil broke during a math test. You would probably feel a lot more stress if you learned that you were moving far away from your friends.

Some stress can help you. Suppose you're ready to run in a race. You may feel nervous. But the stress gives you energy for the job ahead. That kind of stress can help you do your job better.

How do you know that you're feeling stress? On the next two pages you will learn how to identify stress, and how to control it.

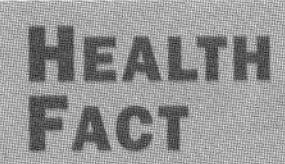

HEALTH FACT

"Stress can give you an energy boost."

It is true. Your body reacts to stress in different ways. Under stress, your body supplies a chemical called *adrenaline* into your blood. This gives you extra energy.

LIFE SKILL

MANAGE STRESS

What Would You Do?

Your friend's family does not allow him to go to the mall without an adult. Why might teasing your friend into going to the mall anyway cause stress?

THE STRESS STORY
Many events can cause stress. You cannot control them all.
But you can learn to recognize the signs of stress.
You also can learn how to control
stress in healthful ways.
TROUBLE THINKING CLEARLY
TROUBLE SLEEPING
FEELING TIRED ALL THE TIME
HEADACHE
FASTER BREATHING
DRY MOUTH
FASTER HEARTBEAT
SWEATING
FEELING NERVOUS OR UPSET
STOMACHACHE
FEELING COLD ALL OVER

Ways to Manage Stress

Be Physically Active

Being active burns up extra energy that builds up under stress. It takes your mind off the situation and helps you calm down.

Relax Being quiet can also help. Find a place to sit or lie down quietly. Rest until you feel relaxed.

Think How important is this event—really? It may look big. But maybe it doesn't matter all that much.

Plan Planning can help you avoid stress. Maybe you feel stress about tests. Plan several study times before your next test.

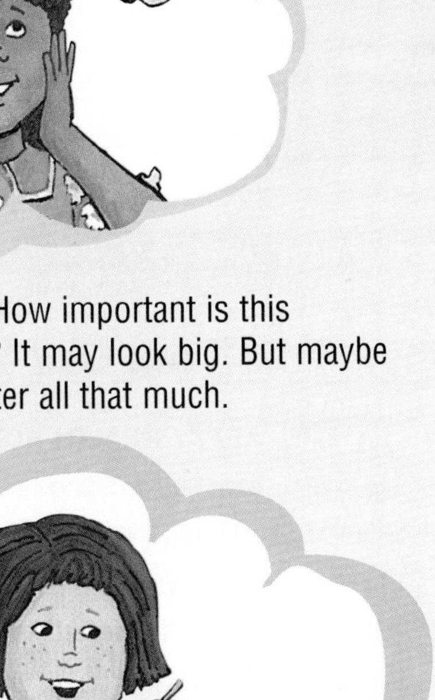

Keep Healthy Eat right, stay active, and get enough sleep. Good physical health helps you manage stress.

Share Tell your parents, a trusted adult, or even a friend about your feelings. They may help you manage the stress. Knowing that people care can also help.

HEALTH ACTIVITY

Stress Check

MANAGE STRESS

1 For the next two days, keep a record of any stressors that happen.

2 Next to each stressor, write whether the stress you felt was "big" or "small." Then write down what, if anything, you did to manage the stress.

3 Look over your notes. If you wish, share one comment from your notebook with the class.

LESSON WRAP UP

Show What You Know

1. What is a stressor? Give an example.

2. What are three signs of stress?

3. **THINK CRITICALLY** You feel stress because you are the pitcher in the softball game tomorrow. What can you do to help you manage your stress?

Show What You Can Do

4. PORTFOLIO **APPLY HEALTH ACTIVITY** **Manage Stress** Write about a situation that caused stress. Tell how you would manage the same stress now that you know more about it.

5. LIFE SKILL **PRACTICE LIFE SKILLS** **Practice Refusal Skills** Suppose a friend asked you to break a family rule. How could saying "no" help you manage the stress?

HANDBOOK LIFE SKILLS pp. 268–279

YOU CAN MAKE A DIFFERENCE

TECHNOLOGY

Shower Your Stress Away

Get a massage—from your shower!

People are always looking for new ways to relax. Taking a vacation is always nice, but what if you just don't have the time? You might consider stepping into the shower. You could step out again feeling stress-free.

Today some shower heads are run by computer. They can be programmed to give you a gentle massage as you get clean. You can arrange to have an all-over massage, or a massage that moves from your toes up to your head.

You can send water pounding onto your neck and shoulders, where much of the body's stress is stored. You can even have special water jets massage the soles of your feet.

Some of these treats can be very expensive. A simple, pulsing shower head does not cost very much, however. With relaxation as close as your tub, who needs a vacation?

MANAGE STRESS

TRY A LITTLE REFLEXOLOGY

Reflexology is foot massage to calm all parts of the body. You can try it yourself. Take off your shoes. Press each toe between your thumb and fingers and count to three. Then press your thumbs into the arch of your foot. Rub gently. Try this when you have trouble falling asleep—it often works!

CHAPTER

3 REVIEW

VOCABULARY

Write the word from the box that best completes each sentence. Use each word only once.

appreciation
conflict
cooperation
personality
self-concept
self-esteem
stress
stressor

1. The picture of yourself in your mind is your __?__. (Lesson 1)
2. If you feel very good about yourself, you have high __?__. (Lesson 1)
3. Working together shows __?__. (Lesson 2)
4. If you and a classmate are having trouble getting along, there may be a __?__ between you. (Lesson 3)
5. The way the body responds to emotional and intellectual pressure is called __?__. (Lesson 4)

REVIEW HEALTH IDEAS

Use your knowledge of emotional and intellectual health from Chapter 3 to answer these questions.

1. What are emotions? Give three examples. (Lesson 1)
2. What makes up your self-concept? (Lesson 1)
3. When you say that you appreciate someone, what do you mean? (Lesson 2)
4. How can you show consideration for a new classmate? (Lesson 2)
5. What are two skills that make cooperation work? (Lesson 2)
6. What are some healthful ways to show emotions? (Lesson 3)
7. Why is a compromise often the best way to resolve a conflict? (Lesson 3)
8. Why is hitting a poor way of resolving conflicts? (Lesson 3)
9. Give an example of how stress can help you perform your best. (Lesson 4)
10. If you feel stress, should you keep it a secret? Explain. (Lesson 4)

APPLY HEALTH IDEAS

1. Why is it important to understand that there are some things that you can't do well? (Lesson 1)
2. What are two ways you might show consideration toward people at school? (Lesson 2)
3. Why do you think planning is a good way to manage stress? (Lesson 4)
4. PORTFOLIO **SET GOALS** Set a goal for how you will react the next time you feel stress. Write down a plan for how you will make that goal work. For example, you might write "I will relax by jumping rope until I start feeling better."
5. LIFE SKILL **RESOLVE CONFLICTS** Write about four friends solving a problem through cooperation. How does cooperation take care of the problem?

What are some good ways to show consideration of others?

Take a survey of family members and neighbors. Ask each person to name three actions that he or she thinks show consideration of others.

When you are finished, look at the responses. Use them to write a "Top Ten" list of ways to show consideration. If any responses come up often, put them high on the list.

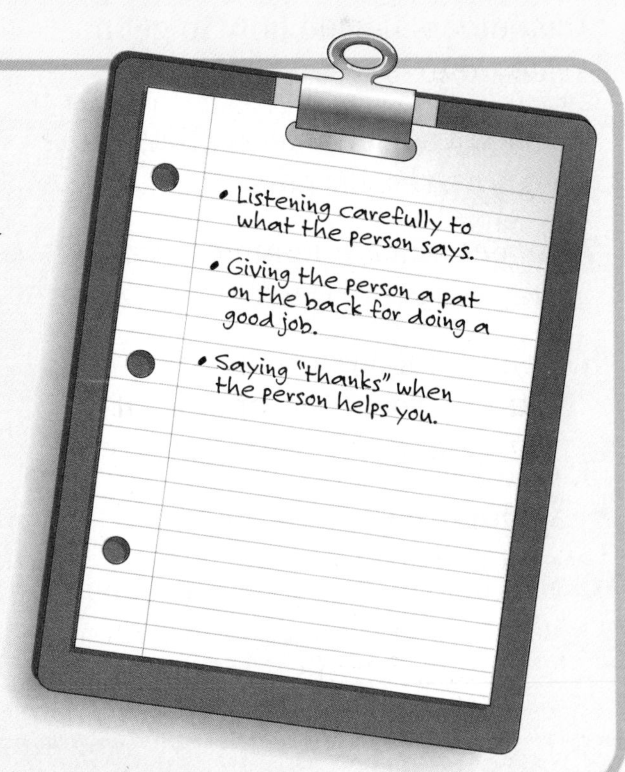

CHAPTER

3 TEST

Write the word or phrase in parentheses that makes each statement true.

1. Your personality, strengths, weaknesses, and emotions make up your (self-concept/self-esteem).
2. Thinking about what your friends like about you helps (weaken/improve) self-esteem.
3. One way to get along well with other people is to (ignore/appreciate) the ways in which they differ from you.
4. The students showed a lot of (competition/cooperation) as they cleaned up the vacant lot.
5. A (plan/contract) helps group members decide how to get a job done.
6. When you settle a conflict, you (ignore/resolve) it.
7. In a conflict, counting to ten is a way to (cooperate/calm down).
8. Your pet dying can be a big (stressor/emotion).
9. One sign of stress is feeling (calm/tired) all the time.
10. Staying (physically active/angry) can help you manage stress.

Write a sentence to answer each question.

11. What are some ways to improve self-esteem?
12. How can having high self-esteem affect your physical health?
13. Describe one way to show appreciation and consideration.
14. How can members of a group show cooperation?
15. Describe one healthful thing you can do if you feel angry.
16. What is a conflict?

17–19. Name three ways in which stress can affect the body.

20. Why might a person try to manage stress by going for a walk?

Performance Assessment

How good are you at resolving conflicts? Write about something you might do or have done to help resolve a conflict.

Family and Social Health

CHAPTER 4

One of the three parts of good health is having healthy relationships with:

- family.
- classmates.
- friends.

Chapter Contents

1 A Healthy Family 84

2 A Healthy Classroom 88

3 Healthy Friendships 92

School Counselor 97

Chapter Review 98

Chapter Test 100

LESSON

1 A Healthy Family

In this lesson, you will learn:

- about families and how they grow and change.
- ways that family members work together to make a family healthy.

VOCABULARY

respect (ri spekt′) a feeling that someone is valuable

responsibility (ri spon′sə bil′i tē) something you are expected to do; a job

QUICK START You want to watch TV. The rest of the family is helping get dinner ready. What should you do?

You have probably been helping out at home since you were little. Helping each other is an important part of family life. In this lesson, you will learn about different kinds of families. You will also learn how families work at being healthy.

How are these family members helping one another?

Families

What comes to mind when you hear the word *family*? Families are made up of people who are related. But families are very different from each other.

Families come in many sizes. Some are small—perhaps two parents and a child or just one parent and a child. Other families are larger, with two parents and several children.

Sometimes a family includes relatives such as grandparents, aunts, uncles, and cousins. These people may live together. Or some members may live far from others.

Family members may be related by birth, like a parent and child. They may be related by marriage, like a husband and wife. Some people join their families through adoption or foster care.

Over time, families change. A child may be born or adopted. An older child may get married. A family member may move away. Divorce and remarriage also change a family.

The most important thing about families is that family members care about each other. They talk together, work together, and play together. They appreciate what they do for each other. They love each other because of who they are.

How are these families different? How might they be alike?

MAKE DECISIONS

What Would You Do?

Write down names of as many family members as you know. Now suppose that they all come to a party. Which family members would you decide to try and get to know better? Why?

HANDBOOK LIFE SKILLS pp. 268–279

Work can be fun, especially if family members cooperate.

A Healthy Family

A person works at staying healthy. So do families. Here are four ways they work at it.

- Respect—if you have **respect** for a person, you feel that he or she is valuable. Members of healthy families have respect for each other—no matter how old, or young.
- Responsibility—family members take responsibilities seriously. A **responsibility** is something that you are expected to do. Providing a safe place to live is a parent's responsibility. Doing your homework is one of your responsibilities.
- Cooperation—family members show *cooperation* by working together. They work together for the same purpose or goal. They solve problems together. They have fun together, too.
- Rules—rules about safety, bedtime, and so on, help family members work together. As an adult, you will have other rules. Following family rules shows that you are growing up. In fact, following family rules is part of everyone's responsibility.

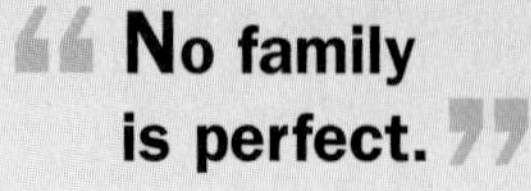

Health Fact

"No family is perfect."

This is true. Sometimes people wish they were part of someone else's family. Think for a minute. We see only part of that other family. Members of that family probably have problems to solve, too. They probably disagree at times. So don't wish for a different family. Instead, help your family be the best it can be. The ideas on this page can help.

HEALTH ACTIVITY

Relative Resolutions

LIFE SKILL
RESOLVE CONFLICTS

1 Work with a group of classmates. Think of your group as a family. Have each group member play the role of a family member.

2 Together, choose a conflict—a scene that would need some family problem-solving. Make some notes about it. One example is a brother and sister who want to play with the same toy.

3 Act out how a healthy family might resolve the conflict. Share your ideas with other groups.

LESSON WRAP UP

Show What You Know

1. Describe three different groups that are all families.

2. Name three ways in which a family might change over time.

3. **THINK CRITICALLY** How is obeying family rules a way of showing respect?

Show What You Can Do

4. PORTFOLIO **APPLY HEALTH ACTIVITY** **Resolve Conflicts** Think of a conflict that brothers and sisters might have. Write down two ideas to help them solve their problem.

5. LIFE SKILL **PRACTICE LIFE SKILLS** **Obtain Help** Think of places in your community that can help families. Check your local newspaper or library for ideas. Find places where families can have fun, learn, or solve problems together.

HANDBOOK **LIFE SKILLS** pp. 268–279

LESSON 2

A Healthy Classroom

In this lesson, you will learn:

- about adults who help make school a safe and good place to learn.
- ways to work to make a classroom a healthy place to learn.

VOCABULARY

school personnel (skül pûr′sə nel′) adults who work at your school; want to help you learn

guidance (gī′dəns) advice (or other help)

attitude (at′i tüd′) a way of feeling that affects the way you behave

QUICK START A teacher tells you to stop running in the hallway. "It's a school rule," he says. Why is there a rule about running? Why does the teacher remind you about the rule?

In many ways, a class is like a family. People work together to get things done. They also have different responsibilities. They care about each other and want the best for each other. In this lesson, you'll look at some ways people work together to make the classroom a healthy place to learn.

Crossing guards help keep you safe.

Many adults work together to make school a healthy place for students to learn in.

Who's Who at School?

Who makes a classroom *healthy*? Students who work hard do. So do the **school personnel**, adults who work at a school. They want to help students learn.

The principal works with teachers and aides to keep the school running safely. A school nurse gives health advice and takes care of students who become ill or hurt. Guidance counselors help students solve problems by giving **guidance**, or advice.

Secretaries answer phones and keep track of school information. Librarians can help students find books, magazines, tapes, and so on. Crossing guards help keep everyone safe when crossing the streets around school.

OBTAIN HELP

What Would You Do?

Bill, a new student, feels lonely. To whom can he go for help?

CULTURAL PERSPECTIVES

Find a Pen Pal

What is it like to go to school in another part of the world? There's an interesting way to find out. You could become pen pals with a student your age in another country! If you would like such a pen pal, write to this organization for information:

Student Letter Exchange
630 Third Avenue
New York, NY 10017

INFOGRAPHIC

Words to Learn By

Working together is important for everyone at school—students as well as school personnel. People who work together for a healthy classroom remember these words.

COMMUNICATION

- Sharing ideas is a wonderful way to learn. So be a part of class discussions.
- Talk about things that you have learned and things that you want to learn.
- When you need help, remember to ask your teacher.

COOPERATION

- An **attitude** is a way of feeling that affects how you behave. People who have a cooperative attitude work together to solve problems.
- Teachers and students need a cooperative attitude. They help each other understand their ideas. They share each other's skill—and get things done together.

RESPECT

- Show respect for other students and their property. All students have valuable skills and ideas.
- At school, remember that your teacher and classmates are valuable. Listen to them. Show by your actions that they are important.

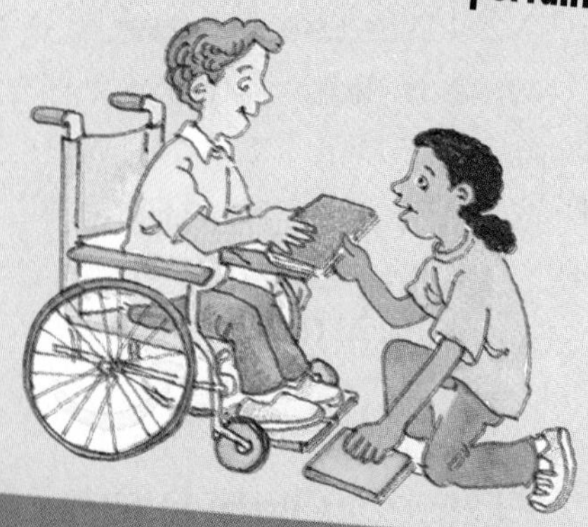

RESPONSIBILITIES AND RULES

- You have responsibilities at home and at school.
- Student responsibilities include being on time, paying attention, working with classmates, and completing assignments.
- It is also your responsibility to follow school rules, including raising your hand before speaking.

HEALTH ACTIVITY

Rule Review

LIFE SKILL SET GOALS

You will need: oaktag, markers

1 Work in a small group. Brainstorm goals that would lead to a school where everyone works together. Write them down.

2 Turn the goals into a list of school rules. Remember that you want everyone to enjoy learning. You also want to keep everyone safe.

3 Choose five rules you think are most important. Make a poster that lists them. Discuss ways to improve how to follow these rules.

LESSON WRAP UP

Show What You Know

1. Name the job of one adult who works at school. Then describe that job.
2. Responsibility is an important part of a healthy classroom. Why is that true? In your explanation, name two student responsibilities.
3. **THINK CRITICALLY** Think about the jobs of a guidance counselor and a school nurse. How are these two jobs alike? How are they different?

Show What You Can Do

4. PORTFOLIO **APPLY HEALTH ACTIVITY** **Set Goals** Write a skit to show how following a rule can make it easier to meet the goal of having a healthy classroom. Perform your skit for the class.
5. LIFE SKILL **PRACTICE LIFE SKILLS** **Obtain Help** Who are people at school you can go to for help? Who can help you if you are ill and get hurt? Who can help you learn?

LESSON 3

Healthy Friendships

In this lesson, you will learn:

- about things that make friendships healthy.
- ways to make and keep friends.
- ways to deal with the stress of peer pressure.

VOCABULARY

friend (frend) someone who is close to you; someone whom you care about and who cares about you

peer pressure (pîr presh′ər) a kind of stress in which people your age try to make you do what they want

QUICK START You're upset about something that happened at school. You want to talk to someone about it. Why might a friend be a good choice?

A **friend** is someone who is close to you. A friend is someone whom you care about—and who cares about you. Friends work and play together. They share good times. They share their problems. They help each other feel good about themselves.

Does that make friendship sound like work? Good friendships may take work—but they're worth it!

How can you tell that these girls are friends?

You can learn a lot from an older friend.

Friends Are Special People

Friends can help you feel good about yourself. They can also help your physical health. For example, playing tag with a friend is a good way to be physically active. A friend will try to stop you from doing something dangerous or unhealthy.

It takes a special person to be a friend. Think about these ideas. A friend:

- understands and cares about you.
- listens to you, even when you don't agree.
- shares things—time, ideas, and skills.
- is kind and helpful.
- is honest and can be trusted.
- respects you and your family.

It's great to have different kinds of friends. Friends may be older or younger than you. They may have disabilities. They may be relatives. They may come from other countries or be of other races. It's fun to have different kinds of friends. We can learn from them all.

HEALTHWISE CONSUMER

Making A New Friend

The library is a great place to make new friends. You might check for notices about interesting events. You might find newspapers that list local activities for your age group. Events and activities that interest you might also interest a friend-to-be!

Finding New Friends

Do you ever wonder, "How can I make friends?" Many friends first meet because they share an interest or hobby. To find a friend, try looking for someone who likes to do something that you like to do.

Keeping Good Friends

The best way to keep friends is to have respect for them. Find time for old friends when you meet new ones. Introduce them to each other.

Still, conflicts sometimes happen, to the best of friends. If you and a friend are having a conflict, talk honestly about your feelings. Sometimes you have to compromise or "meet each other halfway." You may have to ask an adult you trust for help. Work together!

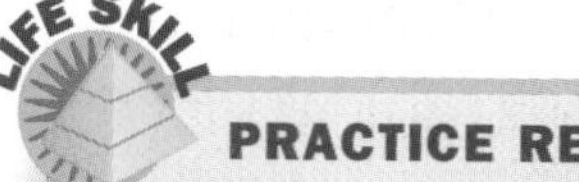

PRACTICE REFUSAL SKILLS

What Would You Do?

Some classmates are making jokes about a new student. They don't want you to be friendly. How could you say "no" and help the new student feel welcomed?

Facing Peer Pressure

Peer pressure is a kind of stress. It happens when your peers try to get you to do what they want. Your *peers* are people your own age. Some are your friends. Some are not.

Peer pressure can be helpful. Your friends may try to help you. But peer pressure can be harmful, too. Some peers are not real friends at all. They may suggest something that would put you in danger. They may try to talk you into doing something that you believe is wrong. If that happens, what should you do? Here are some ideas.

- Think before you act. Sometimes peers will try to bully and embarrass you. They may say "Everyone's doing it." or "A real friend would do it." Think before you act. Would a real friend put your health or safety at risk?

- Remember your values. Think about your family's ideas about right and wrong—and your own. For example, is honesty an important value to you? Then don't let peers pressure you into lying. Do you respect other people? Then don't let peers pressure you into ruining their property.

- Be brave enough to say "no." Explain why you won't follow your peers. Suggest something else that you could do together. If you have to, walk away from them. It's not easy. You might be teased. But what you think about yourself comes first. Show that you care about what's right. Show that you care about other people and about yourself. Then you will really feel good about yourself!

HEALTH ACTIVITY

Plan A or Plan B?

1 With a partner, think of an example of peer pressure at school. For example, what if one classmate tried to talk another into sneaking out of school? Take notes about your example.

2 Describe your example to the class. Have the class suggest two plans, Plan A and Plan B, for handling the peer pressure.

3 Act out the two plans. Which plan offers the better way to manage the stress of peer pressure?

LESSON WRAP UP

Show What You Know

1. Name three things that are true of people who have healthy friendships.

2. Peers who pressure you to do things you don't want to do are not real friends. Do you agree? Why or why not?

3. **THINK CRITICALLY** How can you make a new friend without losing the friends that you already have?

Show What You Can Do

4. PORTFOLIO **APPLY HEALTH ACTIVITY** **Manage Stress** Write a "recipe" for handling peer pressure—such as, 1/2 cup of honesty, 2 ears, 1 tablespoon of bravery. Share your recipes.

5. LIFE SKILL **PRACTICE LIFE SKILLS** **Practice Refusal Skills** Write a list of things healthy friends don't do, such as fight. Make a poster called "Good Friends Don't . . ." that shows people how not to lose friends.

HANDBOOK LIFE SKILLS pp. 268–279

YOU CAN MAKE A DIFFERENCE

CAREERS

School Counselor

Peggy Hanselman, School Counselor

Q: What kind of training did you need to do your job?
Ms. Hanselman: I went to college for four years and then to graduate school. I studied how people behave in groups and how the human mind works. I also studied how to solve problems and how to listen to people.

Q: What skills are most important in your job?
Ms. Hanselman: This is a great job if you love people. It's also important to be patient, organized, and to have a sense of humor.

Q: When do students use your services?
Ms. Hanselman: All the time! They come to see me about personal problems, family problems, and school problems.

Q: What kind of advice are you asked for most often?
Ms. Hanselman: At my school, students ask most about planning for their future.

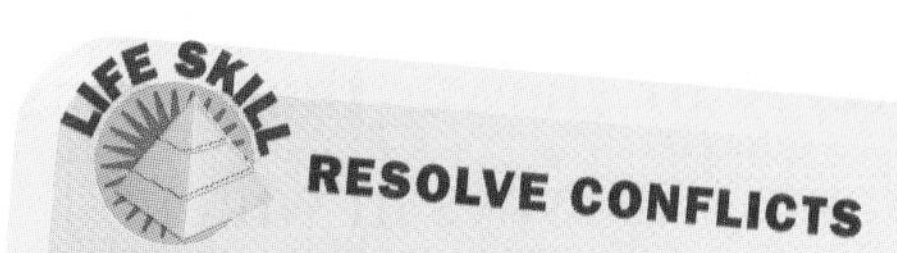

NO FIGHTING, PLEASE

Think of a conflict that might occur between two students. Suppose you are a school counselor and that these two students came to you for help. What could you do to help them resolve their conflict?

CHAPTER

4 REVIEW

VOCABULARY

Write the word or words from the list that best complete each sentence.

attitude
friend
guidance
peer pressure
personnel
respect
responsibility

1. Do you value people and listen to them? If so, you treat them with __?__. (Lesson 1)
2. Helping with household chores shows that you can handle __?__. (Lesson 1)
3. Students who obey school rules show a healthy __?__. (Lesson 2)
4. Does someone want you to be the best you can be? That person is a good __?__. (Lesson 3)
5. If you feel you must do what your "friends" want, you are feeling __?__. (Lesson 3)

REVIEW HEALTH IDEAS

Use what you have learned about family and social health from Chapter 4 to answer these questions.

1. Name two ways in which families can change over time. (Lesson 1)
2. What does cooperation in a family mean? Give an example. (Lesson 1)
3. How can you show respect for your family members? (Lesson 1)
4. Why does a school nurse help students? (Lesson 2)
5. How do crossing guards help keep you healthy? (Lesson 2)
6. Name two ways to keep a classroom healthy. (Lesson 2)
7. Why is it important to follow classroom rules? (Lesson 2)
8. Could someone who is very different from you be your friend? Explain. (Lesson 3)
9. How might you become friends with a new neighbor your age? (Lesson 3)
10. Should you ever walk away from peers who are pressuring you? Explain. (Lesson 3)

APPLY HEALTH IDEAS

1. How might a family change if a son or a daughter gets married? (Lesson 1)
2. One of your classmates is always complaining about school rules. What can you say to her to help improve her attitude? (Lesson 2)
3. "My friend is mad at me," your sister says. "I don't know what to do." What advice would you give her? (Lesson 3)
4. PORTFOLIO **SET GOALS** List ways in which you are a good friend. How could you be an even better friend? Write down one goal. Next week, try to reach that goal. (Lesson 3)
5. LIFE SKILL **PRACTICE REFUSAL SKILLS** Write a skit to show a time when someone would need to say "no." Show a healthful way of saying "no." Perform your skit for the class. (Lesson 3)

Can a relative also be a friend?

Make a list of your relatives. Leave some room after each name for some extra notes. Then, next to each name, write one or two "friendly" qualities of that relative.

When you are finished, review your notes with your family. Which relatives are also your friends?

CHAPTER

4 TEST

Write True or False for each statement. If false, change the underlined word or phrase to make it true.

1. It is important for a friend to be honest.
2. Classmates with a cooperative attitude will try to force their ideas on others.
3. In a healthy family, only the oldest people need to be shown respect.
4. A family can change through adoption, remarriage, and death.
5. Have you met a new friend? If so, you should help your other friends get to know him or her.
6. Keeping everyone safe on the way to and from school is the main job of a principal.
7. A husband and wife are family members by marriage.

8–9. Two good ways of handling peer pressure are to go ahead and do what your peers want and to try to forget what your family would think about it.

10. One way of showing respect in a family is to follow family rules.

Write a sentence to answer each question.

11–12. Complete the following sentence in two ways. A friend should be ___?___.

13. Explain the jobs of two people in your school.

14. What is one good way to find a new friend?

15. Explain one way family members share responsibilities.

16. How can friends work together to resolve a conflict?

17. In what ways can people in a family be related?

18–19. Describe two ways to make your classroom a healthy place.

20. Why is being a good listener a good way to keep a friend?

Performance Assessment

Are you a respectful person? Write down your thoughts. Include ideas about how to be more respectful at home, at school, and with friends.

CHAPTER 5

NUTRITION

Eating healthful foods will:

- give your body energy.
- help your body grow.
- help you stay healthy.

CHAPTER CONTENTS

1 WHY YOU NEED FOOD 102

2 THE FOOD GUIDE PYRAMID 108

3 CHOOSING HEALTHFUL FOODS 114

4 SHOPPING FOR HEALTHFUL FOODS 118

5 FOOD SAFETY 122

YOU CAN MAKE A DIFFERENCE SPACE FOOD 125

CHAPTER REVIEW 126

CHAPTER TEST 128

LESSON

1 Why You Need Food

In this lesson, you will learn:

- what nutrients do for your body.
- how fiber and water can keep your body healthy.

VOCABULARY

proteins (prō′tēnz) nutrients that the body uses for growth and the repair of cells

carbohydrates (kär′bō hī′drāts) nutrients used by the body as its main source of energy

fats (fats) nutrients that give the body long-lasting energy

fiber (fī′bər) material that helps move waste through the digestive system

QUICK START You arrive home hungry after school. What would you like for a snack? Why would you choose that food? Is it a healthy choice?

Food—what comes to mind when you hear this word? You may think about all the foods you like. Maybe you think about a food you don't like, but you've read is "good for you."

Did you ever think about life with no food at all? You couldn't live without food. Your body needs food to work well. Making wise food choices can keep you healthy.

A healthful meal includes many different healthful foods.

Food and Health

"You must have grown a foot since I last saw you!" Someone has probably said this to you before. Without food, you couldn't have grown taller. Food supplies materials needed for your body to grow. Food supplies materials for your bones and skin to grow. Organs like your heart and brain are growing, too—thanks to food.

Food also helps your body heal when it gets hurt. Suppose you scrape your knee. New skin grows to replace the damaged skin. It's food that gives your body the materials it needs to grow new skin.

Food helps your body carry on all its daily life activities such as making new cells. Food helps your body fight illness, too.

Food and Energy

Food gives you energy. Energy gives your body its ability to do its work. It takes energy to kick a soccer ball. You use energy to walk and tie your shoes. You need energy to turn the pages of this book.

Energy also powers activities inside your body. Your heart needs energy to pump blood. Your brain needs energy to think. You couldn't do your homework without energy from food! But to do all these jobs well, your body needs healthful foods.

Your body uses food for growth and energy.

Protein-rich Foods

Nutrients and Your Body

Food does many jobs for your body. Those jobs depend on different nutrients. *Nutrients* are substances in food that your body needs for energy and growth. To stay healthy, your body needs different kinds of nutrients.

Proteins are nutrients that are the body's "building blocks." Your body uses proteins to grow and build muscle. Proteins repair parts of your body after an injury. You can get proteins from fish, meat, chicken, milk, nuts, or beans.

Carbohydrate-rich Foods

Carbohydrates are nutrients used by the body as its main source of energy. Carbohydrates help your body move, breathe, and carry on its other jobs. Carbohydrates are in foods that contain sugar, such as fruits. You also find it in foods that contain starch, such as pasta, breads, and crackers.

Fats are nutrients that give the body long-lasting energy. The body's cells store energy from fats for use over a long time. You don't need a lot of fat each day—but you do need some. Peanuts, many meats, and oils are sources of fat.

High-fat Foods

You only need small amounts of *vitamins* and *minerals*. They help other nutrients keep you healthy. Your body needs vitamins for growth, energy, and disease prevention. Vitamin D, for example, helps prevent a bone disease called rickets. Fruits and vegetables are good sources of vitamins.

Minerals are needed for the body to work properly. A mineral called *calcium* keeps your bones and teeth strong. Milk products and some vegetables are especially high in minerals.

PRACTICE REFUSAL SKILLS

What Would You Do?

Your friend opens a bottle of vitamins. She says, "The vitamins are chewy and sweet like candy. Try one." What should you do?

Less Healthful Foods

Some foods contain few nutrients. For example, snack foods cooked in oil, such as potato chips and corn chips, have a lot of fat. Many people eat more fat than they need. Eating fatty foods can lead to heart disease.

Sweets do not provide a healthful balance of nutrients. Candy, cakes, and soft drinks often have lots of added sugar. Added sugar can cause tooth decay.

Eating lots of sweets and fatty foods can also add to unhealthy body weight. If you fill up on these foods, you aren't eating the healthful foods that provide many nutrients.

Many soft drinks, teas, and coffee also contain caffeine. Caffeine speeds up the way your body works. It can make your heart beat faster. It can keep you awake at night.

The next time you want something sweet, try a food without added sugar, such as an orange. For a low-fat snack, choose nuts or unsalted pretzels. And instead of a drink with caffeine, try fruit juice, water, or milk.

Foods like these give you few of the nutrients that you need for good health.

HANDBOOK LIFE SKILLS pp. 268–279

HEALTH ACTIVITY

SCIENCE CONNECTION

Nutrient Data Base

Nutrients	Foods
Proteins	
Carbohydrates	
Fats	
Fiber	

You will need: used magazines or food circulars, poster board, tape, scissors

1. Make a poster like the one shown at the left.
2. Cut out food advertisements. Which nutrients does each food contain? Does it contain fiber? Tape each food to a row to show one thing the food contains. Write the name of the food in any other rows where it also belongs.
3. Draw an X through any less healthful food that you taped on the poster.

Fiber

Many fruits and vegetables have a lot of fiber. **Fiber** is a material in plant foods that can't be digested. However, fiber keeps the digestive system healthy. It helps move wastes through your digestive system (your stomach and intestines). Beans, whole wheat breads, cereals, and fruits and vegetables are rich sources of fiber.

Foods high in fiber are good for your body.

HEALTH FACT

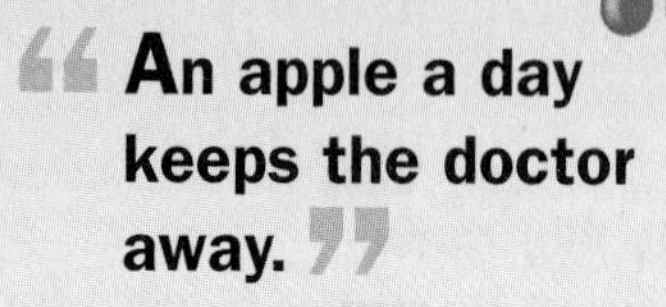

"An apple a day keeps the doctor away."

It is true. Eating apples is a healthy choice. Apples, like many fruits, have a lot of fiber. They have vitamins and carbohydrates. Biting into an apple also helps clean your teeth. But remember, eating apples doesn't mean you'll never need a doctor. You still need to see a doctor for checkups and when you're sick.

Water—The Drink of Life

Did you know that your body is mostly water? If you weigh 60 pounds, about 39 of those pounds are water! Water is important for almost every process in your body. Every cell in your body contains water. Your blood is mostly water. Food mixes with water in your digestive system. You cannot live without water for more than a few days.

Each day you should drink six to eight glasses of water. In hot weather and when playing hard, you should drink even more water.

Your body needs a lot of water.

LESSON WRAP UP

Show What You Know

1. Why does your body need proteins?
2. Why is it important to eat foods with fiber?
3. **THINK CRITICALLY** Why might water be called the "drink of life"?

Show What You Can Do

4. PORTFOLIO **APPLY HEALTH ACTIVITY** **Science Connection** List all the foods you've eaten so far today. Try to name one nutrient in each food. Name more than one if you can.
5. LIFE SKILL **PRACTICE LIFE SKILLS** **Practice Refusal Skills** You are buying a snack. How would you refuse a friend who urges you to buy a candy bar?

HANDBOOK LIFE SKILLS pp. 268–279

LESSON

2 THE FOOD GUIDE PYRAMID

In this lesson, you will learn:

- about the five basic food groups and the Food Guide Pyramid.
- how to use the Food Guide Pyramid to make healthful food choices.

VOCABULARY

food group (füd grüp) a group of foods that contain similar nutrients

junk food (jungk füd) food that has few useful nutrients

Food Guide Pyramid (füd gīd pir′ə mid′) a diagram of the food groups that helps you plan your food choices

QUICK START "Eat your vegetables." Have you ever heard that? Why is it important to eat vegetables?

Think of juicy strawberries or a bowl of tasty spaghetti. Now think about eating nothing but that food, day after day. You'd probably get tired of it. You would probably also get sick. Your body needs many different foods. No single food can supply all the nutrients your body needs to stay healthy. That's why it's important to eat a variety of foods.

Part of the fun of a celebration such as Kwanzaa is eating many different foods.

Foods in the fruit group and in the vegetable group are rich in nutrients and fiber. They are also low in fat.

Food Groups

Foods have been grouped to help plan meals. There are five basic **food groups**. Each group has foods with similar nutrients.

Foods made of grains go into the *Bread, Cereal, Rice, and Pasta Group*. Rice, wheat, corn, oats, and rye are grains. All grains come from plants. Foods in this group are rich in carbohydrates. Cornflakes, oatmeal, and other breakfast cereals belong in this group. So do tortillas made from corn or flour.

Foods in the *Fruit Group* come from plants. Apples, grapes, and plums belong in this group. Foods in the *Vegetable Group* also come from plants. Lettuce, carrots, and broccoli are part of this group. The foods in these two groups contain many nutrients. They are rich in vitamins and minerals. They are low in fat and are rich sources of fiber.

Two more food groups are important sources of protein. One is the *Milk, Yogurt, and Cheese Group*. The other is the *Meat, Poultry, Fish, Dry Beans, Eggs, and Nuts Group*.

All the foods in the Milk, Yogurt, and Cheese Group come from milk. Foods in the Meat, Poultry, Fish, Dry Beans, Eggs, and Nuts group come from animals (meat, poultry, eggs, and fish) and from plants (beans and nuts).

INFOGRAPHIC

THE FOOD GUIDE PYRAMID

The Food Guide Pyramid is a diagram of the food groups. Each food group has a section of the pyramid. The bigger the section, the more servings you need daily.

FATS, OILS, AND SWEETS
Should be limited.
These foods include sweets, butter, margarine, and oils. This section is not one of the five food groups.

MEAT, POULTRY, FISH, DRY BEANS, EGGS, AND NUTS GROUP 2–3 Servings
These foods are high in protein. Your body uses proteins to grow and stay healthy.

MILK, YOGURT, AND CHEESE GROUP 2–3 Servings
These foods provide calcium for strong bones and teeth. They are also a good source of protein.

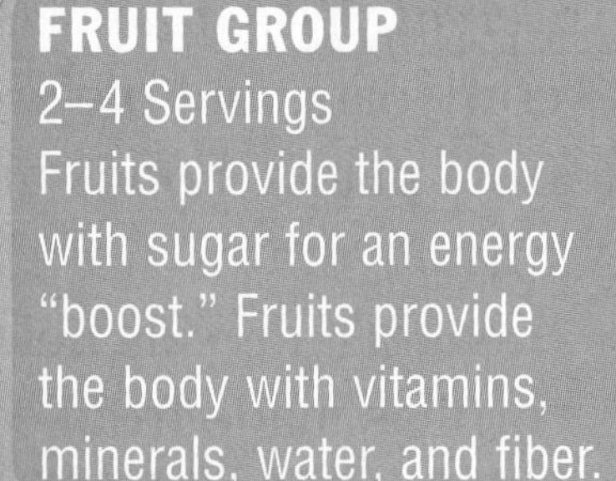

FRUIT GROUP
2–4 Servings
Fruits provide the body with sugar for an energy "boost." Fruits provide the body with vitamins, minerals, water, and fiber.

VEGETABLE GROUP
3–5 Servings
Vegetables are rich in vitamins and minerals. They are high in fiber and low in fat.

BREAD, CEREAL, RICE, AND PASTA GROUP 6–11 Servings
These foods are made from grains. Grains are rich in carbohydrates. Grains also provide protein, fiber, vitamins, and minerals.

KEY
• Fat (naturally occurring and added)
▿ Sugars (added)

These symbols show fats, oils, and added sugars in foods.

Junk Foods

Foods from the five food groups are high in nutrients. In Lesson 1, however, you also learned about less healthful foods. These foods are sometimes called **junk foods**. They are found at the top of the Food Guide Pyramid. They are *not* a food group.

Junk foods are usually high in fat or sugar. Chips fried in oil are high in fat. Frosted cakes and donuts are high in fat and sugar. Hard candy is almost all sugar. Chocolate bars have a lot of fat, sugar, and caffeine.

What's so bad about junk foods? The body needs small amounts of fats. Eating a lot of fats over many years, can put some people at risk of heart disease. Eating lots of sugar and fat can result in unhealthy body weight. Being overweight can lead to other health problems.

Many junk foods also contain a lot of salt. Salt, or sodium, is a mineral needed to balance the water in your body. But a lot of salt can, over time, damage your heart.

Junk food should be only a very small part of what you eat. Most of your food should come from the five food groups.

Any of these fruits and vegetables would make a healthful snack. You can choose them instead of junk foods.

Making Healthful Choices

For each food group, the pyramid suggests the number of servings you should eat every day. The lower a food group is on the pyramid, the more daily servings you should choose.

The number of servings you need also depends on your age. Right now you only need the middle number of servings every day. That means you need about 9 servings of grain foods and 4 servings of vegetables.

A serving is a specific amount of a food. For example, a serving of cooked spaghetti is half a cup. At a meal you might eat a cup and a half of spaghetti. That would be three servings on the Food Guide Pyramid.

Here's how to get three servings from the Fruit Group in one day. A glass of orange juice with breakfast and an apple with lunch make up two servings. With an after-school snack of a half cup of grapes, you have three servings. Healthful foods add up faster than you think. But you need servings from all five groups.

CULTURAL PERSPECTIVES

Celebrating Corn

Native Americans have long prized corn because of the many foods that can be made from it. They often referred to corn as "Sacred Mother" and "Seed of Life." Many Native American groups held special corn ceremonies. The Iroquois, for example, held a four-day Green Corn Ceremony marking the harvest of the first corn of summer. Think about how much you prize corn the next time you eat some popcorn, corn on the cob, or cornflakes.

LIFE SKILL

MAKE DECISIONS

What Would You Do?

You're eating dinner at a restaurant with your family. You know you've eaten only one serving of vegetables today. What healthful choices could you make when you order dinner?

HEALTH ACTIVITY

Fast Food Menu Order

1. The menu shows some foods you could order at a restaurant or cafeteria. Use it to decide what to order for lunch. List your food choices.
2. Look over your food choices using the Food Guide Pyramid. Decide which foods are healthful and which are not.
3. Use the menu to decide on a class lunch. Make it as healthful as possible.

MENU

Beverages

orange juice	$1.00
milk	$ .75
cola	$ .75
milkshake	$1.50

Side Orders

green salad	$1.00
french fries	$1.50
pasta salad	$2.00

Lunch Specials

chicken salad	$3.00
hamburger	$3.00
omelette	$2.50

Desserts

fruit cup	$1.50
ice cream cone	$1.50
low-fat yogurt	$1.50

LESSON WRAP UP

Show What You Know

1. What are three of the five basic food groups?
2. How does the shape of the Food Guide Pyramid help you make healthful food choices?
3. **THINK CRITICALLY** Do you think that one section of the Food Guide Pyramid is more important than another?

Show What You Can Do

4. PORTFOLIO **APPLY HEALTH ACTIVITY** **Make Decisions** Look at a menu from a take-out restaurant. Make a list of the foods that are healthful and that you like. See how many you can find.
5. LIFE SKILL **PRACTICE LIFE SKILLS** **Set Goals** Set a goal to get out of "the same food" rut. Try at least one new fruit, vegetable, or grain each week. Keep a record of your new favorite foods.

LESSON 3

Choosing Healthful Foods

In this lesson, you will learn:

- what makes up a person's diet.
- the importance of a balanced diet.

VOCABULARY

diet (dī′it) everything you eat and drink every day

balanced diet (bal′ənst dī′it) meals and snacks made up of foods from all five food groups in healthful amounts

QUICK START Your class is taking a field trip. You're supposed to pack a snack. What snack would be healthful and easy to carry?

You probably do a lot of different things after school and on weekends. Sometimes you may play sports. Other times, you read or watch TV. A variety of activities is fun—and healthy for your body and your mind. It is the same way with food. To stay healthy, your body needs different nutrients. You can get these nutrients by eating a wide variety of healthful foods.

Healthful foods like apples give you some of the nutrients you need for bike riding and other activities.

A Balanced Diet

It is important to eat a variety of foods from the Food Guide Pyramid every day. Everything you eat and drink every day is your **diet**. You can get the nutrients your body needs if your diet is balanced. A **balanced diet** includes meals and snacks made up of foods from all five food groups in healthy amounts.

The Food Guide Pyramid can help people plan a balanced diet. At the end of the day, count the total number of servings of each group from all your meals. This number should fall within the numbers of servings on the pyramid.

It's easy to plan meals that fit into a balanced diet. Meals should include foods from several food groups. Breakfast might include cereal, milk, and berries. For lunch you might have a hamburger, cucumber salad, and a glass of milk. For dinner you might eat a meal of black beans and rice with green peppers, a glass of milk and for dessert, a fruit salad.

Eating and Emotions

Healthful meals and snacks can be part of a fun day. But sometimes, if people are upset or sad, they may not think carefully about the foods they eat. They may eat more *or less* than they should. They may fill up on junk snacks.

Overeating and undereating are not healthy ways to deal with stressful times. Get help from a trusted adult if you are not following the guidelines set by the Pyramid.

CULTURAL PERSPECTIVES

Basic Foods

Many cultures have basic foods—foods that form a large part of people's diet. Rice, for example, is a basic food in China, India, Japan, and other Asian countries. For many European cultures, foods made from wheat, such as bread and pasta, are basic. The yam is an important food in many West African countries, such as Ghana. What other basic foods do you know about? Identify the food group they come from.

HealthWise Consumer

Fruit Drinks vs. Juices

Did you know that there is a difference between fruit drinks and fruit juices? Fruit juices are made up mostly of real fruit juice. Fruit drinks may have some real fruit juice. But they also have other ingredients such as sugar, water, and flavorings. If you want the real thing, buy orange juice instead of orange drink.

Choosing Healthful Snacks

Most people eat snacks now and then. You might be tempted to choose sweet, fatty, or salty snacks. Remember, though, that every snack is part of your diet. For a balanced diet, you need healthful snacks.

LIFE SKILL

MAKE DECISIONS

What Would You Do?

You've just gotten home from school and you are hungry. What healthful snack could you eat that won't fill you up before dinner?

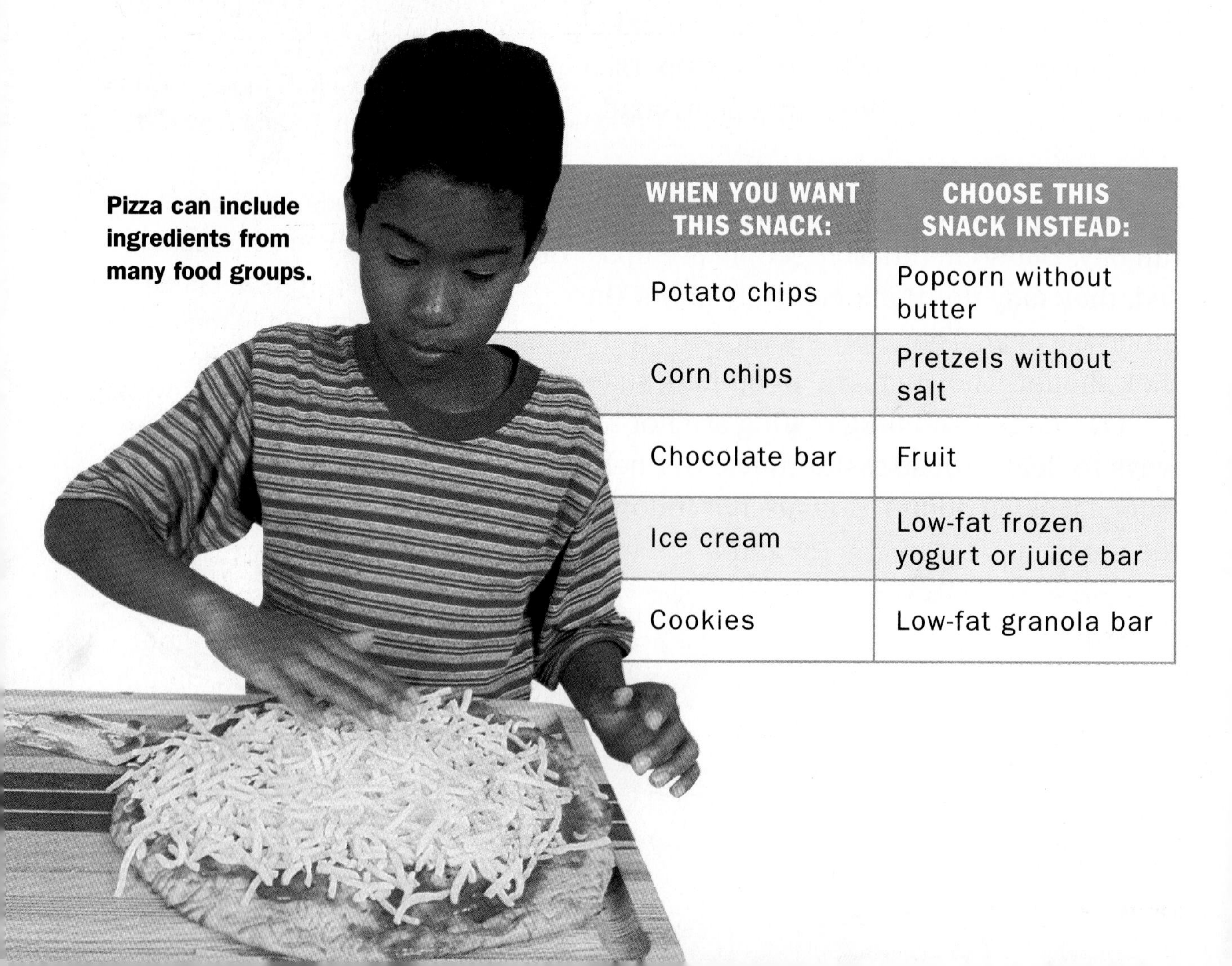

Pizza can include ingredients from many food groups.

WHEN YOU WANT THIS SNACK:	CHOOSE THIS SNACK INSTEAD:
Potato chips	Popcorn without butter
Corn chips	Pretzels without salt
Chocolate bar	Fruit
Ice cream	Low-fat frozen yogurt or juice bar
Cookies	Low-fat granola bar

HEALTH ACTIVITY

Keep Your Balance

1 Your class will be divided into four groups: breakfast, lunch, dinner, and snacks.

2 Write two different menus for your assigned meal or snack. Your goal is to make each meal or snack as healthful as possible. Use the Food Guide Pyramid.

3 Share all the menus with the class. Decide which breakfast menu is more healthful. Do the same for lunch, dinner, and snacks. Have you met your goal of a balanced diet for the day?

LESSON WRAP UP

Show What You Know

1. What makes up a diet?
2. Why is it important to have a balanced diet?
3. **THINK CRITICALLY** Start with a freshly cooked bowl of spaghetti. How could it be served to provide many food groups?

Show What You Can Do

4. **APPLY HEALTH ACTIVITY** **Set Goals** Set a goal to eat a balanced lunch every day. Plan five lunches. List the food groups included in each lunch.
5. **PRACTICE LIFE SKILLS** **Obtain Help** Ask a family member or school dietitian for help in making your diet more balanced. What foods should you eat less of? What foods should you eat more often?

HANDBOOK LIFE SKILLS pp. 268–279

Shopping for Healthful Foods

In this lesson, you will learn:

- about the information on food labels.
- how to make better food choices by reading labels.
- how ads help sell food.

VOCABULARY

ingredient
(in grē′dē ənt) any one of the parts that are mixed together to make food

QUICK START Suppose you are choosing a snack. You see several kinds of crackers. How would you decide which kind to choose?

You're in the supermarket. It's a food feast! There are shelves and shelves packed with cereals. Each is in a brightly colored box. You can find gallons of milk and fruit juices. The freezer holds packages of steaks, chicken, and fish. In another section, dozens of green and yellow squash are piled high. Baskets of plump strawberries and blueberries sit side by side. There are so many tasty foods to sip, chomp, and munch!

There are many cereals to choose from. You can find good-tasting cereals with the nutrients you need.

Food Labels

Most food products come with a label that gives nutrition facts about the product. The food label tells about the nutrients provided in the food. Study this label from a container of low-fat lemon yogurt.

Serving Size: This is the amount of food that makes up 1 serving. Solid foods are measured in grams (g) or in very small units called milligrams (mg).

% Daily Value: The % (percent) symbol tells how much of a day's worth of nutrients is found in the food. 0% means none. 50% means half the amount your body needs every day.

Total Fat: The label gives the total amount of fat in one serving. Use this guide to help you cut back on total fats.

Cholesterol: A fat-like substance. Eat only small amounts of it in foods.

Sodium: You call it salt. The label calls it sodium. Keep your sodium intake low.

Total Carbohydrate: Under this label you'll find out how much fiber and sugars are in the food. Sugars, remember, are carbohydrates.

Yummy Yogurt

Nutrition Facts

Serving Size 1 container (227 g)

Amount per Serving	
Calories	**210**
Calories from Fat	**30**
	% Daily Value*
Total Fat 3 g	**5%**
Saturated Fat 2 g	**10%**
Cholesterol 15 mg	**5%**
Sodium 160 mg	**7%**
Potassium 510 mg	**15%**
Total Carbohydrate 36 g	**12%**
Dietary Fiber 0 g	**0%**
Sugars 35 g	
Protein 10 g	
Vitamin A	**4%**
Vitamin C	**4%**
Calcium	**40%**
Iron	**0%**

INGREDIENTS: GRADE A MILK, SKIM MILK, SUGAR, NATURAL LEMON FLAVOR, PECTIN AND ACTIVE YOGURT CULTURES

* Percent Daily Values are based on a 2,000 calorie diet.

A food label usually includes a list of ingredients. An **ingredient** is any of the parts that are mixed together to make a food. Many foods have several different ingredients. Food labels list ingredients in order, from greatest to least amount. An ingredient list is useful to people who must limit or avoid certain foods. Knowing the nutrition facts about a food can help you choose healthful foods.

HEALTH FALLACY

"Food labeled 'low fat' is always a good choice."

This is not true. People should try to cut down on fats in their diets. However, shoppers need to pay attention to other nutrients and ingredients besides fat. A food low in fat may be high in sugar or salt. So it may still be a poor choice. Read the label.

Food Ads

You have already looked at some food ads in Lesson 1. Companies use advertising to make you want to choose their product.

Many ads give useful information about food. But some ads do not tell you about what's in the food. For example, a sports star in one ad might say that the food is great. Other ads hint that you will have more fun if you eat that food. Ads like these say nothing about the food's nutrients. Don't make a choice until you know all the facts.

Suppose you are buying a snack. How can you make a healthful choice? Look at the nutrition facts label. Ingredients like sugar and salt can be unhealthful if eaten in large amounts. Avoid these foods and foods with a lot of fat.

LIFE SKILL

MAKE DECISIONS

What Would You Do?

You want to buy a snack food. Your choice is wheat crackers or tortilla chips. Both come in packs of equal size. How would you decide which to buy?

HEALTH ACTIVITY

Looking Out for Ads

PRACTICE REFUSAL SKILLS

1 Watch some television ads for less healthful foods. Or find ads in magazines. Make a chart like the one shown. List ads that don't give information about nutrients.

2 Write how each ad tried to get you to choose the food. Did a famous person talk about the food? Did the ad show children having fun? Write these things on your chart.

3 At school, talk about why shoppers should say "no" to ads like these.

Food	Ad	Message
chips	baseball stars eating chips	You should eat the same chips as the baseball star to be more like him.

LESSON WRAP UP

Show What You Know

1. What information can you find on a food label?

2. How can food labels help a shopper to choose more healthful foods?

3. **THINK CRITICALLY** You see a TV ad for frozen pizza. The ad has a catchy tune. You want your family to buy the pizza. What else should you find out about it first?

Show What You Can Do

4. PORTFOLIO **APPLY HEALTH ACTIVITY** **Practice Refusal Skills** Write a letter to a food company about an ad that doesn't give nutrition facts. Tell why consumers should not buy products without this information.

5. LIFE SKILL **PRACTICE LIFE SKILLS** **Manage Stress** Your friend eats a small bag of cookies after school each day. He says it helps him relax. What are some healthier ways to relax?

HANDBOOK LIFE SKILLS pp. 268–279

LESSON

5 Food Safety

In this lesson, you will learn:

- how to recognize spoiled foods.
- safe ways to buy, prepare, or store food.

VOCABULARY

spoiled (spoild) no longer safe to eat or drink

mold (mōld) a type of living thing that grows on food and other moist materials

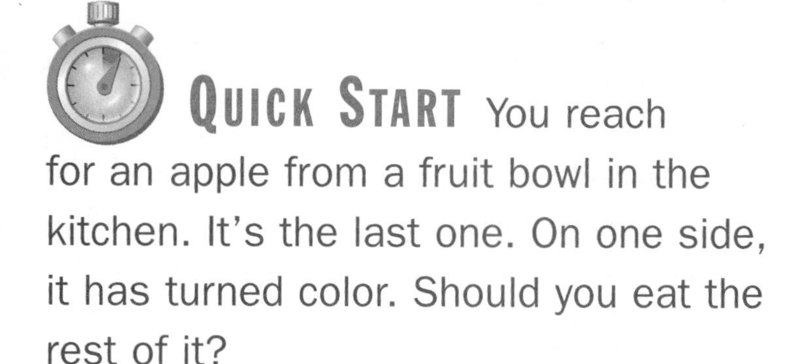

QUICK START You reach for an apple from a fruit bowl in the kitchen. It's the last one. On one side, it has turned color. Should you eat the rest of it?

Have you heard of food "going bad"? When this happens the food is spoiled. **Spoiled** food is no longer safe to eat or drink. A food spoils because germs get on the food and grow.

It's easy to see **mold** on food. It usually looks like a fuzzy green or black spot. Sometimes spoiled food smells funny.

Foods left out by mistake may not be safe to eat.

Being Safe With Food

It's important to know about food safety. Here are some tips to keep in mind when you buy, prepare, cook, or store food.

- Don't buy or use foods in damaged or bulging containers. Tell the store manager.
- After shopping, put dairy, meats, and frozen food products into the refrigerator right away. Cold temperatures slow down the growth of germs that can spoil food.
- Wash your hands before touching food. Germs on your hands can get on the food.
- Make sure knives, forks, spoons, pots, pans, and cutting boards are clean.
- Wash all fresh fruits and vegetables.
- Thorough cooking kills germs in meats, fish, and poultry.
- Refrigerate leftovers right after eating. Wrap them or put them in a container with a tight lid. This prevents food from spoiling.
- Eat leftovers within two or three days. After that, throw them out.
- Never taste a food that may be spoiled.

HEALTHWISE CONSUMER

Shopping for Food

It's important to read food labels carefully when selecting foods. Many products are stamped with a "sell by" or "best used by" date. Paying attention to this information will help you avoid buying or eating food that is no longer safe to eat.

Proper storage of leftovers prevents them from spoiling.

LIFE SKILL

RESOLVE CONFLICTS

What Would You Do?

Your brother likes milk as a snack. But he never puts the milk container back in the refrigerator. When you tell him that this isn't safe, he gets angry. How could you resolve this conflict?

HANDBOOK LIFE SKILLS pp. 268–279

HEALTH ACTIVITY

Food Safety

SET GOALS

1 Families are often in a rush after a meal. People may forget to clean up and store food safely. By working together, however, time can be saved.

2 List some things that need to be done after a meal. Set a goal to follow food safety guidelines.

3 List jobs for different family members as part of a clean-up plan. Take the plan home. Show it to your family. Change it if you need to. Then follow it at home.

LESSON WRAP UP

Show What You Know

1. What are some signs that food has spoiled?

2. What should you do with leftover food?

3. **THINK CRITICALLY** Why is it important to rinse fresh fruits and vegetables?

Show What You Can Do

4. PORTFOLIO **APPLY HEALTH ACTIVITY** **Set Goals** Make a checklist with three goals of how you can prepare and handle food more safely. Check your list at the end of the week to see if you met your goals.

5. LIFE SKILL **PRACTICE LIFE SKILLS** **Make Decisions** Old leftovers are often thrown away spoiled. How can people try to eat leftovers in time to avoid waste and still be safe?

HANDBOOK LIFE SKILLS pp. 268–279

YOU CAN MAKE A DIFFERENCE

TECHNOLOGY

Space Food

Astronauts Sharing a Meal

The first astronauts sucked liquid foods out of plastic tubes. All of their food was ground up like baby food.

Today, astronauts' food is more like the food you might take camping. It comes in several forms. Some foods are heat-processed and stored in tins. Some are freeze-dried or must be mixed with water before they are eaten. A very few "natural form" foods such as carrot sticks or nuts are allowed.

The Space Shuttle menu includes around 70 foods and 20 drinks. Astronauts have different meals each day for six days, then the menu repeats. They eat three meals a day plus snacks. One astronaut removes meals for the crew from storage and heats them in a small warming oven.

Scientists are working to design a better space food. They need to make the food safe and nutritious but also lightweight and tightly packed. Also, the food cannot use much water, and the packaging must withstand a lot of pressure.

MAKE DECISIONS

CHOOSE FRESH FOOD

Suppose you are traveling on the Space Shuttle for a week. You may bring only one piece of fresh fruit or one vegetable for each day. You cannot cook on the shuttle. What would you bring? Why? Make a list and compare it with other students' lists.

CHAPTER

5 Review

VOCABULARY

Write the word or words from the box that best complete each sentence. Use each word only once.

balanced diet
carbohydrates
fiber
ingredient
junk food
protein
spoiled

1. You need __?__ to help move waste through your digestive system. (Lesson 1)
2. Salty chips and sugary donuts are sometimes called __?__. (Lesson 2)
3. To have a __?__, you need to eat a variety of foods from all five food groups every day. (Lesson 3)
4. A(n) __?__ is one of the substances mixed together to make a food. (Lesson 4)
5. Food that is no longer safe to eat is __?__. (Lesson 5)

REVIEW HEALTH IDEAS

Use your knowledge of nutrition from Chapter 5 to answer the following questions.

1. How are carbohydrates and fats alike? different? (Lesson 1)
2. How do vitamins and minerals help keep you healthy? (Lesson 1)
3. How do fiber and water help keep the body healthy? (Lesson 1)
4. Name the five basic food groups. (Lesson 2)
5. Why is eating junk food not a healthy habit? (Lesson 2)
6. Why are fruits and vegetables important to good health? (Lesson 2)
7. Why do you need to eat a variety of foods? (Lesson 3)
8. Why is reading food labels important? (Lesson 4)
9. What are some signs that food may have spoiled? (Lesson 5)
10. Why is it important to wash your hands before touching food? (Lesson 5)

APPLY HEALTH IDEAS

1. If you scrape your knee, proteins play a part in healing the scrape. What do you think the proteins do? (Lesson 1)
2. Suggest a healthful snack from each of the five food groups in the Food Guide Pyramid. (Lesson 2)
3. How healthful is a vegetable soup that lists water as the first ingredient? Explain. (Lesson 3)
4. **MANAGE STRESS** Your friend gets nervous before tests and fills up on "junk food." She says it helps her stay calm. What would you tell your friend? (Lesson 3)
5. **MAKE DECISIONS** You drop a spoon you are about to use. What must you do before you use it? Why? (Lesson 5)

Look at the food label on two of your favorite snacks. Compare the two snacks on a chart like this one. If you have trouble reading the Nutrition Facts, ask an adult to help you. Which one is a more healthful snack? Explain why.

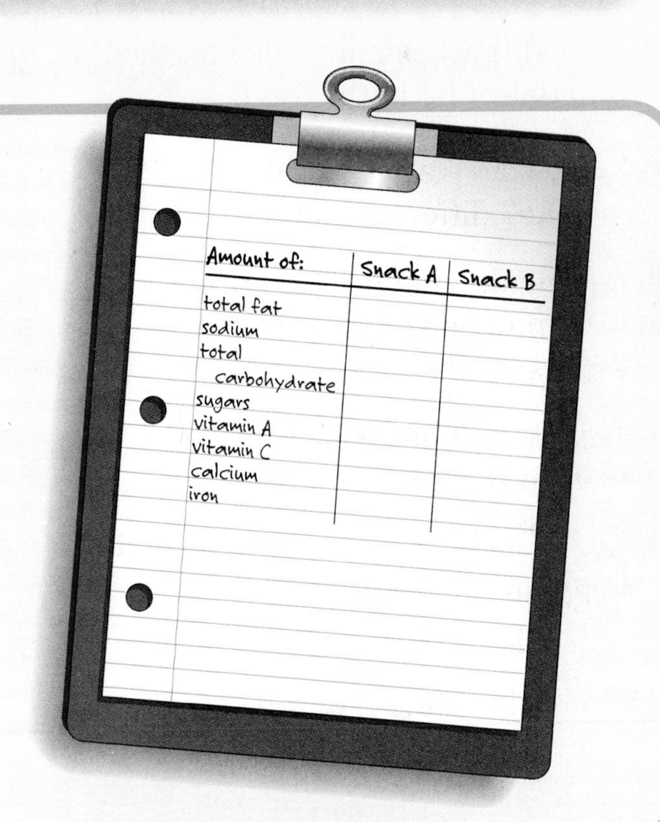

Amount of:	Snack A	Snack B
total fat		
sodium		
total carbohydrate		
sugars		
vitamin A		
vitamin C		
calcium		
iron		

CHAPTER

5 TEST

Write True or False for each statement. If the statement is false, change the underlined word to make it true.

1. Cold temperatures speed up the growth of germs that spoil food.
2. A nutrient is a material in food that your body needs to live and grow.
3. Fats, oils, and sweets are one of the five food groups.
4. Food ads always give information about a food's nutrients.
5. You should try to eat foods mostly from groups at the top of the Food Guide Pyramid.
6. A food label usually tells you the amount of fat in the food.
7. Cheese comes from the Meat Group.
8. A balanced diet provides the body the nutrients it needs for good health.
9. A sugary donut is a more healthful snack than an apple.
10. Fiber helps move wastes through the digestive system.

Write a sentence to answer each question.

11. Why are food labels important?
12. What makes up a person's diet?
13. Why is it important to drink a lot a water?
14. Name a nutrient. Tell how it helps your body.
15. Which food group should make up more servings than any other group? Why?

16–18. Name three food safety tips.

19. How can the Food Guide Pyramid help you have a balanced diet?
20. What is a sign that food is unsafe to eat?

Performance Assessment

PORTFOLIO

Plan and write a menu for a picnic that could be part of a balanced diet. Then explain how you would keep the food safe.

PHYSICAL ACTIVITY AND FITNESS

CHAPTER 6

THE BIG IDEA

Physical activity is an important part of your life. Regular physical activity:

- keeps you fit.
- helps you play, work, and think better.
- helps you feel good about yourself.

CHAPTER CONTENTS

1 PHYSICAL FITNESS IS IMPORTANT 130

2 FITNESS SKILLS 134

3 PHYSICAL FITNESS AND YOU 138

4 SAFETY AND FAIRNESS 144

YOU CAN MAKE A DIFFERENCE HELPING THE COMMUNITY 149

CHAPTER REVIEW 150

CHAPTER TEST 152

LESSON 1 PHYSICAL FITNESS IS IMPORTANT

In this lesson, you will learn:

- about the three parts of physical fitness.
- about ways fitness helps your body, your mind, and your relationships with others.

VOCABULARY

physical fitness (fiz′i kəl fit′nes) the condition in which your body works at its best

strength (strengkth) the ability to lift, push, and pull objects

flexibility (flek′sə bil′ə tē) the ability to bend and move your body easily

endurance (en dùr′əns) being able to continue an activity for a long time without tiring

QUICK START You like to run races with your friends. Sometimes you win and sometimes you lose. How can you prepare yourself to do your best?

Regular physical activity helps keep your body working at its best. *Physical activities* include games, sports, and other actions that involve moving your body. But physical activities keep more than your body healthy. You feel better about yourself when you are active. And physical activities give you a chance to share good times with family, friends, and classmates.

Many physical activities can be shared with friends.

ree Parts of Physical Fitness

'hysical fitness is the condition ıich your body works at its best. g fit helps you work and play easily. It helps keep you from ng sick. It can even help you think clearly.

Vhat does "being fit" mean? It ıs you have strength, flexibility, endurance. These are the three ; of physical fitness.

trength is the ability to lift, ɔush, and pull objects.

'lexibility is the ability to bend ınd move easily.

Endurance helps you continue an ıctivity for a long time without iring.

You work on all these parts just by g active every day. With practice can really improve all of these ;. For example, running in a game g builds strength in your legs. cing or gymnastics keeps you ble. Swimming helps you gain ırance.

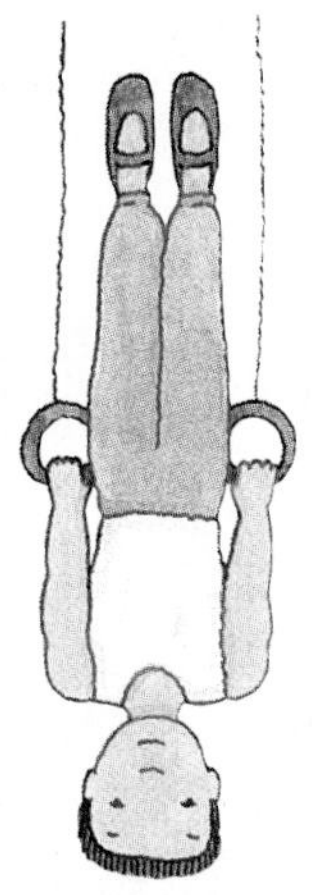

This gymnast's strength helps him support his whole body on his arms.

A basketball player uses flexibility to keep the ball away from players on the other team.

Riding a bicycle is one way to build endurance.

MANAGE STRESS

/hat Would You Do?

ɔur friend is about to run in a ack race. He's afraid he's not ady. What can he do each ay to feel better?

HEALTH ACTIVITY

Power Pictures

You will need: used magazines, scissors, construction paper, glue

1. Cut out pictures of physical activities.
2. Decide which pictures show strength, which show flexibility, and which show endurance. Make a collage for each group.
3. Decide on one activity from each group that is best for you to do. Give reasons for your choices. Explain how often you will do each. Talk to a coach or physical education teacher first.

HEALTH FACT

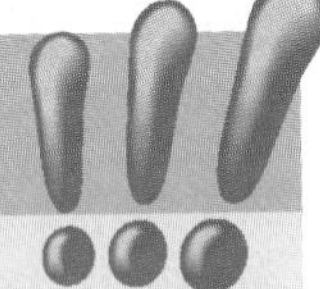

"Body fat can be good for you."

This is true. Your body needs a certain amount of fat to be healthy. Body fat helps your body absorb certain vitamins. Fat also protects your bones and organs in case you fall or get bumped. And in cold weather, body fat helps keep you warm. But too much fat means your heart works extra hard so that your body can carry the extra weight.

Fitness and Physical Health

Being physically active helps your muscles get stronger. The heart is an organ made mostly of muscle tissue. So, your heart gets stronger from physical activity. And as you become more active, your lungs can do a better job.

Your heart, lungs, and blood vessels work together to carry oxygen to all parts of your body. They can do this important job better when you are physically fit.

Being physically active also helps you keep a healthy weight. But remember—you also need a balanced diet for a healthy weight. A strong heart and healthy body weight will help you lead a healthier, longer life.

Fitness and Overall Health

Physical activity also improves your emotional and intellectual health. Taking care of your health shows that you value yourself. Being physically active helps improve your self-esteem. It also helps you deal with stress. It helps you relax and think things through, to solve problems.

Physical activity helps you find out more things about yourself. What are you good at? What can you improve?

Being physically active also improves your social health. Working and playing with others helps you learn something about them. And you'll probably make new friends along the way.

Games, sports, and other activities help people enjoy one another.

LESSON WRAP UP

Show What You Know

1. Explain what physical fitness is and name its three parts.

2. How does physical activity help your body, your mind, and your relationships?

3. **THINK CRITICALLY** Your best friend is not very active. She doesn't like working or playing hard. How could you help her understand that physical fitness is important?

Show What You Can Do

4. PORTFOLIO **APPLY HEALTH ACTIVITY** **Make Decisions** Think about what you do each day. Make some decisions about how you can be more physically active during your day. Write them out.

5. LIFE SKILL **PRACTICE LIFE SKILLS** **Manage Stress** Many employers give their employees time for fitness workouts. List reasons why this is a good idea.

HANDBOOK **LIFE SKILLS** pp. 268–279

LESSON

2 FITNESS SKILLS

In this lesson, you will learn:

- the importance of fitness every day.
- about the six fitness skills.

VOCABULARY

agility (ə jil′i tē) being able to change direction quickly

balance (bal′əns) being able to keep the body in a steady, upright position

coordination (kō ôr′də nā′shən) using more than one part of the body at the same time

power (pou′ər) a combination of strength and speed

reaction time (rē ak′shən tīm) time it takes to notice and respond to something

speed (spēd) being able to move quickly

QUICK START What skills does it take for a soccer player to kick the ball and score a goal?

Every day you can see people using their strength, flexibility, and endurance. A mail carrier walks long distances carrying a heavy sack. A mother bends to pick up her toddler. Children play a game of tug-of-war. Being fit helps people work and play more easily.

Think of all the things you do during the day. Whether you're skating or sweeping the floor, physical activity is an important part of your daily activities.

Carpenters need to be fit to do their jobs well.

To play hopscotch or hula hoops you need agility, balance, and coordination.

Fitness Skills

A *skill* is an ability that can get better with training and practice. To improve your physical fitness, you can work on six skills. Practicing all six skills will improve your overall strength, flexibility, and endurance.

- **Agility** is being able to change direction quickly. For example, you are agile when you jump out of the way during a game of tag. To gain agility, practice activities that need quick movements such as volleyball or tennis.

- **Balance** is being able to hold your body in a steady, upright position. When you stand on one foot, you use the skill of balance. To improve your balance, try skating or gymnastics.

- **Coordination** is using more than one part of your body at the same time. To improve coordination, try soccer or basketball. To kick a ball, you watch the ball with your eyes and kick it with your foot. In basketball, you dribble and run with the ball at the same time.

HEALTHWISE CONSUMER

Games

Games are a good way to build fitness skills. But you don't need to purchase equipment for all of your games at the store. For example, all you need to play hopscotch is a piece of chalk, a stone, and a hard, flat area. Hopscotch builds agility, balance, and coordination. What other games can you play with things you already have or could make?

A baseball player needs a quick reaction time to hit the ball, power to hit it far, and speed to run to base.

CULTURAL PERSPECTIVES

Biking for Fitness and Fun

In many parts of the world, people of all ages use bicycles instead of cars to get around. Bike riders use many of the six fitness skills. People who bicycle use their legs and arms in different ways at the same time (coordination). They keep themselves and their bikes upright (balance). They may need to dodge other bikes or people (reaction time and agility). They often need to push hard with their legs (power).

- **Speed** is the ability to move quickly. You can improve your speed by moving quickly—and running or swimming quickly, as quickly as is comfortable for you.
- **Reaction time** is the length of time it takes to notice and respond to something. To shorten your reaction time, practice batting and catching a softball.
- **Power** is both strength and speed. You use power when you kick a soccer ball or hit a home run. To increase your power, you need to make your muscles stronger. Running makes your legs stronger. Push-ups make your arms stronger. Sit-ups strengthen your stomach muscles.

LIFE SKILL

MAKE DECISIONS

What Would You Do?

Your friend asks you to join an in-line skating club. It's for very good skaters. You aren't a good skater yet. What decision would you make?

HEALTH ACTIVITY

Improving Your Fitness

SET GOALS

1 Think of one thing you do that uses physical activity. It could be something you do every day such as walking up stairs. It could be doing a sport or game you enjoy.

2 List all the fitness skills you use to do this activity.

3 Set a goal to improve each skill you need for the activity. Explain how to reach your goal. You can even come up with your own "moves" to improve the skills.

LESSON WRAP UP

Show What You Know

1. How does physical fitness affect your daily activities?

2. List three fitness skills. Give an example of a way you use each one.

3. **THINK CRITICALLY** How can knowing the fitness skills help you improve your fitness?

Show What You Can Do

4. PORTFOLIO **APPLY HEALTH ACTIVITY** **Set Goals** Think of a fitness skill that you use the least. Write a plan to show how you can improve it by doing everyday activities.

5. LIFE SKILL **PRACTICE LIFE SKILLS** **Obtain Help** With a partner, practice one fitness skill you wish to improve. Help each other to use the skill better and to measure your progress.

LESSON

3 Physical Fitness and You

In this lesson, you will learn:

- how to improve your physical fitness.
- about the parts of a physical fitness routine.
- about guidelines for improving fitness.

VOCABULARY

warm-up (wôrm′up′) gentle body movements like stretching that prepare the body for physical activity

aerobic exercise (â rō ′bik ek′sər sīz′) any nonstop activity that makes you breathe deeply and speeds up your heart rate

cool-down (kül′doun) gentle body movements like stretching done after physical activity to relax the body

Quick Start You want to take part in a walk-a-thon. How can you prepare for the long walk?

The way to get better at something is to do it. If you want to be a faster runner, go out and run. If you want to jump high, practice jumping. If you want to be a better juggler, juggle every day. The key is to do it. You will get faster. Your muscles will get stronger. Your coordination will improve. When you practice skills regularly, you can get better at the activities you enjoy.

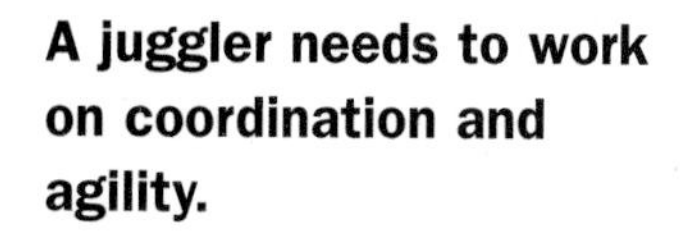

A juggler needs to work on coordination and agility.

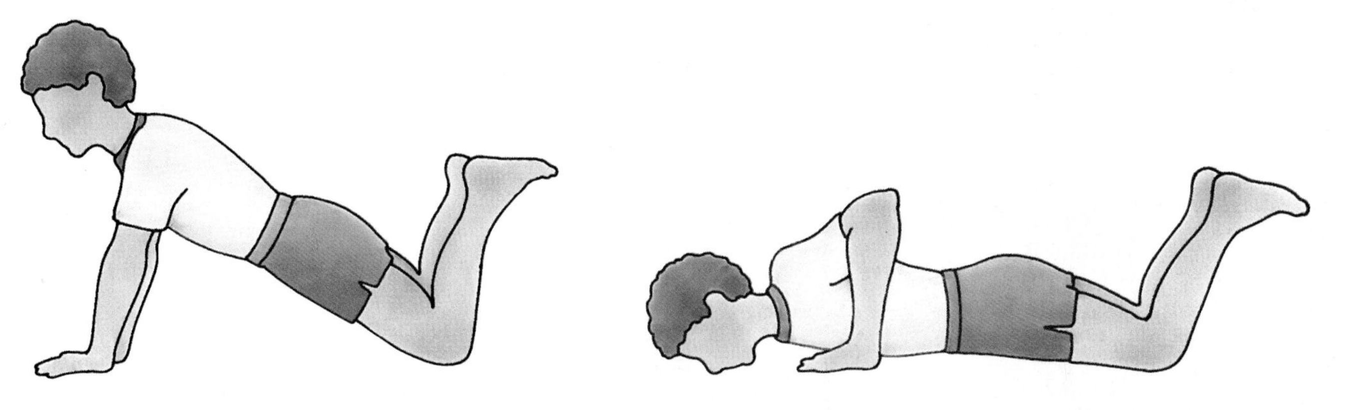

Strength—Push-ups build up strength in your arm and shoulder muscles. Power and balance are important when doing push-ups.

Building Your Physical Fitness

Few people are really good at all the six fitness skills. You may have developed some of them, but you may need to improve others. Try these steps for improving your skills:

- Decide which skills need improving.
- Find activities you enjoy that use those skills. Ask a parent, teacher, or friend to coach you. He or she can show you how to do the activities and then watch you do them.
- Practice the skills by doing the activities over and over.

As you work on improving the six fitness skills, you will develop the three parts of fitness—strength, flexibility, and endurance.

LIFE SKILL

MAKE DECISIONS

What Would You Do?

You want to join the basketball team. But you can't sink a basket. Your fitness skills are not developed enough. Your friend says, "Try another sport." What would you do?

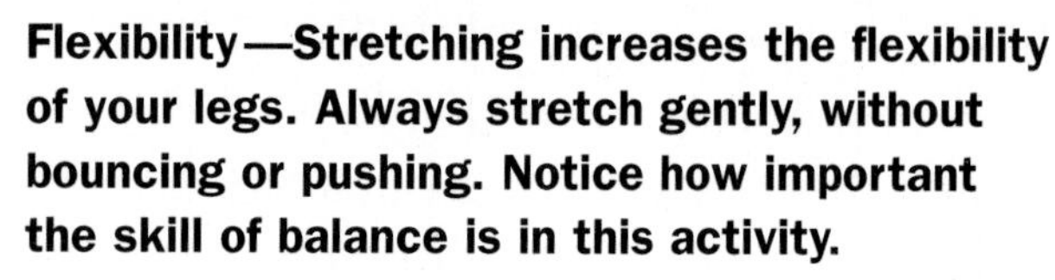

Flexibility—Stretching increases the flexibility of your legs. Always stretch gently, without bouncing or pushing. Notice how important the skill of balance is in this activity.

Endurance—Jumping rope builds endurance. Notice how you use the skills of agility, balance, coordination, and speed.

A Physical Fitness Program

You can put together a program to build your physical fitness. First measure your physical fitness. To do this, try the five exercises that make up the President's Challenge. An *exercise* is an activity that works on a skill or a part of fitness. See pages 286–287 of the Handbook.

These activities will help you learn what parts of your physical fitness you may want to improve. Be sure you work with a coach, physical education teacher, or a fitness-trained adult as you put together your program.

Also, be sure your program follows a three-part routine that includes doing an activity *before* and *after* the exercise itself. See the opposite page for more information about a three-part routine for all physical activity.

A Three-Part Routine

MAKE ANY PHYSICAL ACTIVITY PART OF A THREE-PART ROUTINE

1. Warm Up

Before you do any physical activity, warm up. **Warm-up** activities prepare your body for physical activity. They include gentle movements like stretching that get your heart beating faster. They help keep your muscles from getting injured. Then start your physical activity slowly.

2. Aerobic Exercise

Do physical activity for 20 minutes. You might choose to do aerobic exercise. **Aerobic exercise** is any nonstop activity that makes you breathe deeply and speeds up your heart rate. Jumping rope, jogging, and bicycling are aerobic activities. These activities will help build your endurance.

3. Cool Down

After physical activity, you need to cool down. **Cool-down** activities help your heart return to its usual rate. Gentle stretching helps relax your muscles and prevent cramping.

HEALTH FALLACY

“No pain, no gain.”

This is not true! You don't want to push yourself until your body is in pain. Build up your endurance and strength by doing a little bit more each day. Stretch gently and try to reach a little farther each day. Your muscles may be sore after you do an activity, but they shouldn't hurt during the activity.

Guidelines for Physical Fitness

Follow these suggestions as you put together your physical fitness program.

- Be active every day, but don't overdo it. Carry out your fitness plan three to five times a week.
- Gradually increase how long you perform an activity. Little by little you could build up the time you spend doing an activity.
- Warm up before physical activity and cool down afterwards. If you feel pain at any time, stop the activity.
- Drink a lot of water to replace fluids your body loses when you sweat.
- Wear proper safety equipment and know your limits. See Lesson 4 to learn more.

It is important to drink plenty of fluids—especially water—while you are active.

HEALTH ACTIVITY

A Physical Fitness Program

OBTAIN HELP

1 Brainstorm a list of physical activities that you enjoy. Choose two activities to include as part of a physical fitness program.

2 Talk to a physical education teacher, coach, parent, or trusted adult about the activities you have chosen. Ask them to help you include these activities into a physical fitness program.

3 Make a list of ways that these activities can improve physical fitness. Also make a list of tips for doing the activities.

LESSON WRAP UP

Show What You Know

1. How could you build your physical fitness?

2. Describe the three parts of a physical fitness routine.

3. **THINK CRITICALLY** What do you think is the most important guideline to follow when building physical fitness? Explain.

Show What You Can Do

4. PORTFOLIO **APPLY HEALTH ACTIVITY** **Obtain Help** Write a letter to a friend. In your letter ask if your friend is willing to help you improve your fitness. It'll take time and patience.

5. LIFE SKILL **PRACTICE LIFE SKILLS** **Make Decisions** Role play with a group. Jog in place. Pretend you're all running so you won't be late for school. You feel a cramp in your leg. What should you do?

HANDBOOK LIFE SKILLS pp. 268–279

LESSON

4 SAFETY AND FAIRNESS

In this lesson, you will learn:

- the importance of knowing your own physical abilities and limits.
- about different kinds of safety equipment.
- about being a good sport.

VOCABULARY

safety equipment (sāf′tē i kwip′mənt) protective gear used to reduce the risk of injury

teamwork (tēm′wûrk′) working with other people in a group or on a team to reach a common goal

competition (kom′pi tish′ən) a contest between people or teams

QUICK START You are with a classmate. He wants to get a bike helmet with a certain design. The box says, "Size: Adult." Should your friend get the helmet?

Regular physical activity can help you stay fit your whole life. You can also have fun being physically active. To get the most fun out of physical activity, you need to work and play safely. You also need to get along with others.

What are these bike riders doing to stay safe? Is there anything they should do to be safer?

How Much Can I Do?

How do you know how much physical activity is right for you? You know you are doing the right amount if you feel good while you are doing the activity. You should not be tired the next day from doing too much.

Suppose you want to get better at a physical activity. For example, you want to be able to run farther. Try running a little farther each day. You will feel a little stronger each time. If you feel tired or sore, rest or stop for the day. Otherwise you risk getting hurt.

When you play with others, remember that everyone has different abilities and levels of fitness. Let your friends stop and rest when they need to.

Know your own physical abilities and limits. Take a break when you need one!

PRACTICE REFUSAL SKILLS

What Would You Do?

While playing field hockey, you feel dizzy. You stop to rest. Other team members complain that now the teams are uneven. How can you answer them?

Wearing safety equipment shows that you take your activities and your health seriously.

Gearing Up for Safety

For some activities you'll need to wear safety equipment. **Safety equipment** is protective gear that helps reduce the risk of injury. Remember to ask an adult for help when using safety equipment for the first time. This chart lists safety equipment for some activities you may enjoy.

PHYSICAL ACTIVITY	SAFETY EQUIPMENT	HOW IT PROTECTS
Bike riding	Helmet	Protects skull and brain
In-line skating or skateboarding	Helmet; wrist, elbow, and knee pads	Protects skull and brain; protects wrists, elbows, and knees from bruises, sprains, and breaks
Swimming	Goggles	Protects eyes
Soccer	Shin guards	Protects shins from bruises
Softball batter	Hard-shell helmet with ear covering	Protects skull, brain, and ears
Catcher	Face mask, chest protector, and shin guards	Protects face and throat; pads body to prevent injuries to heart, ribs, stomach, and shins

Being a Good Sport

You can have a good time playing games or doing other physical activities with friends and family members. It's even more fun when you are a good sport. A *good sport* plays in a way that lets everyone have a good time. The best part of being a good sport is that you enjoy yourself more, too. Here are some tips for being a good sport.

- Play fair. Play by the rules. And don't try to change the rules during the game.
- Take turns with others when you are doing an activity such as shooting baskets or diving into a pool.
- Do your own part as well as you can. Let others do their parts. Offer them your encouragement.
- Listen to the coach or team leader.

When you practice teamwork and fair play, everyone wins—and has more fun!

Taking part in team activities improves your physical health and social health. Working with others in a group or on a team to reach a common goal is **teamwork**. Part of teamwork means being polite to your teammates. It means supporting them as well. It means being fair.

All team activities involve competition. **Competition** is a contest between people or teams. When you play in a competition, you do your best to win. But you still need to respect the players on the other team.

If you lose, you may feel disappointed. But try not to feel angry or sad. Don't blame others for losing. Work harder to succeed next time. Everyone will enjoy the game if you all have fun as you play.

HEALTHWISE CONSUMER

Biking Safety

Even if you can ride a bike well, you still need to wear a helmet. Even the best rider needs to be ready for the unexpected. And you need the right helmet. It must fit you. A helmet that is too big can fall off easily. When choosing a helmet, ask the store clerk to help you choose one that's just right for you.

HEALTH ACTIVITY

Work It Out

RESOLVE CONFLICTS

1 Talk about conflicts that can come up during physical activities. For example, what if two people on the same team want to play the same position?

2 Choose a situation. Talk about how players can use teamwork and fair play to resolve the conflict. How can you help others have a good attitude?

3 Role play the situation for others in the class. Show how teamwork and fair play helped resolve the conflict.

LESSON WRAP UP

Show What You Know

1. Explain why you should know your own physical abilities and limits.

2. What kinds of safety equipment would you use for in-line skating? Why do you need to use this equipment?

3. **THINK CRITICALLY** Why are teamwork and being a good sport important when you take part in a sports competition?

Show What You Can Do

4. PORTFOLIO **APPLY HEALTH ACTIVITY** **Resolve Conflicts** Make a booklet showing how teamwork and fair play can help resolve conflicts. Draw pictures and write captions to explain the situations.

5. LIFE SKILL **PRACTICE LIFE SKILLS** **Manage Stress** Some of your friends don't wear helmets when they play baseball. You want to bring your helmet to a game. But you're afraid your friends may tease you. What should you do?

HANDBOOK LIFE SKILLS pp. 268–279

YOU CAN MAKE A DIFFERENCE

HEALTH HEROES

Helping the Community

These children are helping Robert Leathers create a new playground.

Q: How did you become interested in designing playgrounds?

Mr. Leathers: As a child I built treehouses in the woods. In 1970 my children's school needed a playground. I worked with other adults and children to design and build a playground.

Q: How do children help you?

Mr. Leathers: We ask children to make drawings and to write stories about the "perfect" playground. Many communities also have a design team of 30 to 40 children. This team helps research ideas and create the design for each playground.

Q: What is usually the most popular playground item?

Mr. Leathers: Swings.

Q: How do you think future playgrounds will different?

Mr. Leathers: They will be learning centers as well as active play environments.

SET GOALS

PLANNING A PLAYGROUND

If you were part of a design team, what ideas would you want to include in a "perfect" playground? Set a goal to prevent playground injuries. List three ideas that would make a playground a fun and safe place to play.

CHAPTER

6 REVIEW

VOCABULARY

Write the word or words from the box that best complete each sentence.

aerobic exercise
coordination
endurance
physical fitness
power
teamwork
warm-up

1. The condition at which your body works its best is called __?__. (Lesson 1)
2. Continuing an activity a long time without tiring is the skill of __?__. (Lesson 1)
3. Using more than one part of your body at the same time takes __?__. (Lesson 2)
4. Nonstop activity that makes you breathe deeply and speeds up your heart is __?__. (Lesson 3)
5. Working with others to reach a common goal is __?__. (Lesson 4)

REVIEW HEALTH IDEAS

Use your knowledge of physical activity and fitness from Chapter 6 to answer these questions.

1. What are the three parts of physical fitness? (Lesson 1)
2. Describe two ways physical activity affects your health. (Lesson 1)
3. Describe three of the six fitness skills. (Lesson 2)
4. How is physical activity a part of your daily activities? (Lesson 2)
5. What can you do to build your physical fitness? (Lesson 3)
6. List two guidelines for improving fitness safely. (Lesson 3)
7. How do cool-down activities help the body? (Lesson 3)
8. What do you need to reduce injury when in-line skating? (Lesson 4)
9. Why is it important to know your own fitness abilities and limits? (Lesson 4)
10. Why is playing according to the rules important? (Lesson 4)

APPLY HEALTH IDEAS

1. You are riding a bike. How might you use the fitness skills of agility, balance, and coordination? Which of the three parts of fitness are you improving? (Lesson 2)
2. Why is it important to build a physical fitness program around activities you enjoy? (Lesson 3)
3. Explain why being a good sport is important to teamwork. (Lesson 4)
4. PORTFOLIO **MAKE DECISIONS** You and some friends are deciding what to do. One friend suggests watching TV. Another wants to play ball. Explain why playing ball might be the better choice. (Lesson 1)
5. LIFE SKILL **RESOLVE CONFLICTS** Members of your soccer team are arguing with those of another team. Each side claims the other cheats. List ways this conflict could be resolved. (Lesson 4)

Talk to the members of your family. What activities for building fitness does your family enjoy?

Make a list of the activities that everyone likes and can do together. Choose activities that build strength, flexibility, and endurance. Try to do each activity at least once a week.

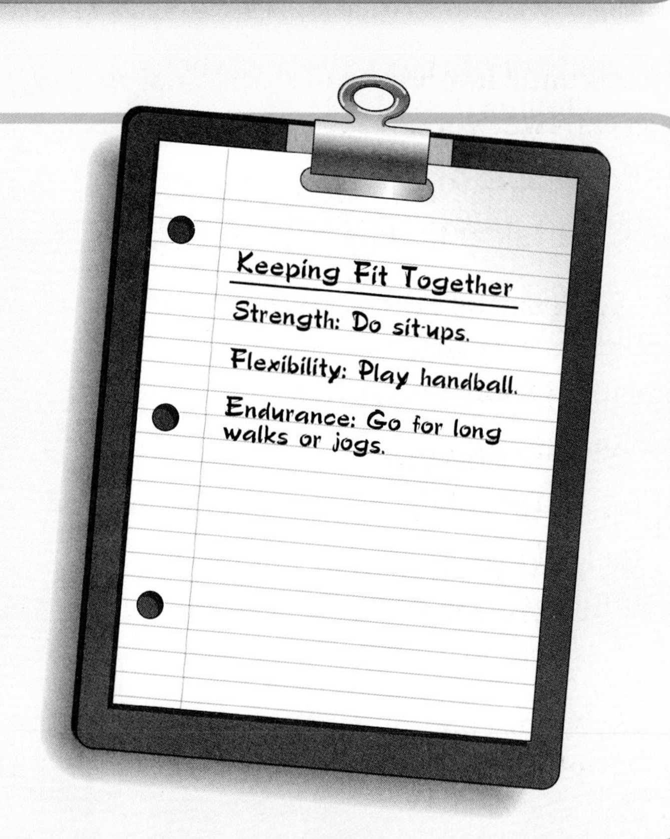

CHAPTER

6 TEST

Write True or False for each statement. If the statement is false, change the underlined word or phrase to make it true.

1. Being physically fit can help you do a physical activity more easily.
2. Push-ups and sit-ups strengthen muscles and build speed.
3. The condition in which your body works at its best is physical fitness.
4. A warm-up activity is a nonstop activity that speeds up your heart rate.
5. Do not push yourself beyond your limits.
6. Teamwork is a contest between two teams.
7. Being able to change direction quickly shows the skill of power.
8. It's best to begin physical activity quickly.
9. The ability to push, lift, and pull objects is called endurance.
10. Physical activity can make you feel good about yourself and improve your self-esteem.

Write a sentence to answer each question.

11. What fitness skills do you use when you dash to first base?

12–13. Name two guidelines to follow when building physical fitness.

14. How do good sports treat their teammates?

15. How does physical activity improve all parts of your health?

16–18. Describe the three parts of a physical fitness routine.

19. Why is it best to go at your own pace when doing physical activity?

20. How does safety equipment reduce your risk of injury?

Performance Assessment

You decide to start a school fitness club. Make a poster explaining the purpose of the club. Tell what kinds of things club members will do. Describe the benefits that club members might gain.

DISEASE PREVENTION AND CONTROL

CHAPTER

7

You can help prevent or control disease by knowing:

- how diseases are caused.
- how diseases can affect the body.
- how you can prevent the spread of disease.
- what you can do to stay healthy.

CHAPTER CONTENTS

1 LEARNING ABOUT DISEASES 154

2 COMMUNICABLE DISEASES 160

3 FIGHTING DISEASES 164

4 HIV AND AIDS 170

5 STAYING HEALTHY 176

YOU CAN MAKE A DIFFERENCE ROBOTS HELP OUT 179

CHAPTER REVIEW 180

CHAPTER TEST 182

LESSON

1 LEARNING ABOUT DISEASES

In this lesson, you will learn:

- about the symptoms of diseases.
- about the causes of diseases.
- about two kinds of germs that can make you sick.

VOCABULARY

disease (di zēz′) an illness; condition that keeps the body from feeling or working well

symptom (simp′təm) a sign of a disease

germ (jûrm) a tiny particle or living thing that can cause disease

bacteria (bak tîr′ē ə) one-celled living things

virus (vī′rəs) a tiny particle, smaller than a bacterium, that can multiply only inside a living cell

QUICK START Think about the last time you were sick. How did you feel? Whom did you tell?

You probably know when your body is working at its best. You can think clearly. You can work and play hard without feeling tired. But sometimes your body doesn't work at its best. You feel sick. In this lesson, you will learn what happens to you when you are sick.

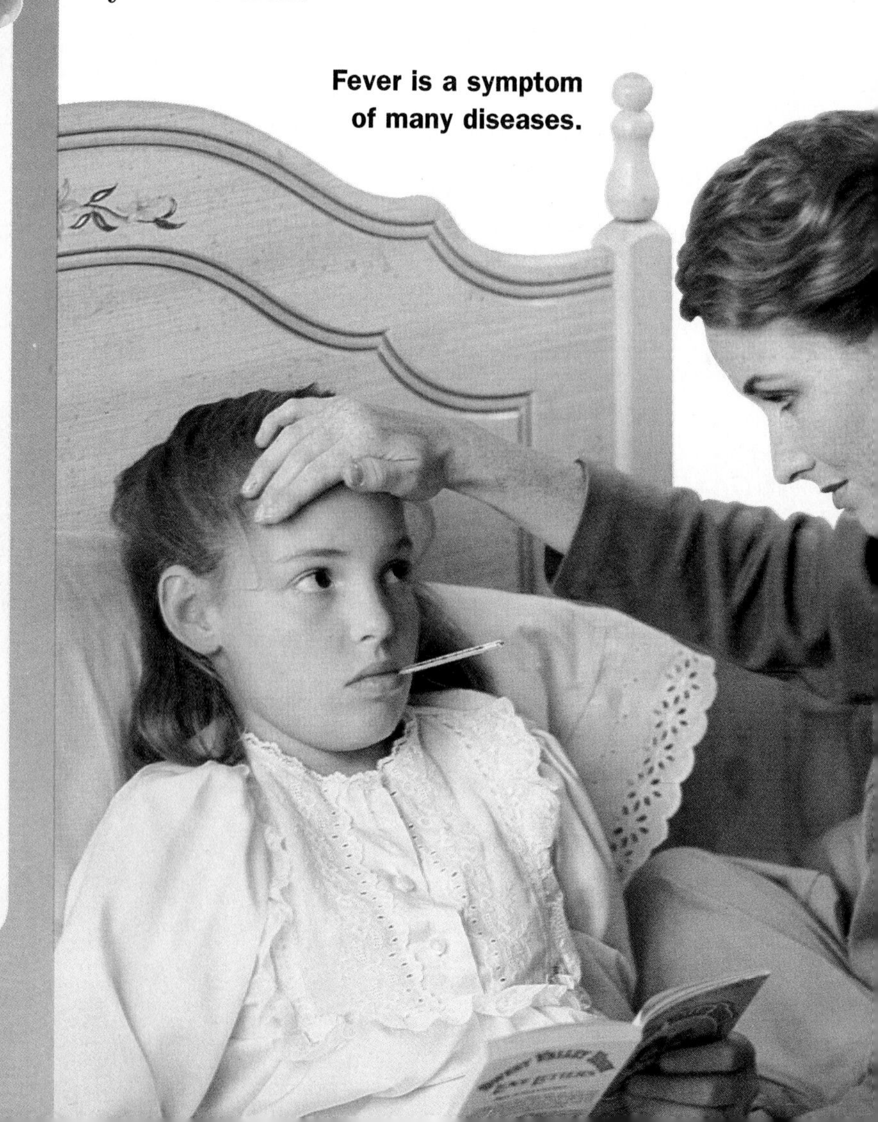

Fever is a symptom of many diseases.

Disease and Your Body

How did you feel the last time you were sick? Tired? Was your throat sore? Did you cough a lot? "Being sick" means having an illness, or a disease. A **disease** is any condition that keeps your body from feeling or working well.

Every disease has its own symptoms. A **symptom** is a sign of a disease. For example, a scratchy throat and sneezing are symptoms of a cold. A fever may be a symptom, too. When you have a *fever*, your body temperature is higher than normal. It shows that your body is fighting the disease.

When You Are Sick

When you're sick, tell an adult who will make a helpful health decision for you. At school, tell a teacher or school nurse. At home, tell your family. Your family may have to take you to a doctor.

Be sure to do your part when you are sick. Your body needs rest—so get a lot of it. It's also important to drink plenty of water or juice and eat healthful foods. Taking special care of yourself can help you feel better faster.

OBTAIN HELP

What Would You Do?

You're at recess. A friend tells you that he has a stomachache and feels sick. How could you help your friend?

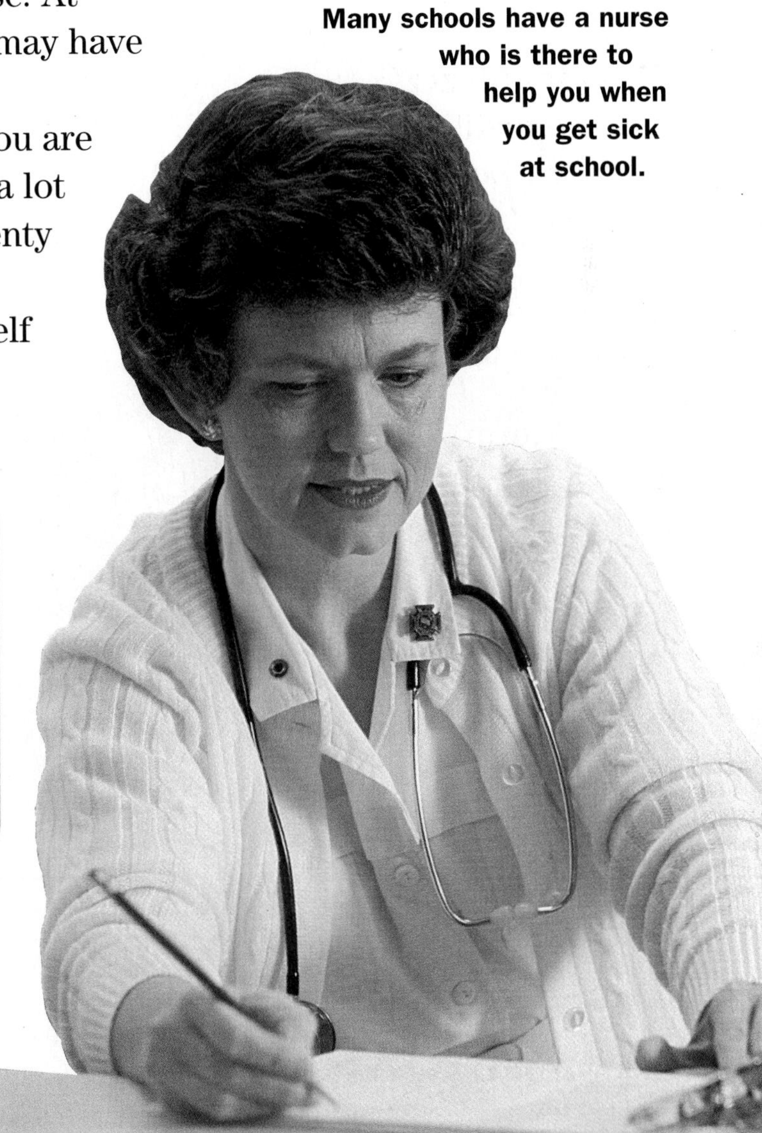

Many schools have a nurse who is there to help you when you get sick at school.

HANDBOOK LIFE SKILLS pp. 268–279

Some Causes of Disease

There are many causes of diseases. Some diseases are inherited. That is, they are passed from grandparents to parents to children by birth. An inherited disease can skip some family members but affect others. Sickle-cell anemia is one example of an inherited disease.

Some other diseases are caused because parts of the body are not working properly. Diseases of the heart and lungs are examples.

Many diseases are caused by contact with germs. **Germs** are tiny particles or living things that can make you sick. They are so small that they can only be seen through microscopes. Germs are everywhere—in the air, water, and soil.

To cause a disease, germs have to get into your body. Germs can enter through a cut, scrape, or burn in the skin. You can also breathe in germs. Most germs enter the body if you touch something with germs on it and then touch your eyes, mouth, nose, or ears.

Different bacteria have different shapes.

E. coli

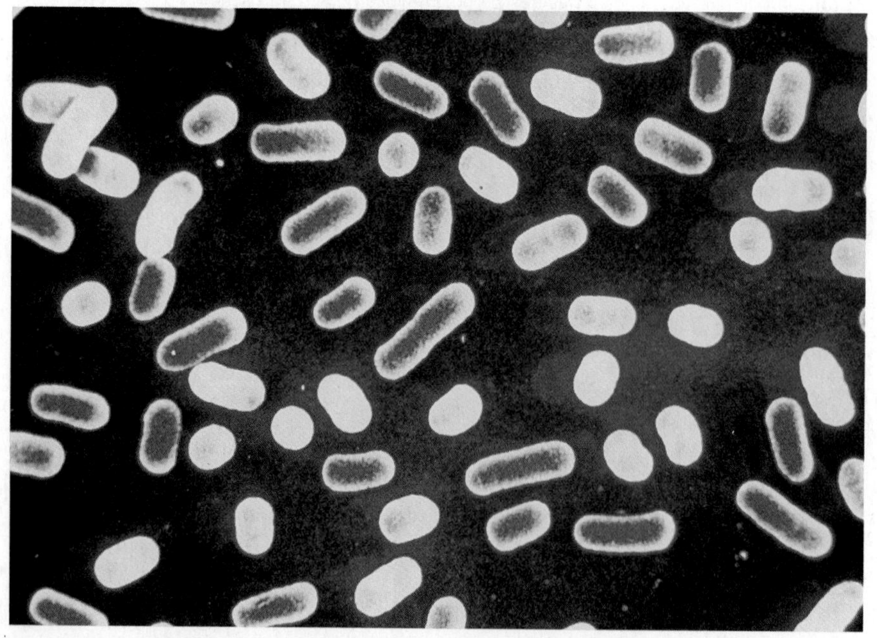

Magnification: 14,300×

Spirillum volutans

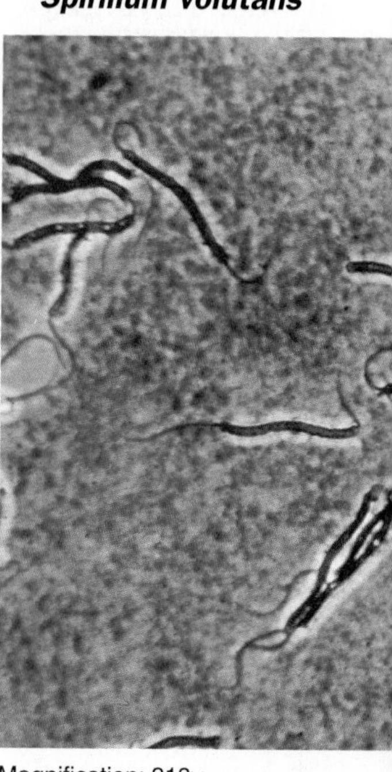

Magnification: 313×

Bacteria

There are different kinds of germs. One kind of germ is called bacteria. **Bacteria** are one-celled organisms. An *organism* is something that is alive.

Once bacteria get inside the body, the conditions are just right for some of them to live. It's warm and moist. And there's plenty of food—from body cells. In time, bacteria grow and multiply. If a lot of harmful bacteria grow in your body, you can get sick. One way bacteria can be harmful is by giving off *poisons*. These poisons can hurt your body cells and cause disease.

Different kinds of bacteria cause different diseases. Two different bacteria cause strep throat and pinkeye.

Usually your body can fight diseases by itself. But sometimes, it needs help. If a disease is caused by bacteria, a doctor may give you a medicine that kills bacteria.

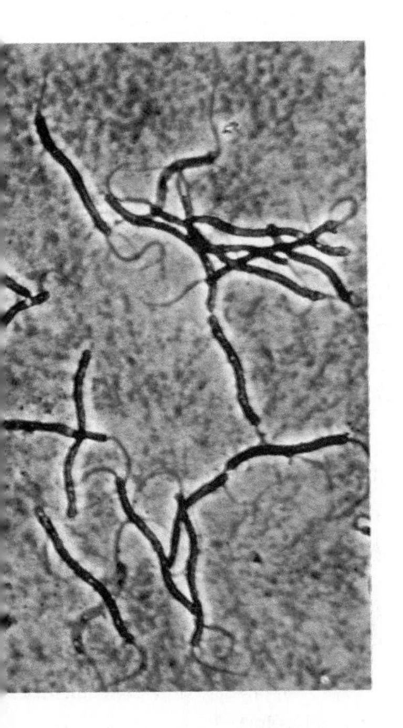

Streptococcus mutans

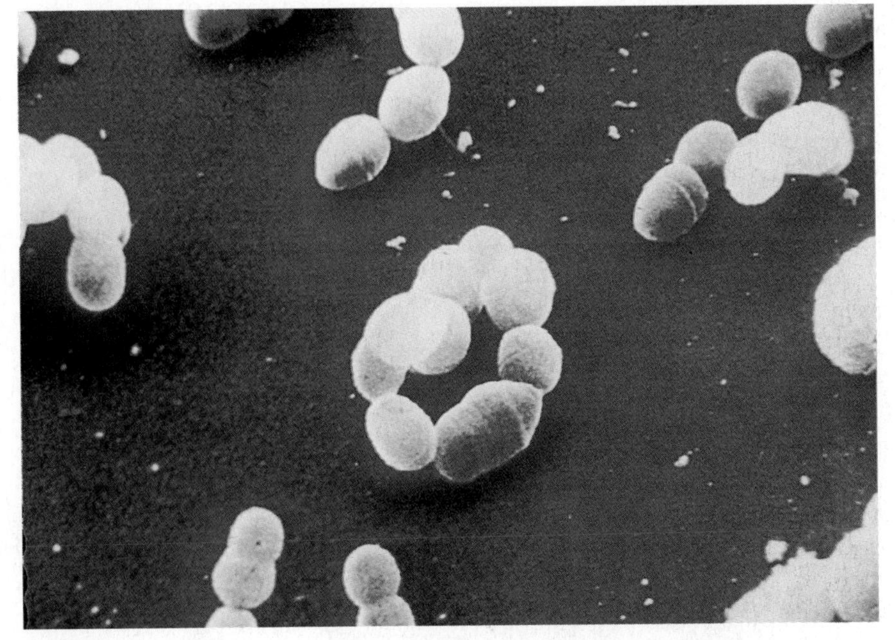

Magnification: 33,350×

HEALTH FALLACY

"Medicine can cure a cold."

This is not true. Researchers have yet to discover a cure for the common cold. However, there are medicines that can relieve the symptoms of a cold. Some medicines lower a fever. Some medicines can ease a cough. Other medicines can dry up a runny nose. It's up to your body to fight the disease.

Viruses

A virus is another kind of germ that can cause disease in people. **Viruses** are particles much smaller than bacteria. They are not really living things. They can multiply inside a living cell.

When a virus enters the body, it gets into a cell. Once in the cell, the virus can multiply quickly. In a short time, one virus can make many more of itself. These new viruses burst out of the cell, killing the old cell. New viruses then invade nearby cells and make more viruses. The process repeats itself. In this way, viruses spread and cause disease.

The common cold is caused by a virus. Chicken pox is another disease caused by a certain virus. Other diseases caused by viruses include measles, mumps, rabies, and the flu.

There are no medicines that can destroy a virus. But certain medicines can keep you from getting a disease caused by a virus. If you do get a disease caused by a virus, your family or doctor may give you medicine to ease the symptoms. But the only cure is to rest and help your body fight the disease.

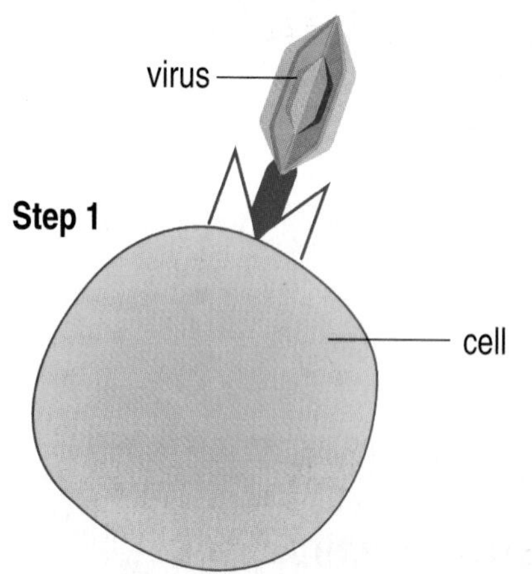

The virus attaches itself to the cell.

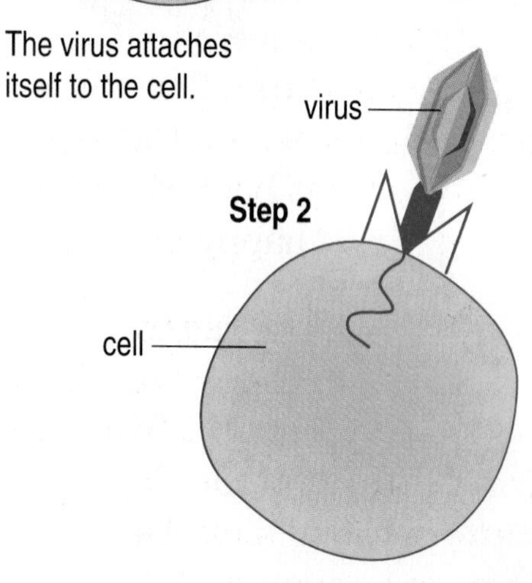

Parts of the virus are emptied into the cell.

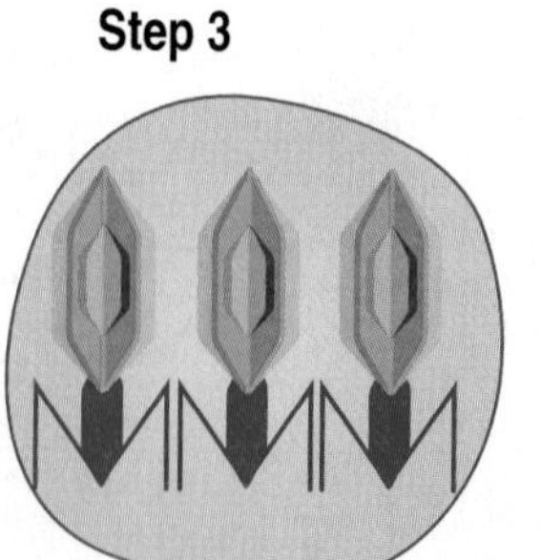

Once inside the cell, the virus makes copies of itself.

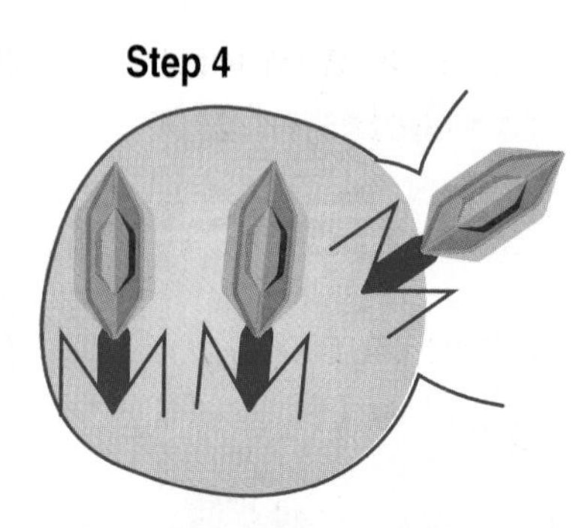

The new viruses break out of the cell. They invade other cells and continue to make more viruses.

HEALTH ACTIVITY

SCIENCE CONNECTION

How Viruses Cause Disease

You will need: index cards

1. Work with a partner. Think about what happens when a virus gets inside a cell. Review the diagram on page 158, then organize the steps into a numbered outline. Write each step on a card.
2. Use the outline as a guide to write a scene or tell a story. Describe what happens to the virus when it attacks a cell. What happens to the cell?
3. Share your scene or story with other students.

LESSON WRAP UP

Show What You Know

1. What is a disease? Give two examples of disease symptoms.
2. Explain two causes of diseases.
3. **THINK CRITICALLY** How are viruses and bacteria different?

Show What You Can Do

4. PORTFOLIO **APPLY HEALTH ACTIVITY** **Science Connection** Make a flowchart to tell a story starting with: "A person touches a doorknob that has bacteria on it." Give the story a "happy ending."
5. LIFE SKILL **PRACTICE LIFE SKILLS** **Make Decisions** You have tickets to see your best friend in the school play. On the day of the show you feel sick. Decide whether or not you will go. Explain your decision.

HANDBOOK LIFE SKILLS pp. 268–279

LESSON

2 COMMUNICABLE DISEASES

In this lesson, you will learn:

- about ways some diseases can be spread.
- about ways you can prevent the spread of diseases.

VOCABULARY

communicable disease (kə mū′ni kə bəl di zēz′) a disease, caused by germs, that can spread to a person from another person, an animal, or an object

QUICK START You have a cold. The doctor told your family you should stay home for a day or two. But you'd like to go out and play with your friends. Why is it important to do what the doctor says?

People say that you "catch" a cold. But what do you catch it from? Usually, you catch a cold from another person. Diseases in which germs are spread to a person from another person are called **communicable diseases**. Bacteria and viruses, remember, are two kinds of germs. Germs can also be spread by animals. They can be on objects and in foods and unclean water too.

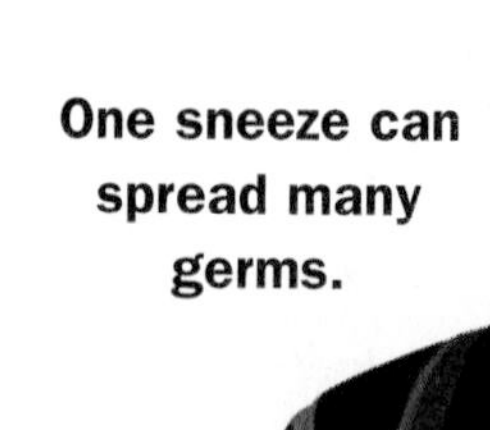

One sneeze can spread many germs.

The Spread of Germs

Many diseases are communicable. If you know how they are spread, you can help avoid catching them. Here are the most common ways communicable disease can spread.

- **Contact with another person or object**—Suppose your sister has a cold. She sneezes into her hand. You might touch her hand. You might also touch an object that she touched, like a toy. The germs can pass to your hands. They could then enter your body if you touch your mouth. They could also enter through a cut or break in the skin.
- **Through the air**—If someone coughs or sneezes, germs get into the air. You can breathe in those germs.
- **Contact with animals or insects**—If you get bitten by an insect or animal, the bite makes a break in the skin. Germs can then enter through the break. Germs can enter in the smallest of openings. For example, a tick bite can spread Lyme disease. Rabies can be spread from the bite of an animal with the disease.
- **From water or food**—Unclean water can contain harmful germs. If you swim in or drink the water, germs can enter your body. You can also bring germs into your body by eating spoiled food or food not cooked thoroughly.

Insects can carry germs to foods.

CULTURAL PERSPECTIVES

No Germs Allowed!

Disease prevention takes different forms in different countries. In some Asian countries such as Japan, it is considered polite to wear a mask over the nose and mouth when ill. This avoids spreading germs to other people. In the United States, masks are used in hospital rooms, or by workers exposed to dust.

Preventing Germs From Spreading

You can help stop germs from spreading.

- Cover your mouth with a tissue when you cough or sneeze. (Use the bend of your elbow if you don't have a tissue.) Throw away the tissue so that no one else touches it.
- Wash your hands before you eat and after you use the bathroom.
- Do not share eating utensils. Don't drink from the same cup or eat from the same plate as someone else.
- Don't share toothbrushes, towels, hats, scarves, combs, or hairbrushes.
- Keep cuts clean and bandaged.

LIFE SKILL

MANAGE STRESS

What Would You Do?

Head lice are tiny insects that live in hair and on scalps. They cause sores. People spread them by sharing hats and other things. Your school has an outbreak. You're scared. How can you feel safe?

HEALTHWISE CONSUMER

Drink to Your Health.

Make sure you buy milk that has been pasteurized. Before milk is sent to the store, it is treated with heat to kill harmful germs. Milk is usually heated to about 145°F for 30 minutes. After that, the milk is quickly cooled to below 45°F. It is stored at this temperature. This process, called *pasteurization*, makes milk safe to drink.

HEALTH ACTIVITY

Germ Buster

You will need: drawing paper, colored markers

1. Make up a cartoon character called Germ Buster. Germ Buster's goal is to stop germs from spreading. List ways Germ Buster can meet this goal.
2. Draw a cartoon strip that shows how Germ Buster meets the goal. Put your cartoons on a bulletin board. Title the bulletin board *The Adventures of Germ Buster*.
3. Talk about how you, too, can meet Germ Buster's goal at home and at play.

LESSON WRAP UP

Show What You Know

1. Name three ways germs can spread.
2. What are two things you can do to stop the spread of communicable diseases?
3. **THINK CRITICALLY** Ben covers his mouth with his hand when he coughs. What's the next thing he should do as soon as possible? Explain.

Show What You Can Do

4. PORTFOLIO **APPLY HEALTH ACTIVITY** **Set Goals** Set a goal to keep from catching or spreading diseases at school. Make a list of things you can do in school to stop the spread of germs.
5. LIFE SKILL **PRACTICE LIFE SKILLS** **Make Decisions** The student next to you on the school bus begins to cough and sneeze without covering his mouth. How might you handle this situation?

HANDBOOK LIFE SKILLS pp. 268–279

LESSON 3

FIGHTING DISEASES

In this lesson, you will learn:

- how your body keeps out germs.
- how your body fights disease.

VOCABULARY

immune system (i mūn′ sis′təm) all the body parts and activities that fight disease

antibody (an′ti bod′ē) a chemical made by the immune system to fight a particular disease

immunity (i mū′ni tē) the body's ability to protect itself or fight diseases caused by germs

vaccine (vak sēn′) a medicine that causes the body to form antibodies against a certain disease

QUICK START Tears, your skin, and your blood all have a job in common. What is it?

Bacteria, viruses, and other germs are all around. Some get inside your body. But you're not sick all the time. Why not? The reason is that your body can fight many germs. In this lesson, you will find out more about how your body protects itself against germs.

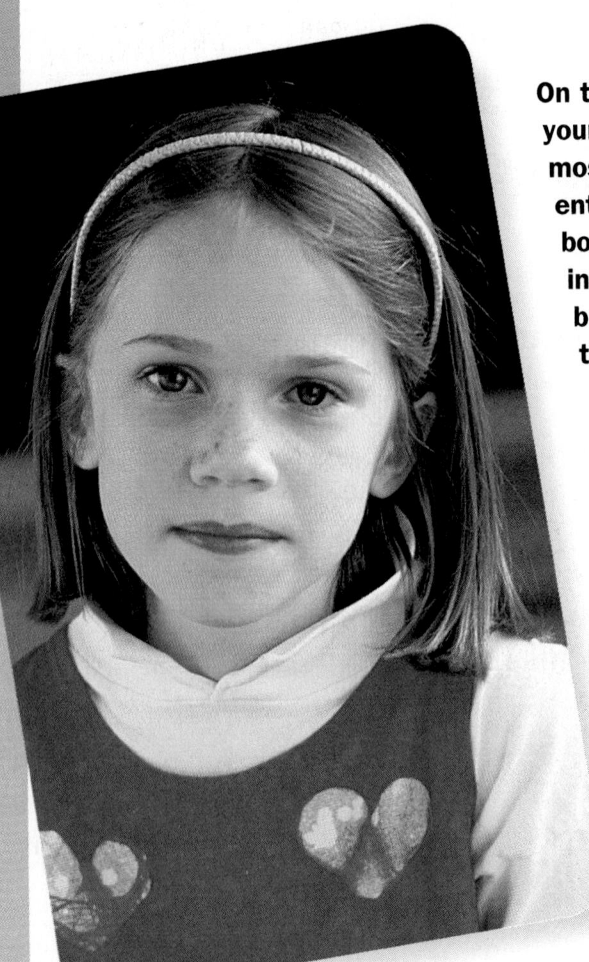

On the outside, your skin stops most germs from entering your body. On the inside, your body also acts to fight disease.

INFOGRAPHIC

GERMS—KEEP OUT!

Certain parts of your body work to keep germs from entering. They are the body's first line of defense against many kinds of germs. Study the picture to find out how each part works.

Nose, Mouth, and Throat

The linings in your nose, mouth, and throat release *mucus*. Mucus and the tiny hairs in your nose and windpipe trap germs. You get rid of trapped germs when you sneeze, cough, or blow your nose.

Stomach Juices

Your stomach juices digest food and also kill many germs that enter your stomach.

Tears

Tears wash germs from your eyes. They also can kill germs.

Saliva

Saliva, the liquid in your mouth, helps digest food. Saliva also helps your body get rid of some germs.

The Skin

The tough outer layer of the skin protects you. Germs can enter only when you have a cut, burn, or scrape.

Cells That Kill Germs

Sometimes germs do get into your body. Like everyone else, you have had some illnesses. Perhaps you've had a cold recently. Have you ever had chicken pox or the measles? These and other illnesses are common among children your age.

Once germs get into your body, the body starts to fight back. Special cells patrol your blood, waiting to battle invading germs. *White blood cells* are cells in the blood that fight bacteria, viruses, and other germs. White blood cells are always present in your blood. They are always ready to do their job.

When germs are in your body, extra white cells are released into the blood. These cells travel to where they are needed. They wrap themselves around the germs and "eat" them.

This boy has chicken pox. Most likely he won't get it again.

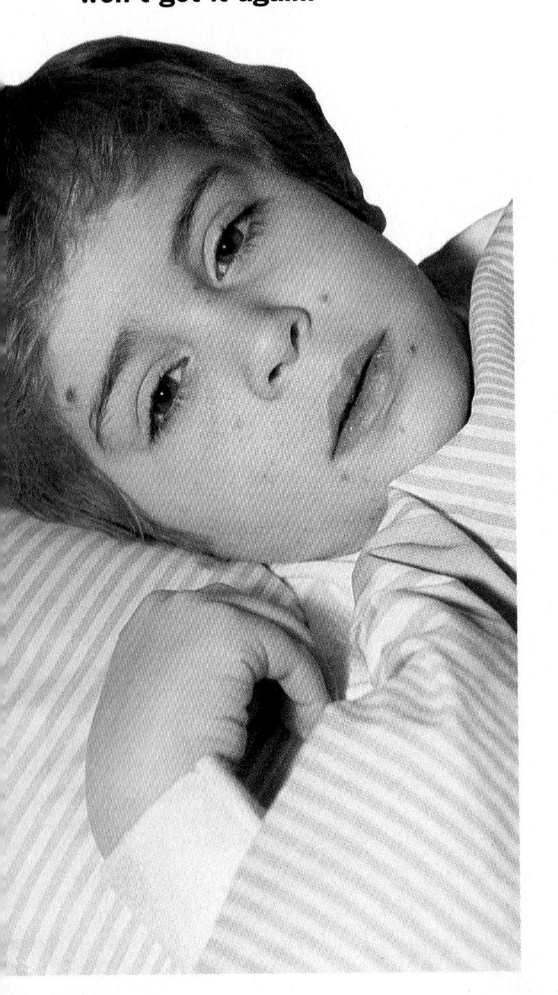

Your Immune System

For some germs, your body pulls out all its defenses. The **immune system** is all the body parts and activities that fight diseases. It works by being able to "recognize" a particular germ whenever it invades. Your immune system is then able to call up just the right weapons each time that germ appears.

For example, a person who has had chicken pox will probably never have it again. The immune system knows how to keep the disease from coming back.

White blood cells are part of the immune system. There are many kinds of white blood cells. Some signal to the others to join the fight. Some make chemicals that stop germs in their tracks—before they make you ill.

How Your Immune System Works

When a germ first enters the body, white blood cells soon launch their attack. You become sick if the germ fights back hard enough. Special white blood cells make antibodies to fight the germ. **Antibodies** are chemicals produced by the body to fight a specific disease. Antibodies are the immune system's main weapons against disease. Each kind of antibody fights only one kind of germ.

Even after the antibodies have destroyed the germ, certain white blood cells "remember" that germ. If the germ returns, these white cells can start antibody production much more quickly. The germ may be killed before it can make you sick. This is called immunity. **Immunity** is the body's ability to protect itself or fight diseases caused by germs.

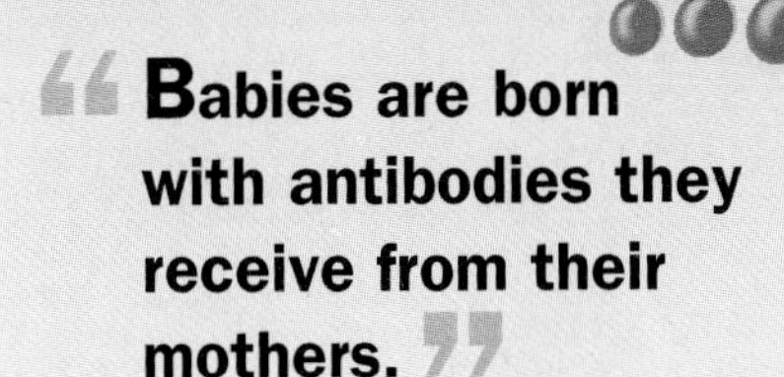

HEALTH FACT

"Babies are born with antibodies they receive from their mothers."

This is true. Inside the mother, a single layer of cells separates her baby's blood from her own. Food and oxygen pass through this layer to feed the baby. Antibodies also pass through the layer of cells. Even after birth, these antibodies protect babies until their own immune systems take over.

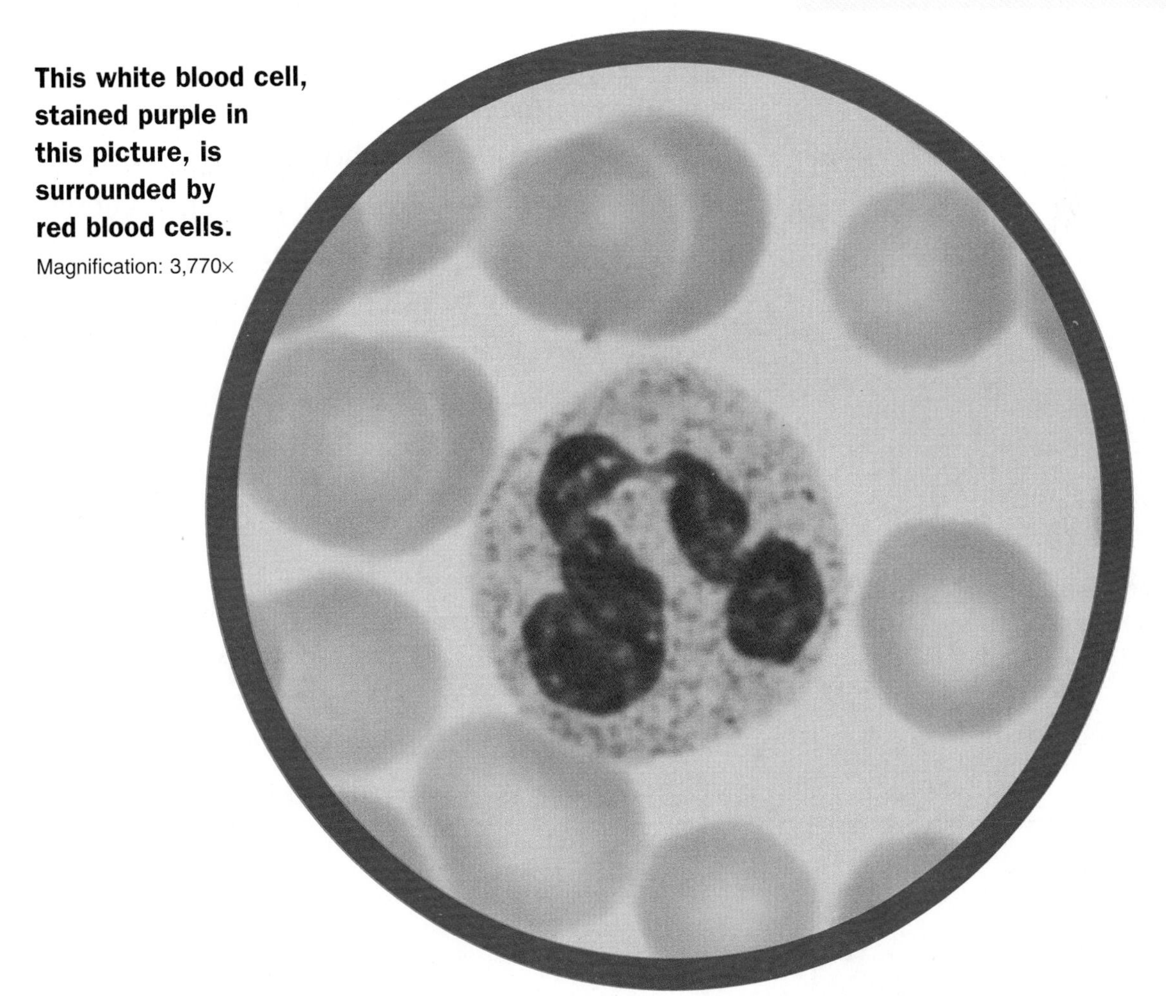

This white blood cell, stained purple in this picture, is surrounded by red blood cells.
Magnification: 3,770×

Vaccines

You've learned about how your body makes antibodies to develop immunity to diseases. Your body can develop immunity without actually having had the disease.

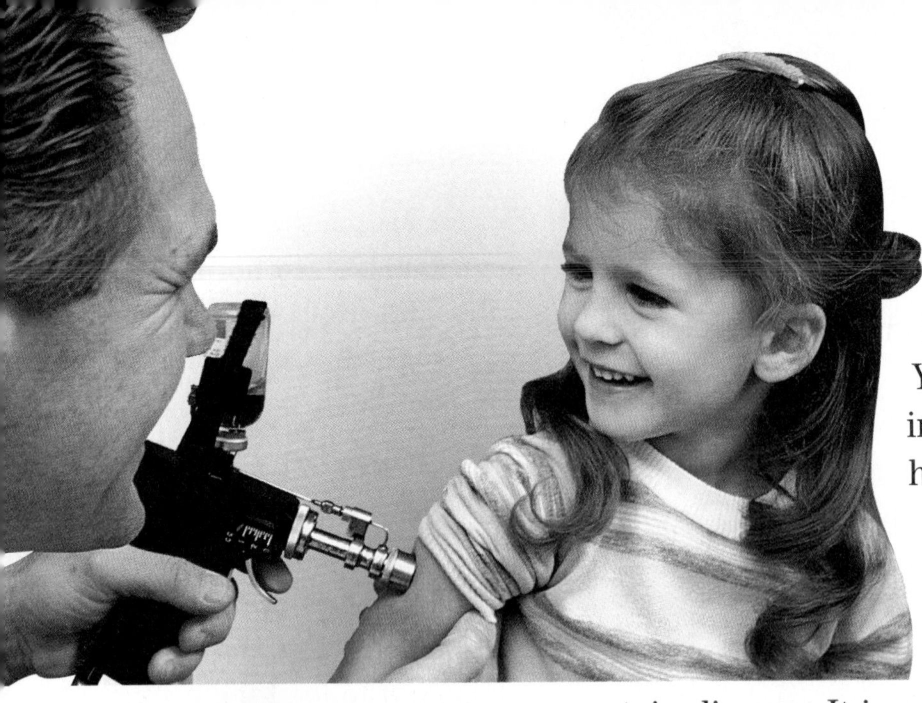

A booster makes sure your body stays immune to a disease.

A **vaccine** is a medicine that causes the body to form antibodies against a certain disease. It is a substance made from weakened or killed germs. A vaccine can be given as an injection or taken by mouth.

Some vaccines give immunity to a disease for life. Others give you immunity for only a short time. For those vaccines you need a booster. A *booster* is an additional vaccine given again in a few years. For example, booster vaccines are given to prevent polio.

Before you started school, you probably had to have vaccines. You got your first vaccines about a year after you were born. These vaccines caused your body to make certain antibodies. You were then protected against diseases such as polio, measles, and whooping cough. Thanks to the vaccines, most people may never get sick from those diseases.

MANAGE STRESS

What Would You Do?

Your younger brother is going for a vaccine. He is worried and afraid. What can you tell him that might help him manage his stress?

HEALTH ACTIVITY

SCIENCE CONNECTION

Body Defenses

1 Work with a group. Review how white blood cells and antibodies attack germs. Think about ways your body stops germs from entering, such as the skin or mucus.

2 Create a skit about how the body might defend against germs that make it past the first line of defense. Show the order of events that might happen.

3 Perform your skit for the class.

LESSON WRAP UP

Show What You Know

1. Explain how two different parts of the body keep germs out.

2. How does the immune system destroy harmful germs?

3. **THINK CRITICALLY** You were with your friend while he was coming down with a cold. Now he is at home sick, but you didn't get sick. Why do you think you didn't get sick?

Show What You Can Do

4. PORTFOLIO **APPLY HEALTH ACTIVITY** **Science Connection** Make a drawing that shows how your body defends against germs. Trace the path of a germ from the skin to the blood. Show what might happen to the germ as it travels through the body.

5. LIFE SKILL **PRACTICE LIFE SKILLS** **Practice Refusal Skills** A classmate offers you a taste of her yogurt bar. Why should you refuse? How would you refuse?

HANDBOOK LIFE SKILLS pp. 268–279

LESSON 4

HIV AND AIDS

In this lesson, you will learn:

- about AIDS and HIV, the virus that causes AIDS.
- about the effects of HIV on the immune system.
- about ways in which HIV can and cannot be spread from one person to another.

VOCABULARY

AIDS (Acquired Immune Deficiency Syndrome) (ādz) a very serious disease in which the immune system is extremely weak

HIV (Human Immunodeficiency Virus) (āch ī vē) the virus that attacks the immune system and leads to AIDS

QUICK START You just heard a news report about a famous person with AIDS. What is AIDS? What causes it? Why is it on the news so much?

AIDS is a very serious disease in which the immune system is extremely weak. AIDS is caused by a virus. This virus weakens a person's immune system. The weakened immune system has trouble fighting off germs.

The letters in AIDS stand for Acquired Immune Deficiency Syndrome. *Acquired* means something that can be gotten. That is, a person can get the virus that causes AIDS from someone else. *Immune deficiency* means the person's immune system is *deficient*. That is, it lacks something that it needs. And a *syndrome* is a group of symptoms that happen with a disease.

You cannot become infected with HIV by shaking hands.

Scientists and researchers like Dr. Ho are working to develop a vaccine to prevent HIV infection.

AIDS and HIV

The virus that causes AIDS is named **HIV**. The letters in HIV stand for Human Immunodeficiency Virus. HIV is the virus that attacks the body's immune system.

HIV destroys one kind of white blood cell, called T-cells. This white blood cell helps to organize the work of the immune system. When T-cells are destroyed, the immune system cannot protect a person against invading germs. The immune system is deficient.

A person with HIV may develop many symptoms including fever, rash, body aches, and weight loss. However, many people with HIV may show no symptoms for a long time. A person can have HIV a long time before coming down with AIDS. The only way people can know if they have HIV is by having a special blood test.

HEALTH FACT

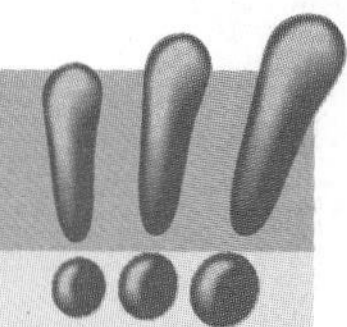

“A carefully planned, balanced diet can help keep a person with HIV healthy longer.”

This is true. In one study, HIV patients ate a variety of healthful foods. They also took vitamins. Some of the people stayed healthy longer than those who weren't as careful about their diet. Scientists believe that a balanced diet can help keep the body's immune system healthy.

When HIV Becomes AIDS

A person with HIV eventually develops AIDS. The immune system breaks down as HIV kills more and more T-cells. At that point the person is said to have AIDS. A person with AIDS has a harder and harder time fighting diseases. The person may develop diseases such as certain kinds of pneumonia and certain cancers. A healthy immune system would have been able to fight off these diseases.

It may take 10 years or longer for people with HIV to develop AIDS. During this time, they can spread HIV.

There is no cure for AIDS at this time. People with HIV can take drugs that help slow the breakdown of the immune system. Other drugs are used to slow down the development of diseases. These drugs can add months or years to the person's life.

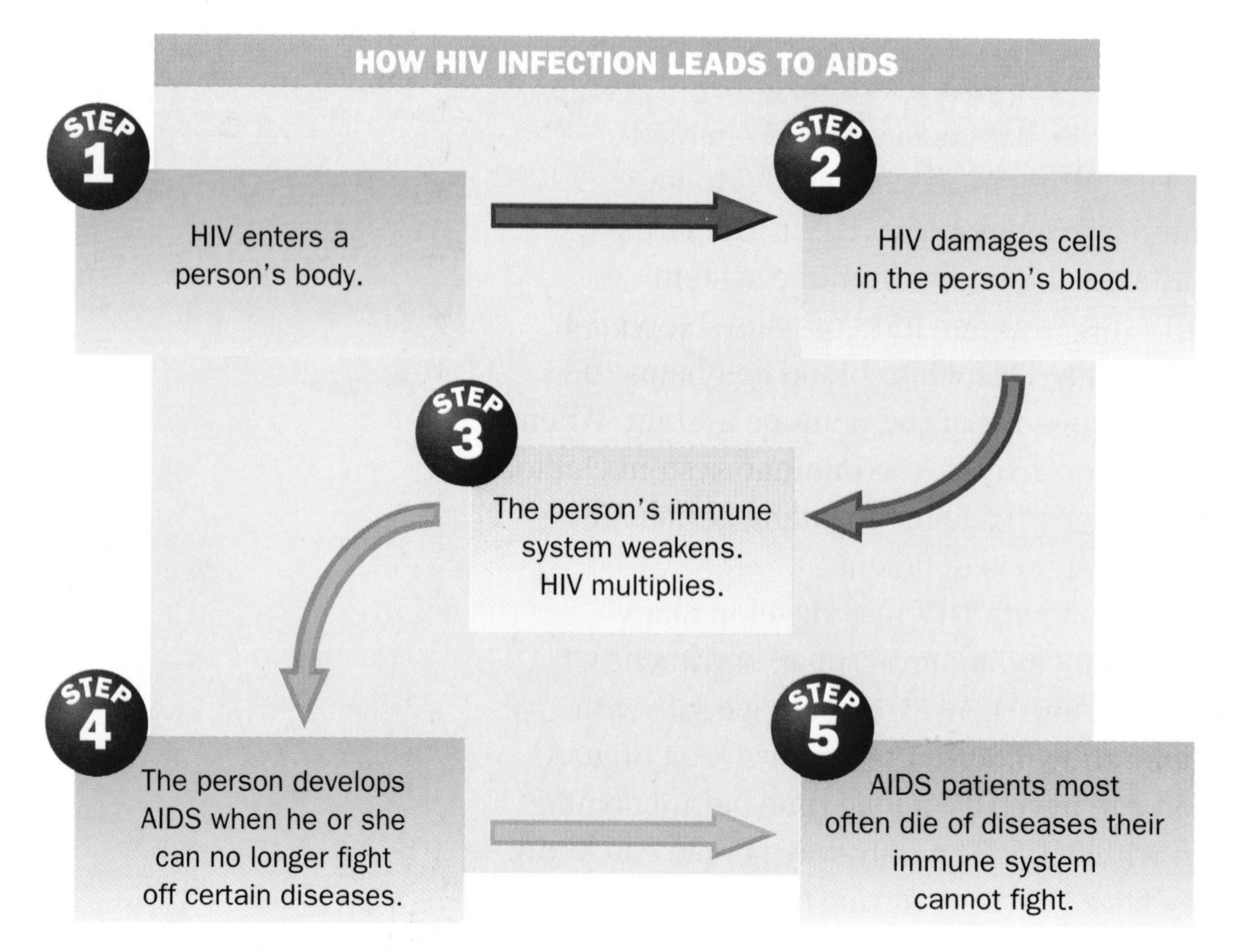

How HIV Is Spread

HIV is a communicable disease. But, unlike a cold, it is spread in very few ways. HIV can only be passed from one person to another through body fluids, such as blood. To avoid the virus, it is important to know how HIV can spread.

- Drug users can get HIV by sharing needles. A used needle may have a tiny bit of blood inside that contains HIV. HIV can be passed to the next person who uses the needle.
- In the past, HIV was sometimes spread when blood was given to a person at a hospital. However, all blood in the United States is now tested for HIV before being given to a sick or injured person. If it contains HIV, the blood is not used.
- A mother with HIV may pass the virus to her unborn baby. The baby may be born with HIV.
- HIV can spread if a person with HIV is bleeding from a cut. Health care workers wear rubber gloves to avoid touching blood. Never touch anyone's blood.

Bringing food to AIDS patients can be very helpful and rewarding community service.

LIFE SKILL

OBTAIN HELP

What Would You Do?

Your class is doing a community service project. Students will deliver meals to the homes of AIDS patients. Should you worry about getting AIDS? Who might you talk to about your concerns?

How HIV Is *Not* Spread

HIV is *not* spread in the following ways.

HIV is not spread through everyday things people do together at school, work, home, or anywhere else.

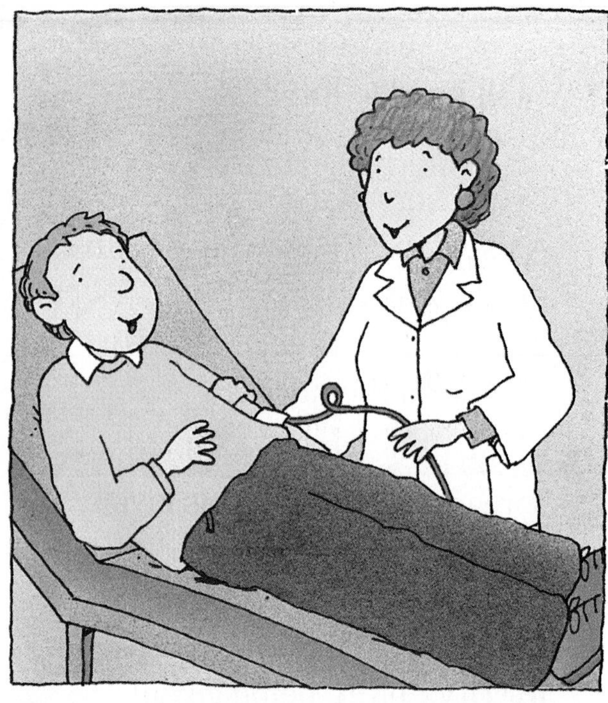

HIV can't be caught by a person *giving* blood. Health care workers use an unused needle to take each person's blood.

HIV is not spread by shaking hands with an infected person.

HIV isn't spread by insect bites.

HEALTH ACTIVITY

HIV and AIDS Slogans

You will need: strips of mural paper

1 Not knowing the facts about a disease can cause stress in many people. Think of ways to give people the facts about HIV and AIDS.

2 Work with a partner to write slogans, or sayings, on banners. The slogans might tell how to avoid getting HIV. Or it might tell how HIV is *not* spread.

3 Share slogans. Discuss how they can help people reduce stress by knowing the facts. Hang your slogans in the classroom.

LESSON WRAP UP

Show What You Know

1. What is AIDS?

2. List one way that HIV is spread and one way it is not.

3. **THINK CRITICALLY** Why do you think people can have HIV for a long time before coming down with AIDS?

Show What You Can Do

4. PORTFOLIO **APPLY HEALTH ACTIVITY** **Manage Stress** Write a short story about a student with HIV. Write about how other students need not be worried about getting HIV from this student.

5. LIFE SKILL **PRACTICE LIFE SKILLS** **Practice Refusal Skills** Suppose a friend has AIDS. Tell what reasons you would give for saying "no" to classmates who want to avoid your friend.

HANDBOOK LIFE SKILLS pp. 268–279

LESSON 5

STAYING HEALTHY

In this lesson, you will learn:

- about ways to strengthen your immune system.

VOCABULARY

stress (stres) the way the body and mind respond to changes around you

QUICK START You can't control everything about your health. But what can you do to stay healthy?

By now you know that harmful germs are everywhere. But you also know how your immune system defends your body against those germs. In this lesson, you will learn how to keep your immune system strong. With a strong immune system your body will be better able to fight disease.

Getting regular checkups is a good health habit.

Make Healthy Choices

The health of your immune system depends a lot on the choices you make. Follow these health habits for a strong immune system.

- Eat a variety of healthful foods that make a balanced diet. Eat foods that are high in vitamins and minerals. Avoid foods high in fat, salt, and sugar.
- Be physically active. Run, swim, bike, or take a walk—every day.
- Get enough sleep and rest. Your body uses this time to repair cells and grow new cells.
- Make responsible choices. Do not smoke, drink alcohol, or take harmful drugs.
- Recognize causes of **stress**, the way you respond to changes. Deal with your stress in healthful ways.
- Get regular checkups. A doctor will check for any signs of disease and treat the disease before it develops. The doctor checks your eyes, ears, throat, heart, and lungs. The doctor checks your height and weight too. If you need a vaccine, the doctor gives it.
- Keep up with the news. Learn about how to deal with health problems in your area.

SET GOALS

What Would You Do?

Which health habit listed on this page do you need to improve the most? Explain why you think so. Set a goal to improve that habit.

HEALTH FACT

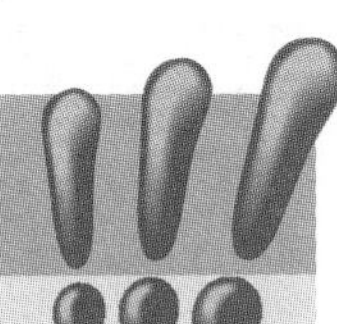

"People are living longer."

This is true. People are living longer, healthier lives. They're taking better care of themselves. Medical discoveries that prevent disease and promote health have also contributed to people living longer. In 1900, people could expect to live to the age of 47. Today, on the average, Americans can expect to reach 75. Researchers predict that by 2010 it will be 77. So keep up the good health habits and you may become a centenarian—a person over 100.

HANDBOOK LIFE SKILLS pp. 268–279

HEALTH ACTIVITY

Your Own Health Log

1 Set up a daily log as shown.

2 During the day, write any decisions you made to help you stay healthy. Write the decisions in the columns they best fit.

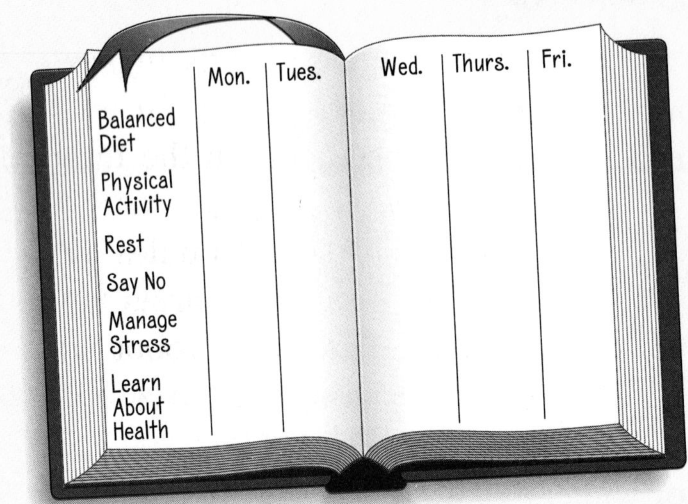

3 What if you didn't make any today? Start making them. They are easy. For example, say "no" to junk foods by eating a healthful snack. Enter that snack under "Balanced Diet" as well. Ride a bike for 20 minutes. Fill up your log in no time.

LESSON WRAP UP

Show What You Know

1. List three health habits that build a strong immune system.
2. For a healthy immune system, which kinds of foods should you eat and which should you avoid?
3. **THINK CRITICALLY** Why is it especially important to keep your immune system strong when you are sick?

Show What You Can Do

4. PORTFOLIO **APPLY HEALTH ACTIVITY** **Make Decisions** Decide which health habits most students in your class need to improve. In a group, write and perform a good-health commercial about decisions students need to make.
5. LIFE SKILL **PRACTICE LIFE SKILLS** **Obtain Help** Find out about medical practices in the past. You might ask a librarian or other adult where you can find materials on this topic.

HANDBOOK LIFE SKILLS pp. 268–279

YOU CAN MAKE A DIFFERENCE

TECHNOLOGY

Robots Help Out

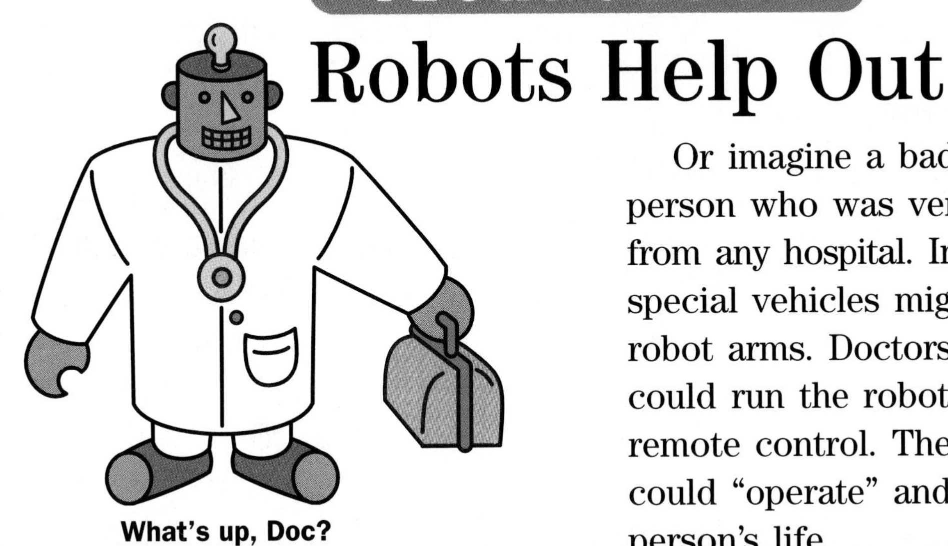

What's up, Doc?

In the future, robots may be a common feature in hospitals. Even today, robots are helping doctors keep people healthy.

If a patient needs a new hip, doctors today might use a big robot named Robodoc to help. Robodoc carves bones so that new hips fit exactly. Robodoc's carving is more precise than any human's could be.

Suppose a patient has a bad stomachache. In the near future, a tiny robot might move through the patient's stomach to find the problem. It might even carry very tiny equipment for doctors to use in surgery.

Or imagine a badly injured person who was very far away from any hospital. In the future, special vehicles might carry robot arms. Doctors miles away could run the robot arms by remote control. The robot arms could "operate" and save the person's life.

Robots will never replace doctors. However, they can make doctors' jobs easier—and help save lives.

SCIENCE CONNECTION

DESIGN A ROBOT

Imagine that you are a robot designer. Choose one thing that a doctor or dentist might want a robot to do. Draw a robot that could help out. Label the robot's parts. Explain how the robot helps the doctor or dentist. Share your drawing with the class.

CHAPTER

7 REVIEW

VOCABULARY

Write the word or words from the box that best completes each sentence.

antibodies
bacteria
communicable disease
germ
HIV
immune system
vaccine

1. A tiny particle or living thing that can make you sick is a __?__. (Lesson 1)
2. A disease caused by germs passed from person to person is a __?__. (Lesson 2)
3. The body's __?__ fights diseases. (Lesson 3)
4. Chemicals made by the immune system to fight a disease are called __?__. (Lesson 3)
5. The virus that causes AIDS is called __?__. (Lesson 4)

REVIEW HEALTH IDEAS

Use your knowledge of disease prevention and control from Chapter 7 to answer these questions.

1. Germs cause some diseases. What are some other causes of diseases? (Lesson 1)
2. Describe two different kinds of germs? (Lesson 1)
3. Describe three ways germs can spread. (Lesson 2)
4. Name two ways you can stop the spread of communicable diseases. (Lesson 2)
5. Explain how two parts of the body work to protect it from germs. (Lesson 3)
6. What do white blood cells do to keep you healthy? (Lesson 3)
7. Explain how antibodies keep you from becoming sick. (Lesson 3)
8. What does HIV have to do with AIDS? (Lesson 4)
9. Name two ways HIV is not spread and two ways it can be spread. (Lesson 4)
10. What are two choices you can make to keep your immune system strong? (Lesson 5)

APPLY HEALTH IDEAS

1. What can people do to get over a cold? (Lesson 1)
2. How might germs get onto a pencil and into your body? (Lesson 2)
3. Why are the eyes, nose, mouth, and skin called the body's first line of defense? (Lesson 3)
4. PORTFOLIO **MAKE DECISIONS** Write an ad explaining how getting a vaccine keeps you and those around you healthy. (Lesson 3)
5. LIFE SKILL **PRACTICE REFUSAL SKILLS** Your best friend wants you to be "blood brothers." You would each scratch a finger, then rub the two scratches together to let the blood mix. How can you say "no" while making it clear that you still want to be friends? (Lesson 4)

Germs spread quickly in a family because family members spend so much time together. What could your family do to slow or prevent the spread of germs? List your ideas below.

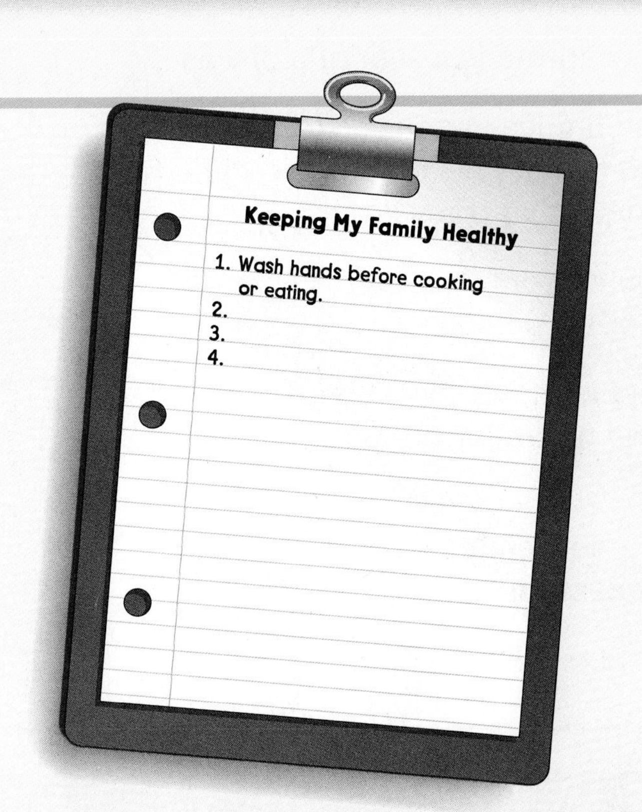

CHAPTER

7 TEST

Write True or False for each statement. If a statement is false, explain why.

1. Good health habits can lessen your chances of getting a communicable disease.
2. You can only develop immunity by having the disease.
3. AIDS is caused by harmful bacteria.
4. Diseases caused by viruses can be cured with medicine.
5. If you have antibodies against chicken pox, then you have immunity.
6. You can breathe in germs.
7. A symptom is a sign of a disease.
8. The linings in your nose, mouth, and throat give off a liquid called mucus that traps germs.
9. You can only get germs from another person.
10. A person can have HIV a long time before developing AIDS.

Write a sentence or two to answer each question.

11. What is AIDS?
12. Explain two causes of disease.
13. You are about to sneeze. What should you do? Why?
14. How can washing your hands protect your health and the health of others?
15. How does a vaccine keep you safe from a disease?
16. What are two parts in the body's first line of defense?
17. How does HIV attack the body's immune system?
18. What is a symptom? Give two examples of symptoms.
19. How is HIV spread? Describe one way.
20. How can a virus attack a cell?

Performance Assessment

PORTFOLIO

Describe how a germ might enter your body and be destroyed by the immune system.

ALCOHOL, TOBACCO, AND DRUGS

CHAPTER 8

You can make choices about your health. It helps to know:

- how drugs can be used to treat and prevent illnesses.
- how drugs can be harmful when used incorrectly.

CHAPTER CONTENTS

1 MEDICINES AND SAFETY 184

2 TOBACCO AND HEALTH 190

3 ALCOHOL AND HEALTH 196

4 OTHER DRUGS 202

YOU CAN MAKE A DIFFERENCE CHANGING PEOPLE'S LIVES 207

CHAPTER REVIEW 208

CHAPTER TEST 210

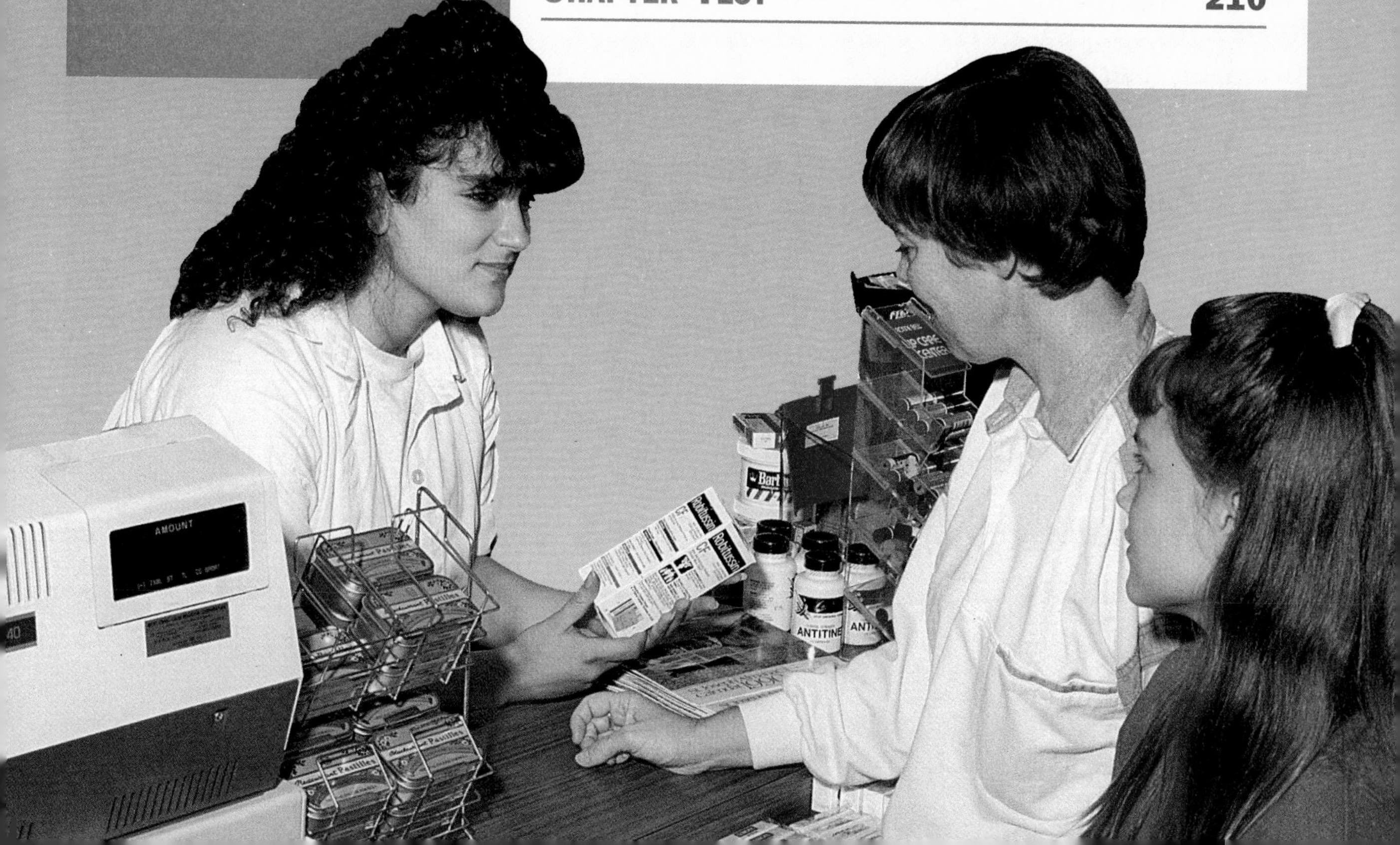

LESSON

1 MEDICINES AND SAFETY

In this lesson, you will learn:

- how medicines can be helpful, when used safely.
- how people can buy medicines safely.
- how medicines can be used safely.

VOCABULARY

drug (drug) a substance, other than food, that causes changes in the body

medicine (med′ə sin) any drug used to prevent, treat, or cure an illness or injury

prescription (pri skrip′shən) a doctor's order to prepare medicine

over-the-counter medicine (ō′vər thə koun′tər) medicine that can be bought without a prescription

QUICK START One morning you wake up with a sore throat. What should you do?

Look around your class. Is anyone out sick today? When you're sick, one way to get better is to stay home and rest. Eating healthful foods and drinking plenty of water also helps.

Sometimes you need more than rest and the right foods to get well. Then your parents or a doctor might give you something to help you feel better or to fight the illness. In this lesson, you will learn about the safe use of substances that can help you get well.

You should only take medicines that a parent or other trusted adult gives you.

Drugs and Medicine

Have you ever had the flu? Your parents may have bought something at the drugstore to help you feel better. A **drug** is a substance, other than food, that causes changes in the body. Some drugs are used to treat, cure, or prevent illness. This kind of drug is called a **medicine**.

For example, some medicines lower fever. Some relieve a cough or clear up a stuffy nose. Some relieve headaches or body aches. Medicated lotions help clear up rashes. Vaccines are medicines, too. They are given to prevent diseases, such as measles and mumps.

Some medicines are used for treating injuries. For example, burn ointments help heal burned skin.

Used safely, medicines can be helpful. However, some drugs are always harmful, no matter how they are used. They are not medicines. You must always say "no" to them. They are never safe. You will learn about these drugs later in this chapter.

CULTURAL PERSPECTIVES

Medicines of the Rain Forest

The Amazon rain forest is home to half of all the different kinds of plants in the world. The native people of the rain forest have used the bark, berries, and leaves of these plants as medicines for thousands of years. Today, scientists are studying these plants and their traditional uses to create new treatments for diseases.

Types of Medicines

If you're sick, a doctor may give you medicine. The doctor writes a **prescription**, an order to prepare medicine for a particular person. This order is written for only one person—the *patient*. No one should take medicine meant for someone else. A medicine good for one person might cause harm to another person. Or it may not help another person get well.

A *pharmacist* fills a prescription order. A pharmacist is a person trained to prepare medicines. A pharmacist also prepares the labels that go on the medicines. These labels include directions from the doctor about how to take the prescription.

Adults can buy some medicines without a doctor's prescription. These are **over-the-counter (OTC)** medicines. Cold pills and cough syrups are examples. These medicines can be bought just about anywhere health care products are sold.

All medicines, with or without a prescription, must be used with care to prevent harm. Don't take any medicine unless a parent or other trusted adult gives it to you. All medicines must be stored safely at home—high up away from young children—in a medicine cabinet. Never open or play with a bottle of medicine.

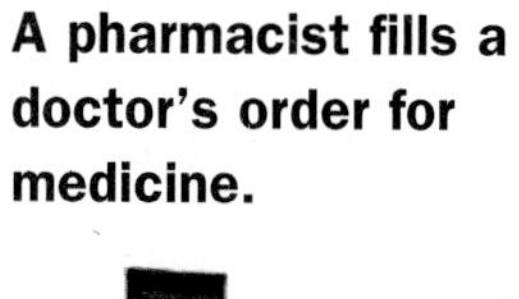

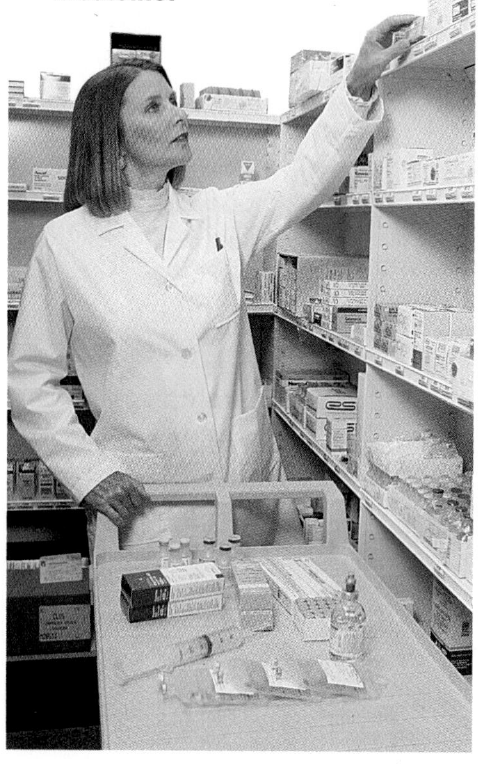

A pharmacist fills a doctor's order for medicine.

OBTAIN HELP

What Would You Do?

You are home alone for a few hours. Your parents are both at work. You begin to feel a headache. What can you do?

Comparing Medicine Labels

Prescription and over-the-counter medicines have valuable information on their labels.

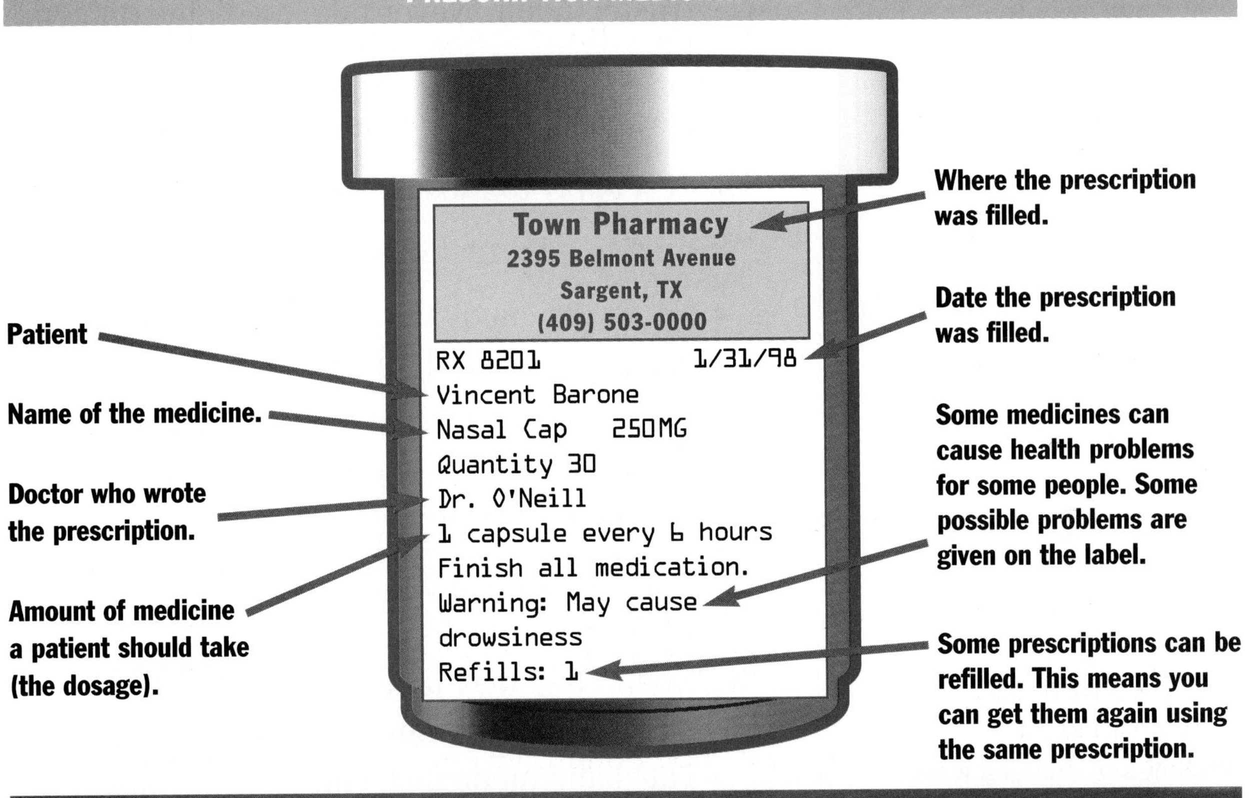

OVER-THE-COUNTER MEDICINE LABEL

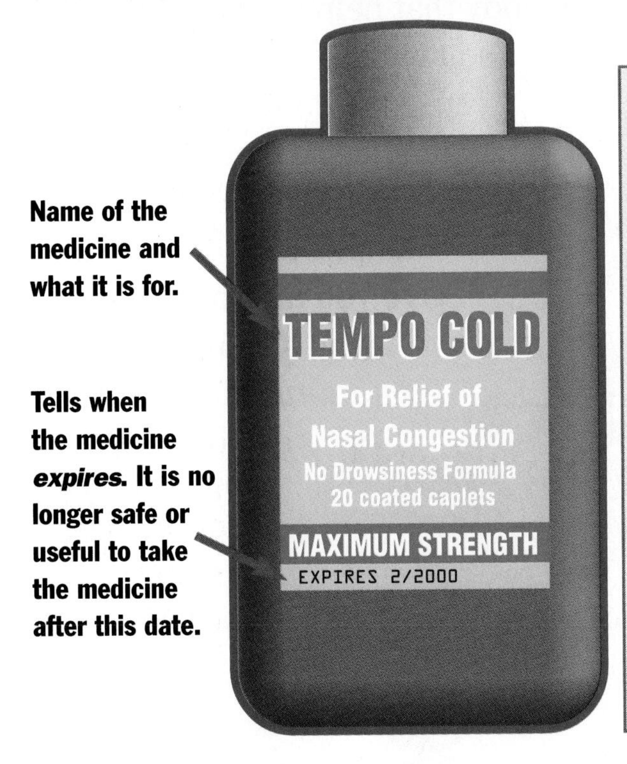

Back Label

MAXIMUM STRENGTH TEMPO COLD CAPLETS Provides hours of relief from symptoms associated with a cold, such as nasal congestion.
DIRECTIONS: Adults and children 12 years and over: 2 caplets every 6 hours, not to exceed 8 caplets in any 24 hour period. Children under 12 years of age: consult a doctor.
WARNINGS: Do not take this product if you have heart disease or diabetes unless directed by a physician.
DO NOT EXCEED DOSAGE.
If nervousness or dizziness occur, consult a physician. Do not take this product for more than 7 days. Consult a physician if symptoms do not improve. Keep this and all drugs out of the reach of children. In case of overdose, seek professional assistance or contact a poison control center immediately.

Tells who should take the medicine, how much to take, and how often.

This warning tells who should not take the medicine. It also warns of possible unpleasant reactions to using the medicine.

HEALTH FACT

"Chicken soup can help when you have a cold."

This is true. Almost everyone gets a cold at some time. Because no medicine really cures a cold, people try other things—like chicken soup. Although chicken soup is *not* a cure, it does provide the body with protein. Protein helps the body heal itself. Chicken soup is also a warm liquid, which helps relieve the stuffiness from a cold.

Medicine Safety

Here are some safety rules about medicines. The first two apply to you directly.

- Take medicine only from a parent or other trusted adult. Never take medicine on your own, or from a friend.
- Never take anyone else's medicine.

The rest apply to those giving you medicine.

- Follow all directions on the medicine label.
- Never use medicine after the date it expires. If it's old, throw it away.
- Never buy an OTC medicine if the safety seal has been broken.

These safety rules prevent *drug misuse.* This means using any medicine improperly. Sometimes people don't follow all directions on the label. They may take too much or too little. Misusing medicines can be dangerous.

The same medicines can affect people in different ways. Usually medicines cause changes in the body that help people. But sometimes medicines can cause unwanted changes, too. These changes are called *side effects.* For example, a medicine can give you a rash or make you sleepy. Report *any* side effects to an adult right away.

Resting and drinking a lot of fluids are the best things you can do for a cold.

HEALTH ACTIVITY

Medicine Safety

1 Design a medicine safety poster. Make decisions about how to include:

- three medicine safety rules.
- where medicines can be stored at home.
- trusted adults who can give you medicines.

2 Compare your poster with other students' posters. Decide on a class list of safety rules and safe places to store medicine.

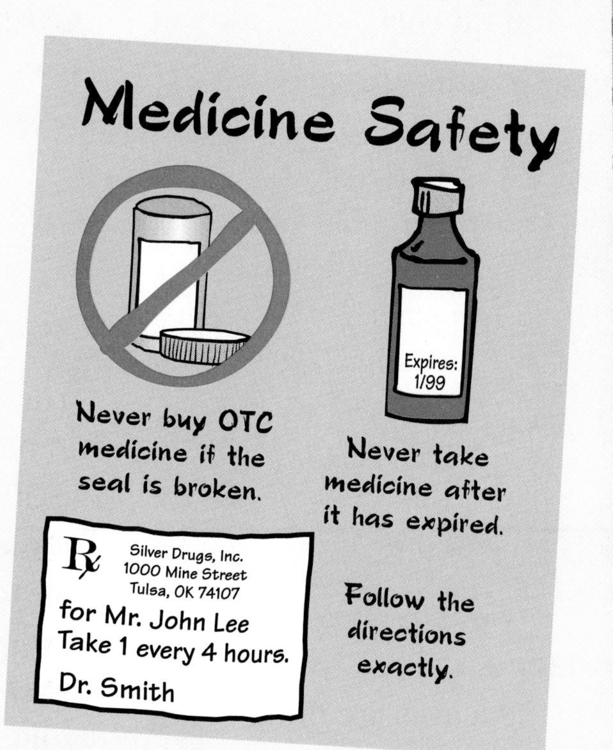

LESSON WRAP UP

Show What You Know

1. How can medicines be helpful, if used properly?
2. How does a prescription medicine differ from an over-the-counter medicine? How are their labels different?
3. **THINK CRITICALLY** Why shouldn't anyone buy an over-the-counter medicine if the safety seal is broken?

Show What You Can Do

4. PORTFOLIO **APPLY HEALTH ACTIVITY** **Make Decisions** Ask a parent to read the label of an OTC drug with you. How does it help an adult to decide to use the drug or not? Record your answers.
5. LIFE SKILL **PRACTICE LIFE SKILLS** **Obtain Help** With an adult family member, interview a pharmacist. Ask what he or she thinks are the most important safety rules about medicines. Write the responses.

HANDBOOK LIFE SKILLS pp. 268–279

LESSON 2

TOBACCO AND HEALTH

In this lesson, you will learn:

- how tobacco products can harm the body.
- how tobacco smoke can harm nonsmokers.
- how smoking is being restricted.

VOCABULARY

tobacco (tə bak′ō) a plant; its leaves are dried and made into cigarettes, cigars, or smokeless tobacco

nicotine (nik′ə tēn′) a harmful drug found in all tobacco products

dependence (di pen′dəns) a strong need for something

passive smoke (pas′iv smōk) breathing in smoke from other people's cigarettes

QUICK START You find a pack of cigarettes on the playground. Why should you turn them in to your teacher?

You've learned about medicines, drugs that can be helpful if used safely. Cigarettes, on the other hand, contain harmful substances. They are never safe. Many smokers think they have to smoke for years before cigarettes can do any harm. They think they can stop smoking whenever they want. These smokers are mistaken.

The harmful effects of cigarettes start right away. And cigarettes contain a drug that makes a person want to keep smoking. Smokers harm their own health and the health of people around them.

Smoking is not allowed in many places because it is harmful.

What Happens With Each Puff

Inside every cigarette are leaves from the **tobacco** plant. Tobacco leaves are dried and used to make cigarettes, cigars, and other products. Tobacco contains a harmful drug called **nicotine**. Nicotine causes:

- the heart to beat faster than it should.
- blood vessels to narrow. The heart pumps harder to get blood through narrow vessels.

When tobacco burns it makes a sticky brown liquid called *tar*. In time, tar builds up and coats the lungs. This makes it hard for the smoker to breathe and for oxygen to get to the rest of the body. People who smoke a pack of cigarettes each day get about 1 cup of tar in their lungs each year. Tar in smoke also causes bad breath and stains fingers yellow.

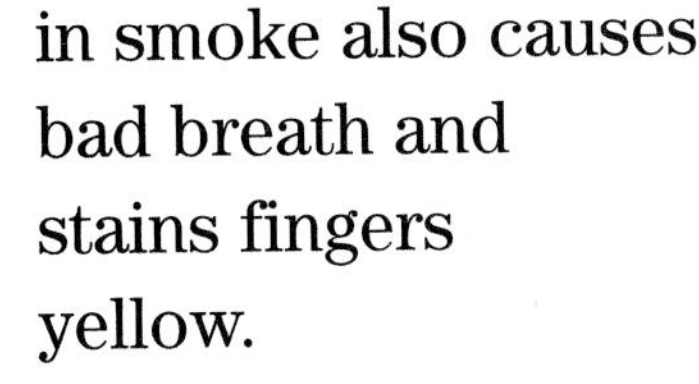

HEALTH FACT

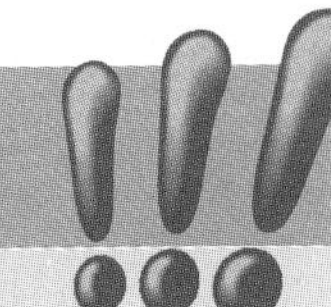

"Cigarette smoke contains poisons."

This is true. The smoke from a cigarette includes more than 4,000 chemicals. Many of these are poisons, substances that can be deadly. There is not enough poison in a single cigarette to kill a person. But most smokers smoke many cigarettes, each day for years. In time, the poisons have a deadly effect.

Using tobacco is harmful. Show others that you care about your health by never starting to smoke.

Smoking and Health Problems

The effects of each cigarette build up over time. One out of four smokers will eventually die from the effects of smoking.

Smoking makes the heart work harder. So smokers have a greater risk of heart disease and heart attack. Smoking also causes lung problems. People who smoke are more likely to develop lung, mouth, and throat cancer.

Quitting the Habit

It is easy to start smoking, but it is very hard to stop. People who smoke develop a habit. That means they smoke because they are used to it. In a short time, smokers develop a dependence on cigarettes. **Dependence** is a strong need for something—in this case, for the drug nicotine. When smokers become dependent, it is very hard to quit. The smoker who quits may get headaches. The person may become shaky and grouchy, or may not be able to think clearly. But, in time, these feelings do go away.

Smokers try to quit in many different ways. Some quit slowly and some quit all at once. Some people join groups to help them quit. The simplest rule about cigarettes is "Don't start in the first place."

HealthWise Consumer

Don't Be Fooled!

Many cigarette ads make smoking look fun and healthy, so young people might start smoking. Companies know that if people start smoking young, they often keep smoking all their life. Ads also show smoking as a grown-up way to act. Young people who see the ads and see adult friends or relatives smoking may fall for the trick. But don't be fooled. Smoking is a deadly habit.

Passive Smoke

Smokers harm more than just themselves. They also harm the people around them. How? The smoke from a burning cigarette goes into the air. So does the smoke that a smoker breathes out. If you are near the smoker, you will inhale the cigarette smoke in the air. Breathing in other people's cigarette smoke is called **passive smoke**.

Passive smoke can affect your health. It can make your eyes water or make you cough. But the effects of passive smoke can cause more serious health problems. The smoke contains nicotine and tar. Breathing in other people's smoke can lead to heart and lung problems. It can be as harmful as smoking cigarettes.

Smokeless Tobacco

Some people use tobacco products that they don't smoke. These are called *smokeless tobacco*. Chewing tobacco is a loose form of tobacco leaves that users chew or hold inside of their mouth. Snuff is a powdered form of tobacco that is also held in the mouth.

Like regular tobacco, smokeless tobacco contains nicotine. The nicotine enters the blood through the mouth or the nose. It causes the same heart problems as cigarettes. Smokeless tobacco can harm you in other ways.

- stains teeth and causes bad breath
- lessens sense of smell and taste
- makes lips and gums crack or bleed
- causes cancers of the lip, tongue, mouth, and throat

Smokeless tobacco causes many of the same health problems as smoking, and can cause other problems besides.

Is Smoking Legal?

The answer to this question is "Not always." Smoking is being banned more and more. For example, smoking is banned in most public areas. It is banned on airplanes. Companies ban it at the workplace.

It is illegal to sell cigarettes to anyone under 18. This includes selling cigarettes by vending machines. And cigarette ads and packs must carry warnings about the dangers of smoking.

Your Right Not to Smoke

When it comes to smoking, there's only one word you need to say. That word is "no." The simplest way to protect your own health is by not smoking.

What if an older student or even a friend your own age offers you a cigarette? Simply refuse the offer. Stand up for yourself and your good health.

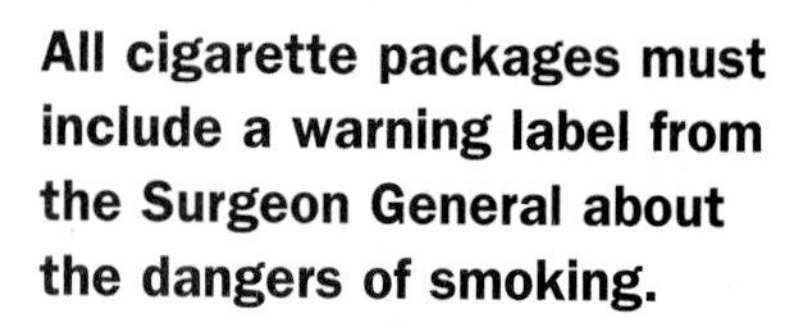

All cigarette packages must include a warning label from the Surgeon General about the dangers of smoking.

MAKE DECISIONS

What Would You Do?

You are in a restaurant. An adult in a nonsmoking section is smoking nearby. You don't want to breathe in her smoke. What could you do?

HEALTH ACTIVITY

Working on Warnings

PRACTICE REFUSAL SKILLS

You will need: construction paper, tape, markers, glue

1. Design warning labels or stickers about the dangers of smoking.
2. With your partner, role play refusing to smoke. In the role play, one partner gives a reason for smoking. The other partner uses the label to explain why smoking is harmful to the body.
3. Reverse roles and role play again.

LESSON WRAP UP

Show What You Know

1. Name two ways cigarettes can harm a smoker. Name two ways smokeless tobacco can harm a person.
2. How can cigarette smoke harm nonsmokers?
3. **THINK CRITICALLY** Why do you think people passed laws to require warning labels on cigarette boxes?

Show What You Can Do

4. PORTFOLIO **APPLY HEALTH ACTIVITY** **Practice Refusal Skills** Prepare a short skit with a friend. In the skit, show what you would do if a friend offers you a cigarette. Present your skit to the class.
5. LIFE SKILL **PRACTICE LIFE SKILLS** **Obtain Help** Many organizations offer information about the dangers of tobacco—for example, the American Cancer Society. At the library, find out where you can learn more.

LESSON 3 ALCOHOL AND HEALTH

In this lesson, you will learn:

- how alcohol can harm the body.
- how alcohol can affect the way a person acts.
- why it is important to know the dangers of alcohol.

VOCABULARY

alcohol (al′kə hôl′) a drug in beer, wine, and liquor and in some medicines

QUICK START Several teenagers are drinking and making a lot of noise. Why do you think the neighbors demand that they stop?

On the news, you hear that someone was arrested for "drinking and driving." *Drinking* here means "drinking beer, wine, or liquor." These drinks contain a drug, **alcohol**. It affects how the brain and body work.

In small amounts, alcohol is in some medicines. That is one reason why some medicines need to be used with care. But the most common use of alcohol is in drinks. And it is very harmful. How does it affect people? Why do they drink it?

There are many ways for teens to have fun without drinking alcohol.

Alcohol and the Body

What happens when someone drinks alcohol? Alcohol goes into the stomach and then passes quickly into the blood. The blood carries the drug to all parts of the body.

When alcohol reaches the brain, it changes the way the brain works. Alcohol slows down messages sent from the brain to the rest of the body.

These are some of the effects of drinking alcohol.

- It dulls a person's senses of sight, smell, hearing, and taste.
- It slows down a person's thinking. Someone drinking alcohol has a harder time making decisions or reacting to things.
- It upsets a person's balance. Some people become dizzy.
- It slows or slurs a person's speech.
- It causes a person to lose muscle control.

Over time, drinking alcohol causes serious health problems. For example, it harms the liver. The liver helps break food down into a form your body can use. Drinking alcohol can also lead to heart disease and cause some kinds of cancer.

People can become dependent on alcohol. People dependent on alcohol may have trouble keeping a job. They may fight with their family and friends. People who are dependent on alcohol may need help to stop drinking.

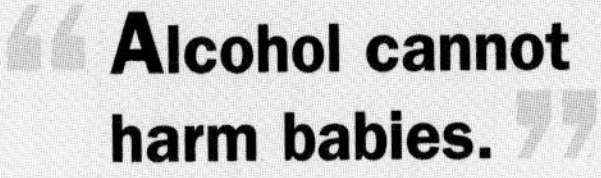

Health Fallacy

"Alcohol cannot harm babies."

This is not true. Alcohol is harmful to adults, teens, and children. And it also harms unborn babies. When a pregnant woman drinks alcohol, the drug passes from her body to the baby's. Alcohol can affect a baby's brain, cause heart damage, and result in other physical problems.

Also, the baby may weigh less than it would if the mother hadn't been drinking alcohol. Underweight babies may develop serious health problems as they grow.

INFOGRAPHIC

How Alcohol Affects the Body

Alcohol can harm almost every part of the body. Here are some of the ways.

Alcohol dulls the senses of sight, hearing, smell, and taste.

Alcohol slows down the way the brain works. Messages from the brain don't reach the rest of the body as quickly as they should. This makes it hard to think clearly and remember what happened.

Alcohol causes heart problems. It damages the muscles that make the heart beat.

Alcohol harms the liver. This damage can kill people who drink a lot.

Alcohol dulls the sense of touch. A person drinking might not feel pain.

Alcohol can cause stomach cancer.

Alcohol Changes How People Act

Alcohol affects the way the brain works. The brain is a control center for a person's thoughts and feelings. Alcohol affects how a person feels, thinks, and acts. Just one drink can make a person become loud and act thoughtlessly. Alcohol can cause people to do dangerous things—such as drinking and driving.

Drinking and driving are a dangerous combination. When people drink alcohol, they have trouble making decisions. They have less control over their muscles. They react more slowly. People who have been drinking alcohol are more likely to have accidents. Almost half of all car crashes are caused by alcohol use.

MANAGE STRESS

What Would You Do?

You are at a friend's house. His teenage brother offers to drive you home. You saw him drinking beer. What would you do?

HANDBOOK **LIFE SKILLS** pp. 268–279

Alcohol and the Law

Laws control the sale of alcohol. It is against the law to sell alcohol to anyone under the age of 21. This is true in every state.

Most states also have laws against driving while under the influence of alcohol. Each year, thousands of car crashes occur because the driver was drinking. Drivers who are caught pay a fine. They may even lose their license.

Saying "No" to Alcohol

Some young people think drinking alcohol makes them seem more grown-up. Some drink alcohol to fit in with other friends who drink. Some think it helps them stay calm when they have a problem. But alcohol is not a healthful choice. Alcohol affects young people even more than it affects adults.

How would you say "no" if offered a drink? You might say, "I can feel good without drinking alcohol." You could mention that alcohol harms your body and your brain. You could explain that drinking is against your family's rules.

It doesn't matter how you choose to say "no." What is important is that you are not fooled by what others say and do. Stick up for your health.

Choosing healthful drinks, like orange juice, will help you stay healthy.

HEALTH ACTIVITY

A Great Act

LIFE SKILL
PRACTICE REFUSAL SKILLS

1 Work with a partner. Think about a situation in which a young person is offered alcohol.

2 Write a story about how the person refuses.

3 Dramatize or act out your story for the class. Discuss the different ways that alcohol was refused. Which way did you find most effective?

LESSON WRAP UP

Show What You Know

1. Name three ways that alcohol affects the body.

2. List two ways that show how alcohol can affect how a person thinks, feels, and acts.

3. **THINK CRITICALLY** Why is it important to understand the dangers of alcohol even if you don't drink?

Show What You Can Do

4. PORTFOLIO **APPLY HEALTH ACTIVITY** **Practice Refusal Skills** Make a bumper sticker that convinces people to say "no" to alcohol.

5. LIFE SKILL **PRACTICE LIFE SKILLS** **Obtain Help** Ask a librarian or a police officer about drinking and driving laws in your town and state. Share what you learn with the class.

HANDBOOK LIFE SKILLS pp. 268–279

LESSON 4

OTHER DRUGS

In this lesson, you will learn:

- how caffeine can affect a person.
- how marijuana, cocaine, and crack harm the body.
- why it is important to live free of drugs.

VOCABULARY

caffeine (ka fēn′) a drug that speeds up body activities

marijuana (mar′ə wä′ nə) an illegal drug made from the hemp plant; it affects thoughts and actions and speeds up the heart

cocaine (kō kān′) an illegal drug made from the coca plant; can have lasting, dangerous effects on the body

crack (krak) a very harmful form of cocaine that can be smoked

QUICK START Someone tells you about a funny movie. People in the movie used illegal drugs. Why would you say, "That's not funny"?

You are skating. Suddenly, you are going faster and faster. You want to stop but cannot. You've lost control. It's scary! You have no control over what is happening—not until you are able to stop yourself.

Some drugs can make people lose control. They can harm the body and the brain. In this lesson, you will find out more about these drugs.

Some drugs are not medicines. They are harmful to your health.

Caffeine and Your Health

What do coffee, tea, cola, and chocolate have in common? They all contain caffeine. **Caffeine** is a drug that speeds up the body's activities. It can make your heart beat faster than it should. Caffeine can make you feel nervous and shaky. It can also keep you awake at night. Too much can cause an upset stomach. It's best to avoid caffeine. Choose caffeine-free drinks and snacks.

These caffeine-free drinks taste good. They're good for your health, too.

Marijuana, An Illegal Drug

Some drugs are *illegal.* It is against the law to buy, sell, or use them. Illegal drugs are dangerous. It is never safe to use an illegal drug.

Marijuana is an illegal drug. It comes from the leaves of a plant—a hemp plant. Marijuana is usually smoked.

Marijuana changes the way the brain works. People who smoke marijuana may forget things. They can get confused and find it hard to think clearly. They take longer to react to things, too. Sometimes smoking marijuana causes people to lose interest in the things around them.

Marijuana also changes the way the body works. Like cigarettes, it can harm the heart and lungs. In fact, marijuana has more tar and other poisons than tobacco. It puts a person at an even greater risk of heart problems and lung cancer.

PRACTICE REFUSAL SKILLS

What Would You Do?

Some older students come by your school. They want you to try smoking marijuana. They say it makes you "feel good." How would you refuse?

HEALTHWISE CONSUMER

Watch Out for Caffeine

It's not hard to avoid caffeine. When you are in a supermarket, check the food labels. Many products are made with little or no caffeine. Look for words like *caffeine-free* or *decaffeinated* on the package. Of course you can always choose juice, milk, or water. You never have to worry about caffeine with these drinks.

HANDBOOK LIFE SKILLS pp. 268–279

Other Illegal Drugs

Illegal drugs can be extremely dangerous for the body. One example is cocaine. **Cocaine** is an illegal drug made from the coca plant. It is a white powder that can be inhaled. It is a very powerful drug.

Cocaine causes the heart to beat very fast. It puts a strain on the heart. Many young people have had heart attacks and died when using cocaine. Users of cocaine often have other health problems, too. They lose weight, can't sleep, and feel nervous.

Another illegal drug is crack. **Crack** is a very harmful form of cocaine that can be smoked. It affects the body within seconds after it is smoked.

One of the most dangerous things about crack and cocaine is that people become dependent, or "hooked," on them very quickly. People who are "hooked" want more of the drug, more often. It is very painful and difficult to stop using crack or cocaine.

Choosing a drug-free life is one of the healthiest choices you can make.

Your Right to Say "No"

You never have to take an illegal drug. Make it clear that it is your right not to take drugs. Send a clear "no" message to any offer of illegal drugs. You can also:

- tell a parent, teacher, or other trusted adult that someone has offered you drugs.
- point out that illegal drugs can harm your mind and body.
- walk away.

Making a Promise to Yourself

By taking a strong stand against illegal drugs, you are taking responsibility for your health. You won't become dependent on drugs. You won't destroy your body with dangerous chemicals. You will be able to take full advantage of opportunities that come your way.

You have the right to be proud when you say "no" to drugs! It means that you're using the facts about drugs to make a healthy decision. But most importantly it shows that you respect yourself.

Drug-free people make the best friends.

HEALTH ACTIVITY

My Pledge

You will need:
large index card

1. Set a goal never to take illegal drugs.
2. Write your goal as a pledge. In your pledge, give reasons for not taking illegal drugs.
3. As a class, decide how to share your pledges. You might want to post the pledges. Or you might want to read them aloud.

LESSON WRAP UP

Show What You Know

1. Name some effects of caffeine.
2. Why are marijuana and cocaine dangerous? Give two reasons for each.
3. **THINK CRITICALLY** Why do you have the right to say "no" to any illegal drug?

Show What You Can Do

4. PORTFOLIO **APPLY HEALTH ACTIVITY** **Set Goals** Write a letter to a friend. In your letter, explain your goal never to take illegal drugs. Explain why your goal is important to you today and for your future.
5. LIFE SKILL **PRACTICE LIFE SKILLS** **Obtain Help** Near your school you see some students buying drugs. Whom could you tell?

HANDBOOK LIFE SKILLS pp. 268–279

YOU CAN MAKE A DIFFERENCE

HEALTH HEROES

Changing People's Lives

Lloyd Newman and LeAlan Jones

Lloyd Newman and LeAlan Jones grew up in the projects in Chicago, Illinois. In their early teens, they recorded a radio show for National Public Radio. They called their show "Ghetto Life 101." The program got a lot of attention and won a prize.

Lloyd and LeAlan wanted to show how violence affects children. They wrote a radio show about Eric Morse, a young child killed by other children in the neighborhood. The show was aired as a National Public Radio special. The boys hoped that it would lead people to stop this kind of violent crime.

The boys are worried about the role of drugs in the ghetto. Drugs often lead to violence. LeAlan is a spokesperson for the No Dope Express Foundation. He talks about the dangers of drugs. Lloyd and LeAlan are working to change people's lives.

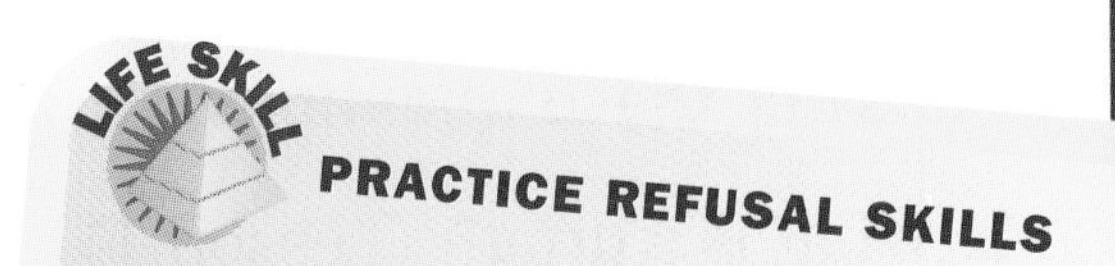

PRACTICE REFUSAL SKILLS

PLAN A RADIO SHOW

Work with three friends. Plan a radio show that tells people how to say "no" to alcohol, tobacco, or drugs. Make sure your show includes reasons for saying "no." Present your show to the class.

CHAPTER

8 REVIEW

VOCABULARY

Write the word from the box that best completes each sentence.

alcohol
caffeine
drug
marijuana
medicine
nicotine
prescription
tobacco

1. A __?__ is a doctor's order to prepare medicine. (Lesson 1)
2. A drug found in all tobacco products is __?__. (Lesson 2)
3. A drug found in wine and beer is __?__. (Lesson 3)
4. A drug found in coffee, tea, cola, and chocolate is __?__. (Lesson 4)
5. An illegal drug that is made from the hemp plant and is usually smoked is __?__. (Lesson 4)

REVIEW HEALTH IDEAS

Use your knowledge of alcohol, tobacco, and drugs from Chapter 8 to answer these questions.

1. What is a drug? (Lesson 1)
2. How can medicines be helpful? (Lesson 1)
3. What are three rules for the safe use of medicines? (Lesson 1)
4. How are tobacco products harmful to people's health? List three ways. (Lesson 2)
5. Why do people find it hard to stop using tobacco? (Lesson 2)
6. Why is passive smoke harmful? (Lesson 2)
7. How does alcohol affect a person's health? (Lesson 3)
8. In what ways can alcohol change a person's behavior? (Lesson 3)
9. What does the term *illegal drug* mean? (Lesson 4)
10. Why are crack and cocaine dangerous? (Lesson 4)

CHAPTER

REVIEW 8

APPLY HEALTH IDEAS

1. Suppose you and your sister both have an earache. Why might one doctor prescribe different medicines for each of you? (Lesson 1)
2. How does tar affect the lungs? (Lesson 2)
3. Why would someone who has been drinking do poorly on a test? (Lesson 3)
4. PORTFOLIO **SET GOALS** Think about a goal you want to reach. Write a paragraph explaining how using tobacco, alcohol, or illegal drugs could stop you from reaching that goal. (Lessons 1–3)
5. LIFE SKILL **PRACTICE REFUSAL SKILLS** Find an ad for cigarettes or alcohol products in a magazine. List two ways the ad tries to get people to use the product. Then write why you will not use this product. (Lessons 2 and 3)

Read the labels on a few food packages. Look to see if the product contains caffeine. If the label lists chocolate, coffee, cocoa, or tea as an ingredient, you can assume that caffeine is in the product.

Make a chart of the products you checked and note if they contained caffeine. Were you surprised to find caffeine in some foods?

Product	Caffeine?
Cola drink	yes ☑ no ☐
Kiwi soft drink	yes ☐ no ☑
Chocolate chip cookies	yes ☑ no ☐
Caffeine-free soda	yes ☐ no ☑
Cocoa breakfast cereal	yes ☑ no ☐

CHAPTER

8 TEST

Write True or False for each statement. If a statement is false, rewrite it so that it is true.

1. It is okay to take over-the-counter medicine on your own.
2. Smoking marijuana can help a person's memory.
3. Caffeine causes the heart rate to slow down.
4. All medicines need an order from a doctor.
5. Alcohol helps people react to things quickly and wisely.
6. Crack is a powerful form of cocaine.
7. There is no nicotine in tobacco smoke.
8. Smoking is harmful only to people who smoke.
9. It is safe to take medicine after the date on which it expires.
10. Alcohol passes quickly into the blood.

Write a sentence or two to answer each question.

11. Why is it difficult for people to stop using tobacco products?
12. How does cocaine affect the body?
13. What are three safety rules about the use of medicines?
14. How does alcohol affect the brain?
15. How can medicines be helpful if used safely?
16. In what ways can alcohol change the way a person thinks, feels, and acts?
17. What is the difference between a medicine and a drug?
18. How does smokeless tobacco harm the body?
19. How can marijuana affect a person's health?
20. What is the difference between an over-the-counter medicine and a prescription medicine?

Performance Assessment

Choose one of the harmful drugs described in this chapter. Make a two-column chart. In one column, list reasons why this drug is harmful. In another column, show ways to refuse it.

SAFETY, INJURY, AND VIOLENCE PREVENTION

CHAPTER

9

THE BIG IDEA

You can prevent many injuries by:

- following safety rules.
- avoiding hazards.
- asking for help when you need it.

CHAPTER CONTENTS

1	INJURY PREVENTION	212
2	VIOLENCE PREVENTION	218
3	INDOOR SAFETY	222
4	OUTDOOR SAFETY	228
5	EMERGENCIES	234
6	FIRST AID	238
YOU CAN MAKE A DIFFERENCE	A NEW USE FOR BALLOONS	243
	CHAPTER REVIEW	244
	CHAPTER TEST	246

LESSON

1 INJURY PREVENTION

In this lesson, you will learn:

- what a hazard is and how to spot a hazard.
- how to prevent injuries by avoiding hazards.
- how to keep safe when you cross a street or ride in a car or bus.

VOCABULARY

injury (in′ jə rē) any kind of physical harm or damage to a person

hazard (haz′ərd) something that creates a dangerous situation or risk of harm

poison (poi′zən) a drug or substance that harms or kills

pedestrian (pə des′trē ən) a person who travels by walking

QUICK START You and your friends are walking to the library together. How can you help everyone stay safe while you're crossing a street?

When you are outside walking or inside playing, think before you act. Think about what can happen because of what you do—or don't do. Sometimes people take chances even when they know there is danger. Don't take chances with your safety. Be "safety smart."

Knowing about safety can keep you from getting hurt. It can help you have a good time, too.

What Is a Hazard?

A burned finger is an injury. An **injury** is any kind of physical harm or damage to you or another person. To prevent injuries, think before you act—avoid hazards. A **hazard** is something that creates a dangerous situation or risk of harm. For example, a hot iron is a hazard—it can burn your finger.

Many household products can be hazards. Products such as bleach, insect spray, and glue contain poisons. A **poison** is a drug or substance that harms or kills. Some products such as bleach or glue give off a gas that has a smell. Inhaling this gas or *fume* can make you dizzy or sick.

Keep these rules in mind when using household products.

- Do not use household products by yourself. An adult should help you.
- Household products should be stored properly—in sealed containers.
- Avoid any fumes. While the products are in use, open a window and turn on a fan. Never breathe in the fumes on purpose!
- Never swallow these products. Don't let them get into your eyes or on your skin.

Even very common household products need to be used carefully.

LIFE SKILL

MAKE DECISIONS

What Would You Do?

You are helping your older brother paint a bookcase. He teases you for wanting to read the safety label on the can. He says he has used the paint before and knows what to do. What should you do?

HANDBOOK LIFE SKILLS pp. 268–279

INFOGRAPHIC

BEING SAFETY SMART

Here are some other hazards you can avoid. Just think "play it safe."

FALLS

Falls hurt! Here's how to prevent them.

- Keep rooms, hallways, and stairs clear. Don't leave things lying around that could make you trip.
- Don't try to find your way around in the dark. Turn on a light or use a flashlight.
- Use nonslip mats in tubs and showers.
- Do not run on wet or waxed floors.
- Never use a chair as a ladder.

HEAT HAZARDS

Be "safety smart" about what's hot!

- After using an appliance that produces heat, turn it off. Then unplug it.
- Take special care with heaters. Heaters can keep you warm in the winter. But they can also burn you or start a fire. Keep heaters away from anything that might catch fire.
- Hot water can burn. Test the water before you get into a shower or tub.

ELECTRICAL HAZARDS

Electricity can cause fires. It can give a harmful shock. Here's how to prevent burns and shocks.

- Never use a cord that is cracked or frayed.
- Don't put too many plugs into the same outlet.
- Pull the plug, not the cord, to unplug an appliance.
- Don't use electrical appliances around water.

How is this family being "safety smart"?

Safety Smart Pedestrian

It's important to be "safety smart" about hazards outside the home, too. When you're out walking, you are a **pedestrian**. Pedestrians stay safe by being careful around traffic.

- Cross at the corner. If there is a crosswalk, use it. Obey the crossing guard.
- At the crosswalk, cross only when the light is green or the WALK sign is lit.
- Always look left, right, and left again before crossing the street. Even when the light is green, look all ways before crossing. Watch for cars and bicycles.
- Do not step into the street from between parked cars.
- If you must walk near the road, walk on the left side. Face traffic.
- At night, never walk alone. Walk in well-lit areas. Wear light-colored clothes. This will help drivers see you better.

Safety Smart Passenger

Sometimes you travel by car or bus. Be "safety smart" when you're a passenger, too!

- When traveling in a car, lock the door. That way, you can't fall out.
- Wear a safety belt. If the car or bus stops quickly, you will stay in your seat.
- Keep your hands and head inside the car or bus.
- Don't ride in the back of a moving pickup truck. You could bounce right out!
- Sit quietly when riding in a car or bus. Do not disturb the driver.
- Get in or out of a car on the curb side, not the traffic side.

HEALTH FACT

"Buckle up—it's the law."

This is true. All 50 states now have child passenger safety laws. The reason for these laws is that buckling up saves lives. Seventy-five percent of all car crashes happen close to home. And more than half of those crashes involve driving at slow speeds. That's why it's important to buckle up every time—even if you're only going around the corner.

HEALTH ACTIVITY

Being "Safety Smart"

SET GOALS

You will need: construction paper, markers or crayons

1. With your partner, talk about the hazards listed on pages 213–214. Think of five ways that you can plan to act more safely at home or at school. Set goals for how to do so.
2. Make a "Playing It Safe Handbook." List the five ways you can improve your safety.
3. Exchange handbooks with classmates. Share ideas for being "safety smart."

LESSON WRAP UP

Show What You Know

1. What is a hazard? Name two examples of hazards.
2. How can you be "safety smart" to avoid hazards at home?
3. **THINK CRITICALLY** How could a passenger talking to a driver of a car or bus be a hazard?

Show What You Can Do

4. PORTFOLIO **APPLY HEALTH ACTIVITY** **Set Goals** Think of ways that you can be even safer as a pedestrian or passenger. Make a "safety first" checklist. List five ways you can be safer.
5. LIFE SKILL **PRACTICE LIFE SKILLS** **Obtain Help** Make a list of hazards that you find in and around school, on the bus, and at the crosswalk near school. Ask a teacher to review your list and help you correct the hazards.

LESSON 2

VIOLENCE PREVENTION

In this lesson, you will learn:

- how to deal with anger in healthy ways.
- how to avoid violence.

VOCABULARY

violence (vī′ ə ləns) use of strong physical force to harm someone

weapon (wep′ ən) something that can be used to attack someone, such as a knife or a gun

QUICK START "You make me so angry!" a friend says. "You never keep a promise." You feel angry toward her, too. What a thing to say! What can you do to keep from fighting?

How would you feel if you were blamed for something you didn't do? How would you feel if someone called you a name? In each case, you might feel angry. Anger is a strong emotion. It is okay to get angry—everybody does. What matters is what you do when you get angry.

Everyone feels angry sometimes. It's important to express anger in healthful ways.

Dealing With Your Anger

Sometimes you might be angry with others or even with yourself. Here are some healthy ways to deal with your anger.

- Count to 10 slowly.
- Do something creative. Try painting, playing an instrument, or doing a hobby.
- Do a physical activity. Try jumping rope, skating, or anything you enjoy.
- Talk to a friend or trusted adult to find out what made you angry in the first place. Together, try to solve the problem.
- Write in your journal about how you feel.
- Spend some time alone to "cool off."

When people don't deal with anger in healthy ways, the anger can lead to violence. When people act with **violence**, they use strong physical force to harm someone. The harm can be little or big. It could be a push or a slap. It could mean using a knife or gun.

OBTAIN HELP

What Would You Do?

An older student, a bully, is picking on a friend of yours. It started with name calling. Now they are pushing each other. What should you do?

CULTURAL PERSPECTIVES

"A man kicks a stone in anger only to hurt his own toe."

This short saying comes from Korea. It tells the story of an angry man who kicks a stone. The saying points out what can happen when an angry person acts without thinking. Kicking the stone did not resolve the problem. It only brought harm to the man. How can remembering this saying help you deal with anger?

Manage your anger so you can stay in control of your actions.

Resolving Conflicts

People may get angry when they have a conflict. A *conflict* is a strong disagreement between people. It can become violent. Try to avoid violence and resolve a conflict.

- Watch for signs that someone may become violent. Pushing and shouting are signs. Prevent violence before it starts.
- Talking calmly can help prevent violence. Listen to one another. You don't have to agree. You just need to understand one another's feelings. An adult can help.
- Sometimes you can't stop a person who wants to be violent. The safest thing may be to walk away from that person. You also may need to report what happened to a trusted adult.

It's not always easy to avoid fights, but it is possible. Deal with anger before it reaches the danger stage.

Weapons and Violence

Sometimes violent people use weapons to hurt other people. A **weapon** is something such as a knife or gun used to attack someone. Weapons can kill people.

To be safe, leave weapons alone. Never play with knives or guns. Never point a gun at anyone—not even a toy gun. In fact, you should never pick up a gun, even if you believe it is unloaded. If you see a gun, tell an adult.

Using a weapon is no way to settle a conflict. To settle a conflict, use your head—not a weapon.

HEALTH ACTIVITY

Vote Against Violence

RESOLVE CONFLICTS

1. With a partner, think of a scene that could become violent. (For example, a friend runs into a classmate's bicycle and breaks the reflector.) Jot down some notes about the scene and its conflict.
2. Add some notes about a plan for resolving the conflict and keeping the scene from becoming violent.
3. Present the scene for the class. Then have a class discussion. Discuss whether students think that your plan would work. What other ideas do students have?

LESSON WRAP UP

Show What You Know

1. Describe two healthy ways to deal with anger.
2. What are two things people can do to avoid violence?
3. **THINK CRITICALLY** Why is using violence never a good way to solve a problem?

Show What You Can Do

4. PORTFOLIO **APPLY HEALTH ACTIVITY** **Resolve Conflicts** You are asked to help two friends settle their differences. Make a list of tips for yourself to follow so that you can help your friends.
5. LIFE SKILL **PRACTICE LIFE SKILLS** **Manage Stress** You try to help break up a fight. But you get pushed around. Now you feel angry and upset. How can you handle the way you feel in a healthy way?

HANDBOOK LIFE SKILLS pp. 268–279

LESSON

3 INDOOR SAFETY

In this lesson, you will learn:

- how to keep safe from fire at home.
- how to keep safe when you are home alone.
- how "good" and "bad" touches are different.

VOCABULARY

smoke detector (smōk di tek′tər) a fire safety device that sounds an alarm when there is smoke

QUICK START A TV news story shows a house on fire. The story also tells how the family got out safely. How might the family have acted to get out safely?

Be "safety smart" at home too. Being safe at home is up to you—and every member of your family. If you work together, you will know what to do to stay safe in a fire. Together, you can come up with rules to help you stay safe when you are home by yourself.

Fire destroys homes and can hurt or even kill family members. Be "safety smart"—follow fire safety rules.

Do you have any fire safety equipment in your home? What equipment do you have? Do you know how the equipment works?

Fire Safety Rules

Fires can start in many ways. Stored rags, paper, or chemicals can catch fire. Frayed electrical cords and gas leaks from the stove can cause a fire, too. Fires can even break out while cooking. For example, a fire can start if grease touches a burner on the stove.

You and your family can help keep each other safe from fire. Here's how.

- Never play with fire. Keep away from matches, lighters, fireworks, and anything with a flame.
- Old papers should be disposed of safely—they should be recycled. Oil soaked rags should be thrown away. Chemicals should be in sealed containers.
- If the smell of gas is coming from the stove, tell an adult immediately. It could be a gas leak.
- Check with your family that there is at least one smoke detector on each floor. A **smoke detector** is a fire safety device. It sounds an alarm when there is smoke. Be sure to know the sound. Homes should have a *fire extinguisher*, too. It sprays chemicals that can put out a fire.

HEALTHWISE CONSUMER

It's a Life Saver

Never borrow the batteries from a smoke detector, no matter what. Smoke detectors can save lives—if they have power.

Most smoke detectors need fresh batteries every few months. Most make a beeping noise when the power is low. As a rule, try changing the batteries when your family resets the clocks in the spring and fall.

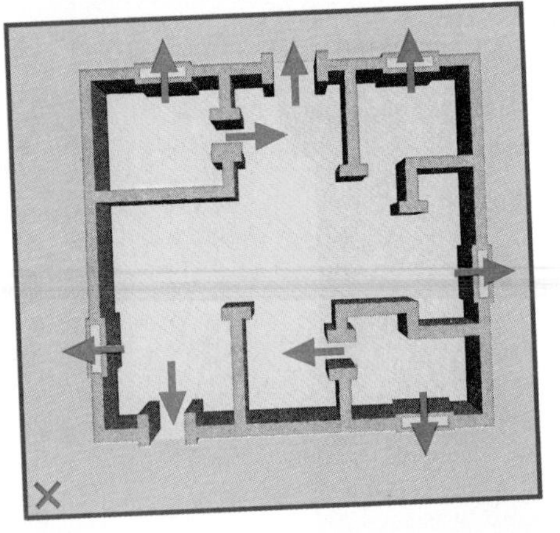

A fire escape plan shows more than one way to get out of each room. "X" marks the spot to meet outside.

A Fire Escape Plan

What would you do if there was a fire in your home? It is important that your family have a fire escape plan. A *fire escape plan* is a map of the inside of your home that shows different ways out of every room. It should also include a place outside for family members to meet. Practice the plan so everyone knows the escape routes.

Safety During a Fire

Follow these rules to be safe in case of fire.

- Stay calm but quickly leave the building. Then call for help. Never go back for any reason.
- Crawl low under smoke. The most smoke-free air will be near the floor. Cover your mouth and nose with a wet cloth to keep from breathing in smoke.
- Feel any door before opening it. If it is warm, the fire is nearby. Keep the door closed. Use another way out.
- If there is no other exit, line the door with towels or blankets to keep smoke out. Go to a window, open it slightly, and call for help.
- If your clothes catch fire, follow the steps shown at the left: STOP where you are, DROP to the ground, and ROLL around to put out the fire.

SET GOALS

What Would You Do?

Do you know where the school fire exits are? Do you know how the fire alarm sounds? Set a goal to improve your fire safety at school.

Home-Alone Safety Rules

When you are home alone, be "safety smart."

- Don't play with matches, knives, or other hazards. They are very dangerous—whether or not someone else is home.
- Don't play with any machines that you are not usually allowed to touch. Never touch a weapon—home alone or not.
- Keep a list of important telephone numbers by the phone. Include numbers for your parents and other trusted adults. (You will learn about emergency numbers in Lesson 5.) Call someone right away if anything makes you feel unsafe.
- If you answer the telephone, never tell a stranger you are alone. Find out from your family what you should say. For example, you might say: "My mom can't come to the phone right now. Do you want to leave a message?" If the stranger keeps asking questions, hang up.

When you are home alone you may need an adult to help you. Always keep a list of emergency numbers handy.

HEALTH ACTIVITY

To Tell or Not to Tell?

PRACTICE REFUSAL SKILLS

1. Work with a partner. Talk about times when a stranger might call on the phone or come to the door.
2. Pick a situation and act it out. Have the stranger try to find out if you are home alone. Refuse to give the stranger any information. Then change roles and act out the scene again.
3. Talk about what happened. What were the best ways to refuse to give information to the stranger?

- Never open the door to strangers. Your family may not want you to say anything. Or use a family password. That's a word known only to you, your parents, and anyone else you are allowed to let in. If someone at the door doesn't know the password, don't let the person in.
- If the stranger won't go away, then use the telephone to call for help. Call your parents or guardian if you have a number for them. If they are not available, then call the police or 911. Tell them what is happening and that you are afraid. Follow the directions they tell you to stay safe until they arrive. Remember never to open the door.

"Bad" Touches and "Good" Touches

A "bad" touch makes you feel uncomfortable and unhappy. It can come from a person you know or from a stranger. It is something that you would not do to someone else. It is something that another person should not do to you.

If someone touches you in a bad way, tell the person to stop. Do not be afraid to say "Don't do that" to an adult who makes you feel uncomfortable by touching you. If the adult doesn't stop, get away from the person or yell for help. Then be sure to report the person to an adult you do trust, such as a parent or a teacher.

A "good" touch makes you feel happy about yourself and the person who is touching you. A hug from a grandparent or holding hands with a friend are "good" touches. Be glad when you get a "good" touch. And give a "good" touch once in a while, too!

How can you tell that this is a good touch?

LESSON WRAP UP

Show What You Know

1. How can you help your family to stay safe from fire at home?
2. How might a password help you stay safe when you are home alone?
3. **THINK CRITICALLY** What is the difference between how a good touch and a bad touch make you feel?

Show What You Can Do

4. PORTFOLIO **APPLY HEALTH ACTIVITY** **Practice Refusal Skills** Create a home-alone comic strip. Show how to be safe if a stranger calls. Show how to refuse to tell the stranger your name or that you are home alone.
5. LIFE SKILL **PRACTICE LIFE SKILLS** **Obtain Help** Where are the best places in a home for smoke detectors and fire extinguishers? Ask an adult to help you make a list of the best places.

HANDBOOK **LIFE SKILLS** pp. 268–279

LESSON

4 OUTDOOR SAFETY

In this lesson, you will learn:

- rules to keep you safe around water.
- rules to keep you safe when bicycling.
- rules to keep you safe during different kinds of weather.

VOCABULARY

personal flotation device (PFD) (pûr′sə nəl flō tā′shən di vīs′) life preserver; device that helps a person float in water

frostbite (frôst′bīt′) injury caused when uncovered skin freezes from very cold weather

QUICK START You and some friends are at a swimming pool. Two friends start to wrestle at the edge of the pool. Why should you tell them to stop?

Whether you're in a backyard or a community park, being active outside can be a lot of fun. Many people enjoy outside activities such as swimming, boating, biking, and running.

Following safety rules will help you keep safe and have more fun outdoors. Be "safety smart" and use the rules to prevent injuries.

What are these students doing to stay safe while they ride?

Water Safety

SPLASH! If you swim or boat it's important to know about water safety.

- Swim with a buddy. If one of you has a problem in the water, the other can help or get help.
- Swim only in places with a lifeguard or other adult swimmer watching. Obey all swimming rules and signs for that place.
- Don't swim too far or for too long. If you feel tired, get out of the water. If you are not a good swimmer, don't swim in water that is over your head.
- If you hear thunder or see lightning, get out of the water fast. Lightning can injure swimmers by moving through the water from a long way off.
- Be safe around water, not just in it. Don't play near the edge of a pool, on a dock, or anyplace else where you could fall into the water.
- When on a boat, always wear a life preserver or **personal flotation device** (PFD). A life jacket or vest is a PFD. These devices will help you float if you fall into the water.
- Never go boating or fishing without an adult. Don't stand up in a small boat or play in a dangerous way.

HEALTH FALLACY

"Personal Flotation Devices (PFDs) are only for poor swimmers."

This is not true. Even good swimmers should wear a PFD when on a boat. Most drownings caused by boating mishaps occur when PFDs are not worn. Suppose, for example, you were to fall into the water. You might hit your head and not wake up. A PFD would keep you floating until help arrives.

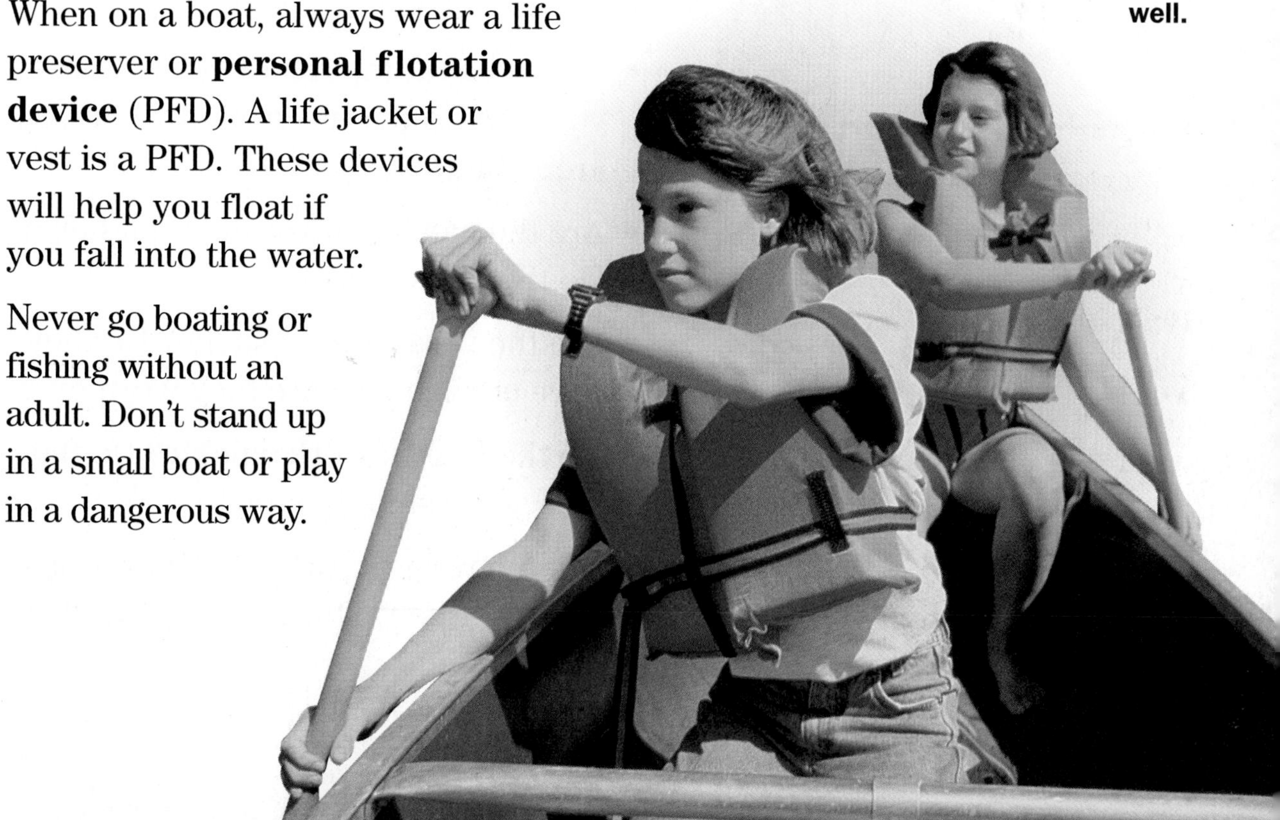

Wear a personal flotation device if you can't swim well. Always wear one on a boat, even if you can swim well.

Use the hand signals shown below whenever you ride your bike.

Bicycle Safety

Biking is a favorite outdoor activity for many people. To stay safe while biking, follow these rules.

- Wear a helmet. (In many places it's the law.) Wear shoes so that your feet won't slip off the pedals.
- Watch for pedestrians and traffic. Obey all traffic signs. Walk your bike across intersections.
- Ride in the same direction as traffic. Ride single file, never side by side.
- Signal all turns and stops. Unless you're signaling, keep your hands on the handlebars.
- Don't let anyone ride on the handlebars or behind you on your bike fender.
- Use lights and reflective clothes at night.

Bicycle Safety Checklist

Make sure your bike is in good working order. Give it a safety check.

- Is the seat at the right height? Can your feet touch the ground while you are sitting?
- Are the handlebars at the right height? Do they move easily?
- Are the tires in good shape? Do they have enough air? Are they worn out?
- Do the brakes work quickly? Do they give you a smooth stop?
- Are the reflectors clean? Do you have a horn or bell? Does it sound loud and clear?

Skating and Skateboard Safety

You may not always be able to avoid falling while on skates or a skateboard, but follow these tips to help yourself avoid injury.

- Wear a helmet, light gloves, and elbow, knee, and wrist guards.
- Keep your speed under control. Know how to stop and how to fall.
- Don't skate or skateboard in traffic. Watch for pedestrians.

Playground Safety

Playgrounds are a great place to have fun. But they are also a place where many children get injured. Here are ways to be "safety smart."

- Stay in the playground area. Play in areas that are clear of hazards such as rocks and nails.
- Do not use broken equipment.
- Use equipment that is the right size for you. For example, smaller swings are meant for smaller children.
- Construction sites and empty buildings are not play areas. Stay away from places where garbage is dumped, too. These *contaminated* areas are unsafe and off limits!

Construction sites are not safe places to play.

LIFE SKILL

MAKE DECISIONS

What Would You Do?

You and a friend are biking to the library. A quick route there is to ride on the street. A longer route is on a bike path on the sidewalk. Which route would you take? Why? How would you decide?

HANDBOOK **LIFE SKILLS** pp. 268–279

Being Weather Wise

Cold weather, hot weather, wet weather—weather can change. It's always a good idea to be "safety smart" and weather wise.

You need to know how to act safely in severe weather. TV and radio weather reports can help you plan. The National Weather Service may tell you when severe weather will strike and what to do.

Strong winds can be very dangerous. A *tornado* is a whirling, funnel-shaped storm that has extremely high winds. To stay safe in a tornado, go to a place with no windows, such as a basement. In a *hurricane*, very heavy rain comes with high winds. Before a hurricane strikes, people may be told to go inland from a coast.

Thunderstorms and blizzards can be dangerous too. A *thunderstorm* produces lightning. If you have to be outside, keep away from trees, water, and anything metal. A *blizzard* is a very heavy snowstorm with high winds. As in any severe weather, stay inside during a blizzard.

Hot Weather Safety

- Dress in loose, lightweight clothes. Wear light-colored clothes to reflect harsh sunlight. Wear a big hat to shade your face, scalp, ears, and neck.
- Drink plenty of liquids to replace water lost through sweating.
- Use a sunscreen to keep your skin from burning.

Cold Weather Safety

- Wear layers of clothes to help hold in your body's heat. Dark outer clothes absorb sunlight and keep you warm.
- Cover up in the cold. Wear a hat, gloves, and a scarf to hold in body heat. Uncovered skin can freeze in very cold weather. This is called **frostbite**. Frostbite can be a serious injury.

HEALTH ACTIVITY

Safety Slogans

LIFE SKILL SET GOALS

You will need: colored markers, plain or colored paper, string, paper puncher

1 Join one of three groups: Water Safety, Bicycle Safety, or Weather Safety. Talk about specific hazards for your group.

2 Each member sets a goal to be more "safety smart" in an important way. Members write their goals as slogans.

3 Work together. Make banners for your group's slogans. Discuss the safety goals shown on each group's banners.

LESSON WRAP UP

Show What You Know

1. Name three rules for staying safe around water.

2. Suppose that you are riding a bicycle. Draw the correct hand signals you would use for a left turn, a right turn, and a stop.

3. **THINK CRITICALLY** You may not have very hot or cold weather where you live. You may not have storms. Why is it still important to learn safety rules for all kinds of weather?

Show What You Can Do

4. PORTFOLIO **APPLY HEALTH ACTIVITY** **Set Goals** Write a letter asking for advice about reaching a safety goal. For example, "Dear Dr. Safety: How can I stay safe in hot weather?" Then write Dr. Safety's answer.

5. LIFE SKILL **PRACTICE LIFE SKILLS** **Obtain Help** Find out about the kinds of severe weather or other possible natural hazards in your area. What sources in the library can help you find out?

HANDBOOK LIFE SKILLS pp. 268–279

LESSON 5

EMERGENCIES

In this lesson, you will learn:

- how minor injuries are different from serious injuries.
- how to get help in an emergency.

VOCABULARY

emergency
(i mûr′jen sē) a serious situation in which help is needed right away

minor injury
(mī′nər in′jə rē) physical harm to a person that can be treated easily

serious injury
(sîr′ē əs in′jə rē) physical harm to a person that requires special emergency help

QUICK START A friend has fallen from a tree. Her leg hurts. Her mother calls an ambulance. How might you help your friend in the meantime?

Have you ever scraped an elbow while playing? Injuries like these happen to everyone. You and your family can usually take care of the problem.

Other kinds of injuries are more serious. If someone stops breathing or has a cut that won't stop bleeding, it's serious. These kinds of injuries need quick action. It's "safety smart" to know what to do if you or someone else is injured.

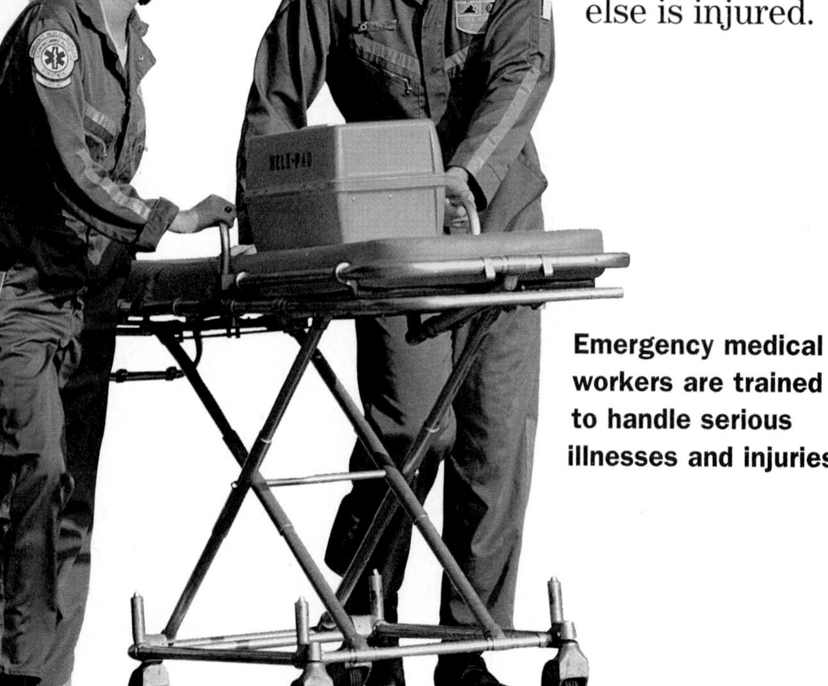

Emergency medical workers are trained to handle serious illnesses and injuries.

What Is an Emergency?

When you think of an emergency, what do you think of? Do you think of flashing red lights and sirens? Do you think of people in a hurry to help?

An **emergency** is a serious situation in which help is needed right away. An emergency can't wait!

All injuries need care. A **minor injury** can be treated easily by you and your family. But a **serious injury** needs special emergency help. The chart shows several types of minor and serious injuries.

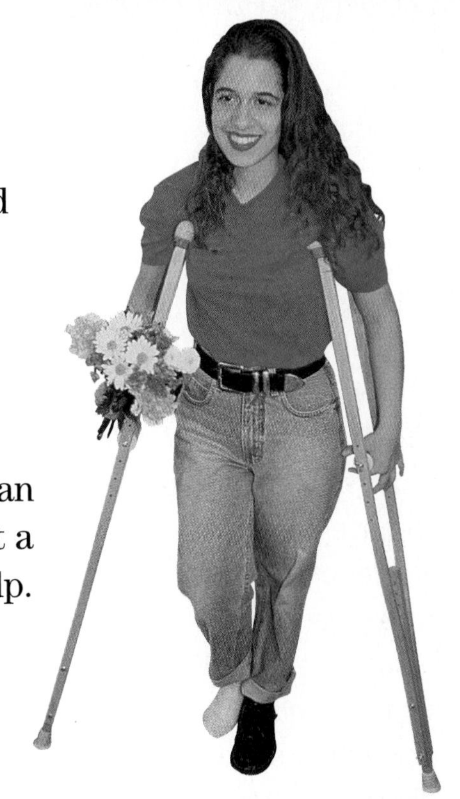

MINOR INJURIES	SERIOUS INJURIES/EMERGENCIES
• scratches, scrapes, small cuts, and nosebleeds • bruises caused by bumping into an object • mild burn that causes the skin to turn pink • a slight headache • a mosquito bite • a mild rash	• a wound that won't stop bleeding • broken or cracked bones • a burn that blisters • hitting head and not being able to wake up • fainting or severe swelling from an insect sting • not being able to breathe • animal bites, especially from snakes, rats, raccoons, and stray dogs

HEALTHWISE CONSUMER

Information, Please!

An injured person who is not awake can't give emergency workers needed health information. For example, an injured person may also have a heart condition. People with health problems often wear medical identification tags. The tags will tell the emergency workers about any medical condition a person may have.

Getting Help

Serious injuries are emergencies. You also need emergency help if a fire starts or you see a crime occur. Firefighters, police officers, and emergency medical workers are there to help.

When you need emergency help, tell a trusted adult right away. If you are alone, call 911. If there is no 911 system in your town or area, dial 0 (zero). Be ready to tell the operator what has happened, who is injured, and where you are.

The person on the phone will tell you what to do. He or she will send help. If medical help is needed, emergency medical technicians (EMT) will be sent.

Until help comes, here's what to do.

- Keep the injured person still. Moving the person might make the injury worse.
- Help the person stay warm. Cover him or her with a blanket.
- Help the person stay calm. Say that help is coming.

MAKE DECISIONS

What Would You Do?

You and a friend are playing in his yard. Suddenly a snake bites your friend. His family is not home. What do you do?

Knowing how to call for help is one of the best ways to prepare for an emergency.

HEALTH ACTIVITY

Can You Help Me?

OBTAIN HELP

1 With your partner, list scenes in which a person might call 911. Each of you choose a scene.

2 Act out calling for help. Have your partner be the emergency operator. The caller should give helpful information. The emergency operator should ask important questions and keep the caller calm.

3 Switch roles. Act out your partner's scene.

LESSON WRAP UP

Show What You Know

1. A friend yells, "Ouch! I cut myself!" How could you tell whether the cut was a minor injury or a serious injury that needed emergency care?

2. Describe what to do in an emergency.

3. **THINK CRITICALLY** Why is it important to keep calm when making a 911 call?

Show What You Can Do

4. PORTFOLIO **APPLY HEALTH ACTIVITY** **Obtain Help** Write a script about someone calling 911 for help and an emergency operator. Use everyday language to make your dialogue sound as real as possible.

5. LIFE SKILL **PRACTICE LIFE SKILLS** **Set Goals** Set a goal to be able to react quickly when an emergency happens. What could you do now to get yourself ready? In your health log write a few sentences telling how you would get ready.

HANDBOOK **LIFE SKILLS** pp. 268–279

LESSON

6 FIRST AID

In this lesson, you will learn:

- the meaning of first aid.
- what supplies belong in a first aid kit and what they are used for.
- proper first aid treatment for some minor injuries.

VOCABULARY

first aid
(fûrst′ ād′) immediate care given to a person who is injured or ill

QUICK START While washing his hands, your brother let the water get too hot. Now the back of his hand is pink and sore. Would you call 911? How could you help him?

Injuries such as a slight burn or a scrape are minor. You don't need to call 911. But you do need to care for them.

Minor injuries can be treated with first aid. **First aid** is immediate care given to an injured or ill person. First aid can stop an injury from getting worse. It can also help it heal faster. It's important to know how to treat minor injuries. But it's best to try to obtain help from an adult, if possible. In this lesson, you will learn some first aid tips.

A school nurse can give first aid.

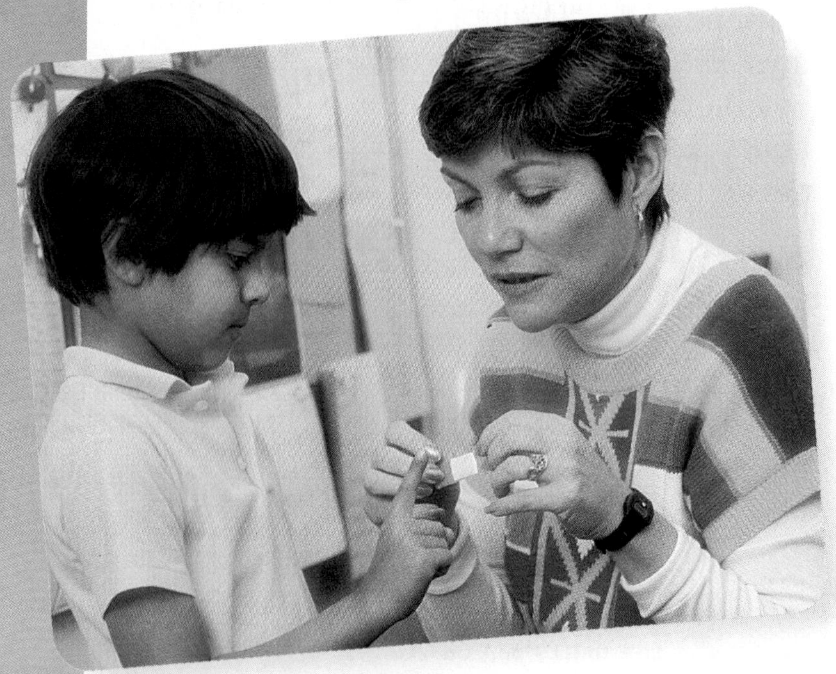

A First Aid Kit

First aid kits contain items that can be used to treat some minor injuries. Here are some important supplies to include in a first aid kit.

- Soap—for cleaning cuts, scrapes, and insect bites. Soap can also be used to wash sap from poisonous plants off the skin.
- Ointment—a cream that helps cuts and scrapes heal. Rub the ointment on after the cut or scrape is cleaned.
- Bandages—to cover a cut, scrape, or burn after it has been properly cleaned. There are types of bandages such as adhesive strips, gauze pads, and tape.
- Tweezers—to remove splinters or ticks from skin.
- Latex gloves—contact with blood can spread germs from one person to another. If you give first aid to another person, be sure not to touch their blood. Latex gloves will act as a barrier between yourself and the other person's blood.

LIFE SKILL

MANAGE STRESS

What Would You Do?

Sometimes a person who is called on to give first aid gets tense. How could a person manage this kind of stress?

HEALTH FACT

"You should check and refill your first aid kit on a regular basis."

It is true. It's a good idea to check your first aid kit regularly. Keep emergency phone numbers up-to-date. Refill any items that have been used. Replace any out-of-date items, such as ointments. A first aid kit is only useful if all the needed supplies are there.

First Aid for Minor Cuts and Scrapes

Wash the injured area with soap and cool water. Pat the area dry with a clean cloth. Then cover it with a clean, dry cloth or bandage.

First Aid for Nosebleeds

Many things can cause nosebleeds—such as an injury or even being in a place with very dry air for a long time. They can also happen when you have a cold. If you have a nosebleed, sit down and lean slightly forward. Bow your head low, pinch your nose closed, and breathe through your mouth. After five minutes, if the bleeding doesn't stop, get help.

First Aid for Minor Burns and Sunburn

Run cool water over the burn or place the burned area under cool water in a sink or bowl about ten minutes. Cover the burn loosely with a clean, dry bandage or cloth. If a blister has formed, leave it alone. Don't try to break it open.

Most nosebleeds are not serious and are usually easy to control.

Bites and Stings

Most insect bites and stings can be treated as a minor injury. If stung, use your fingernail to scrape out the stinger. Do not use tweezers to pull the stinger out. If you are stung or bitten, wash the injured area with soap and cool water. Then apply lotion for bites or stings. If there is pain and swelling, cover the area with ice or a cold wet cloth.

Some people may have a serious reaction to an insect bite or sting. For example, a person may get a rash or have trouble breathing. If this happens, the problem needs special help.

Reactions to Poisonous Plants

Poison ivy, oak, and sumac plants can be dangerous. These plants have oil on their leaves. You can get a blistery rash by touching the leaves of these plants. If you do touch them, wash the oil from your skin immediately. Use a lot of soap and cool water. Then clean the area with rubbing alcohol.

Apply a cream or lotion to help stop the itching. See a doctor if you have more than just a rash.

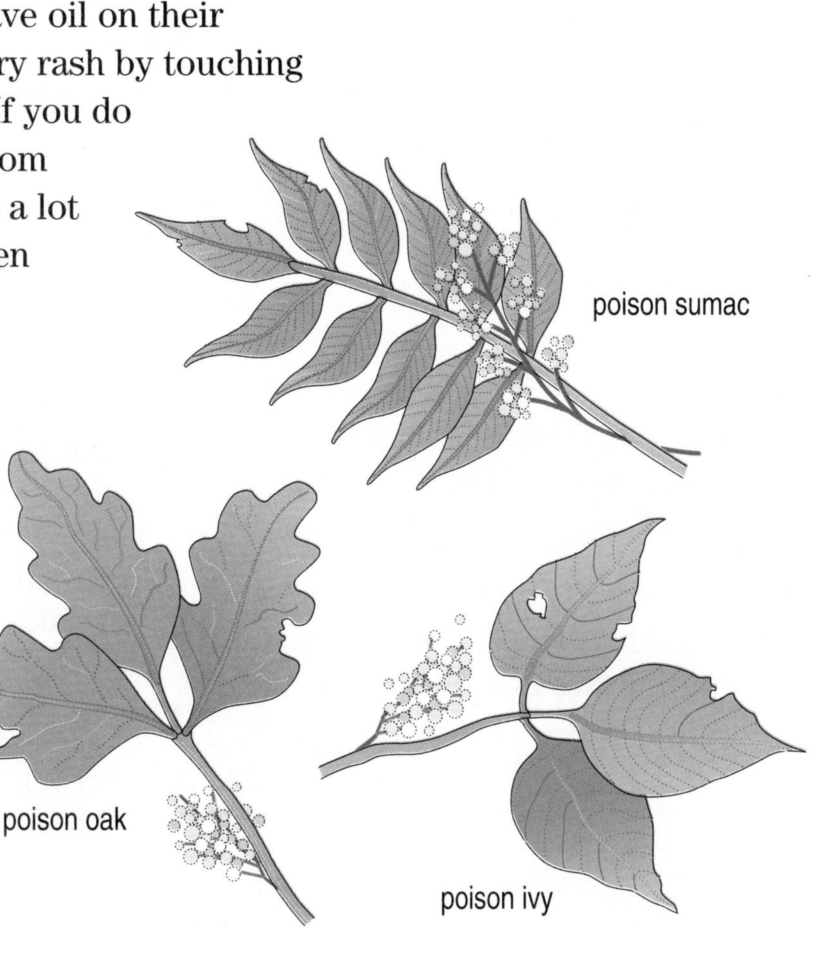

HEALTH ACTIVITY

First Aid—and Fast!

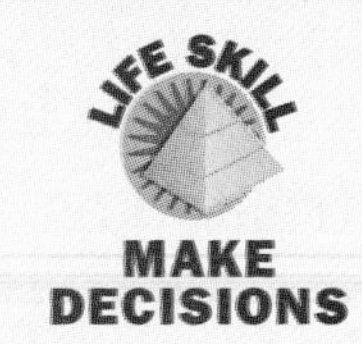

You will need: a classroom first aid kit

1. Think of a situation in which you might be injured and need first aid. Decide if it is a minor injury that can be treated with first aid. Or, does it need special emergency care?
2. If it is a minor injury, decide how to treat it with first aid. If it is an emergency, decide how you would get help.
3. Act out what you decide.

LESSON WRAP UP

Show What You Know

1. What is first aid?
2. Name two items that should be part of a first aid kit. What does each do?
3. **THINK CRITICALLY** Why do you think that the first step in treating many minor injuries is to wash the injured area?

Show What You Can Do

4. PORTFOLIO **APPLY HEALTH ACTIVITY** **Make Decisions** Pretend that you work at a first aid station at a camp. Write a diary entry for one day. Describe the injuries you saw. Tell what action you decided to take and why.
5. LIFE SKILL **PRACTICE LIFE SKILLS** **Obtain Help** What kind of first aid is needed if someone is choking? With a partner, find out about the Heimlich maneuver. Ask an adult to describe how it is done.

HANDBOOK LIFE SKILLS pp. 268–279

YOU CAN MAKE A DIFFERENCE

TECHNOLOGY

A New Use for Balloons

How could balloons help save lives?

Swallowing a balloon can be very dangerous—unless a doctor helps you do it. If something got stuck in your throat, a balloon—in a doctor's hands—could save your life.

Getting something stuck in the throat used to mean a trip to the hospital and an overnight stay. A doctor would have to put the patient under to get the object out.

Now doctors might use a balloon to solve this problem. First they look for the stuck object with an X-ray. Then they push a thin balloon tube into the patient's throat past the stuck object. As they push, they watch the patient's throat on an X-ray machine. They inflate the balloon and pull it back up. The stuck object comes out with the balloon. The whole thing takes just about 15 minutes.

You don't always need big machines and powerful tools to cure people. Sometimes the simplest ways are the best!

MANAGE STRESS

HELP YOURSELF RELAX

Suppose you need the balloon procedure to remove a coin you have swallowed. The doctor tells you to relax, but it's a little scary! What could you do to calm yourself down? Work with a friend. List three things you could do.

CHAPTER

9 REVIEW

VOCABULARY

Write the word or words from the box that best complete each sentence. Use each word only once.

emergency
first aid
frostbite
hazard
minor injury
smoke detector
violence

1. Anything that could cause an injury is a ___?___. (Lesson 1)
2. The use of strong force to harm someone is called ___?___. (Lesson 2)
3. A fire safety device that sounds an alarm when there is smoke is a ___?___. (Lesson 3)
4. A wound that won't stop bleeding should be treated as a(n) ___?___. (Lesson 5)
5. A person who scrapes an elbow might get immediate care called ___?___. (Lesson 6)

REVIEW HEALTH IDEAS

Use your knowledge of safety, injury, and violence prevention from Chapter 9 to answer these questions.

1. Why can bleach, glue, and other household products be hazards? (Lesson 1)
2. Name two things you can do to be a "safety-smart" pedestrian. (Lesson 1)
3. How can you act safely to avoid violence? (Lesson 2)
4. What should you do if an angry person becomes violent? (Lesson 2)
5. What should you include in a fire escape plan? (Lesson 3)
6. Describe two ways to keep safe when home alone. (Lesson 3)
7. How can you tell that a bicycle is safe to ride? (Lesson 4)
8. If you call 911 in an emergency, what will happen? (Lesson 5)
9. Why should soap and latex gloves be parts of a first aid kit? (Lesson 6)
10. What first aid should you give to someone who has a minor burn? (Lesson 6)

APPLY HEALTH IDEAS

1. Name two things that a person could do to be more careful about everyday hazards. (Lesson 1)
2. Why is it important to keep an up-to-date list of emergency telephone numbers by the phone? (Lessons 3 and 5)
3. When bicycling, why do you need to obey traffic signs that car drivers have to obey? (Lesson 4)
4. PORTFOLIO **OBTAIN HELP** Suppose you see someone at school or in the community with a weapon. Tell what you would do to stay safe and keep others safe. (Lesson 2)
5. LIFE SKILL **RESOLVE CONFLICTS** Make an illustrated first aid booklet. Decide how to treat three minor injuries such as cuts, burns, and bee stings. (Lesson 6)

Make a list of safety rules from this chapter that can apply to hazards in your kitchen at home. Think of fire hazards, electric hazards, poisons, and so on. Do the same for your bathroom. Then use your lists to check out these rooms. Talk to your family about how to make these rooms safer. Repeat for the other rooms of your home.

HANDBOOK LIFE SKILLS pp. 268–279

CHAPTER

9 TEST

Write the word or phrase in parentheses that makes each statement true.

1. If you see lightning while swimming, (get out of the water/call for help).
2. Shaking the spelling bee winner's hand is a (good/bad) touch.
3. If an object is out of reach, climb on a (ladder/heavy chair) to get it.
4. When waiting to cross at the green in a crosswalk (run across/look left, right, and left again).
5. To keep from touching a wounded person's blood use (latex gloves/wet towels).
6. When home alone, do not open the door for anyone who does not know the family (password/address).
7. One healthy way to deal with anger is to (count to 10 slowly/slam doors).
8. If stung, remove the stinger by (scraping it out with your fingernail/using tweezers).
9. In cold weather, clothing that is (dark/light) in color can help keep you warm.
10. A bee sting that causes a person to faint is a (minor/serious) injury.

Write a sentence to answer each question.

11. Describe what you should do if your clothes catch fire.
12. Why is talking calmly a healthy way to avoid violence?

13–14. What are two examples of household hazards?

15–16. Name two rules for bicycle safety.

17. What is first aid and why is it important to know?

18–19. Name two ways you can help a seriously injured person.

20. What first aid would you give to someone with a rash from a poisonous plant?

Performance Assessment

PORTFOLIO

Who do you think is the most important person for keeping you safe? Explain your answer.

COMMUNITY AND ENVIRONMENTAL HEALTH

CHAPTER **10**

You can help your health by:

- knowing about the people and places in your community that provide health care.
- working together with your community to keep the environment healthy.

CHAPTER CONTENTS

1 COMMUNITY HEALTH CARE 248

2 A CLEAN ENVIRONMENT 252

3 PROTECTING PLANET EARTH 258

YOU CAN MAKE A DIFFERENCE BEARABLE TIMES 263

CHAPTER REVIEW 264

CHAPTER TEST 266

LESSON

1 COMMUNITY HEALTH CARE

In this lesson, you will learn:

- about jobs of health care workers.
- about health services in your community.

VOCABULARY

health care (helth kâr) services that keep people healthy; includes preventing and treating problems

immunizations (im′yə niz ā′shənz) vaccines that protect people from diseases

clinic (klin′ik) a local place where people can get many kinds of medical treatment

health department (helth di pärt′mənt) part of the government that works to prevent the spread of disease

QUICK START Suppose you fell and broke your arm. Where could your parents take you for treatment?

Your neighborhood is the area where you live. Your neighborhood is part of a larger community. A *community* is a place where many people live and work together. People in a community work together to meet their needs. One of the most important needs is to stay healthy.

Some people make community health their job. They treat illnesses and injuries. They teach people good health habits and how to stay safe. These services—including treatment and prevention—provide **health care** to a community.

Health care workers help people in a community stay healthy.

Community Health Care Workers

Health care workers prevent and treat health problems. They are hard at work in many places in the community.

- *Family doctors* help people who are ill to get better. They also help prevent people from becoming ill. One way they do this is by providing immunizations. **Immunizations** are the vaccines that protect a person from diseases such as measles.
- At a **clinic**, you can find doctors and other health care workers, all in one place. They provide many kinds of treatment. Clinics are located throughout a community.
- *Hospitals* provide special care and equipment that people cannot get at a doctor's office or clinic. At hospitals, health care workers offer medical services such as delivering babies, performing surgery, and giving special medical tests.

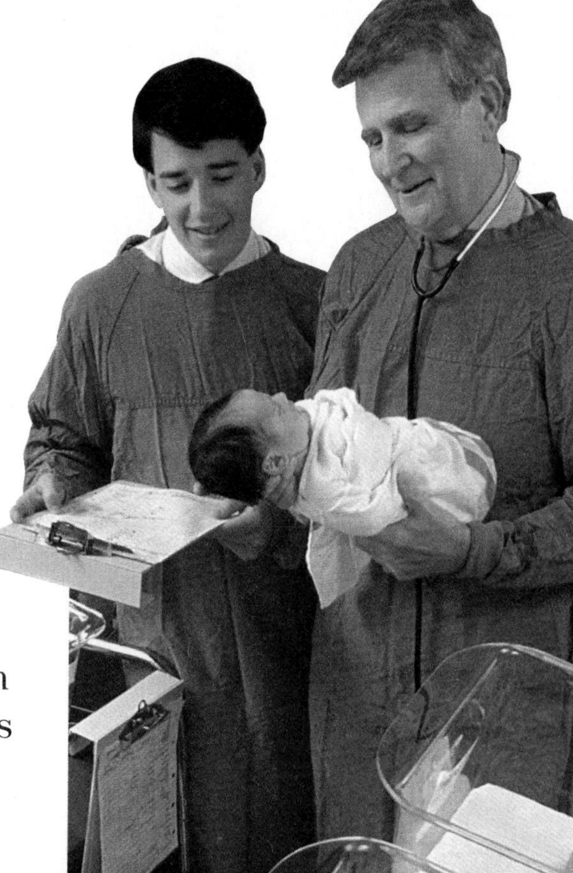

HEALTH CARE WORKERS AND THEIR JOBS

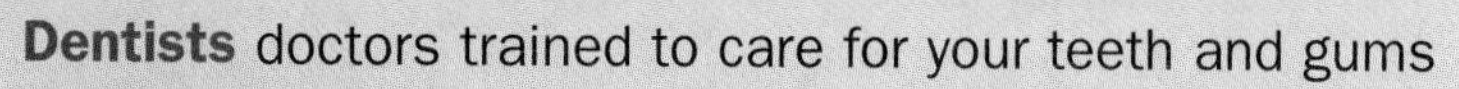

Worker	Job
Doctors	trained to find out what is causing an illness; treat people who are sick or hurt; prescribe medicine; give immunizations
Specialists	doctors trained to treat a specific health condition; for example, a pediatrician is a specialist trained to treat children
Dentists	doctors trained to care for your teeth and gums
Nurses	trained to care for patients and help doctors; school nurses care for students in schools
EMS Workers	trained to treat sick or hurt people who need immediate care; drive ambulances and get people to hospitals for doctors' care
Pharmacists	trained to prepare medicine and fill doctors' prescriptions

HEALTHWISE CONSUMER

Community Drugstores

Most communities have several drugstores—some large, some small. What's the difference?

Most large drugstores offer many choices of medicines at advertised prices. Your family might save money by shopping there. Small drugstores may offer more personal service because the pharmacist knows your family. The best way for a family to choose is to try both and see which better meets its needs.

Health Departments

Health departments provide many services. They are part of the government in the area or the state. Their goal is to prevent the spread of disease in a community.

Health department workers teach people good health habits. They keep records of births, deaths, and diseases. They set guidelines for people to follow to stop the spread of disease. Health departments also help make sure buildings are clean and safe.

Sanitarians are special health department workers. They check that the community's food is safe to eat. They make sure restaurants and stores prepare and store food safely.

LIFE SKILL

OBTAIN HELP

What Would You Do?

You are playing in the schoolyard. Suddenly you fall and scrape your knee. Where would you go for help and why?

Health care workers help a doctor to improve a patient's health. Their jobs include keeping records, planning diets, and running tests for illnesses.

HEALTH ACTIVITY

Where's the Care?

LIFE SKILL
OBTAIN HELP

You will need: index cards, telephone book, push pins

1 Work with a partner. Look in the yellow pages of a telephone book under *Health*, *Hospitals*, *Medical Services*, or *Physicians*. Find four places that provide health care in your community.

2 Write the name, address, and phone number for each place on an index card.

3 Post your index cards on a bulletin board titled "Health Care in Our Community."

LESSON WRAP UP

Show What You Know

1. Name two kinds of health care workers and tell what they do.

2. What are two of the duties of a local health department?

3. **THINK CRITICALLY** What is a difference between the health care you can get at a hospital and the health care you can get at a doctor's office?

Show What You Can Do

4. PORTFOLIO **APPLY HEALTH ACTIVITY** **Obtain Help** Some health groups depend on people to give their time and money to help the group do its job. The American Heart Association is an example. Find out about these groups. Tell the class what you learned.

5. LIFE SKILL **PRACTICE LIFE SKILLS** **Set Goals** Set a goal to learn more about health care workers. With your family, visit some to talk about their jobs.

HANDBOOK LIFE SKILLS pp. 268–279

LESSON 2

A Clean Environment

In this lesson, you will learn:

- how workers, guidelines, and laws keep a community healthy.
- how people in a community can reduce pollution.
- how communities work to keep the environment safe and clean.

VOCABULARY

environment (en vī′rən mənt) everything around you, including the air, water, and land

pollution (pə lü′shən) something that makes the air, water, or land dirty or impure

recycle (rē sī′kəl) to do something to garbage so that it can be used

QUICK START Your community is having a cleanup day. People will clean the sidewalks and parks. Why might you want to help?

Everyone in a community wants the **environment**—everything around the community including the air, water, and land—to be clean and healthy. Anything that makes the environment dirty or impure is called **pollution**.

Keeping a community clean is a big job. When everyone works together, that job is much easier to do.

Recycling is one way to help keep the environment clean.

Keeping a Community Clean and Healthy

Workers from the health department and other departments protect a community from pollution.

- They measure soot and smoke produced by cars and factories. *Soot* is black powder that comes from burning fuels. They tell people when levels of dirt in the air are dangerous. They issue warnings to factories to try to reduce the problem.
- They make sure that the water supply is safe to drink and use.
- They make sure that garbage is collected and deposited properly.

Guidelines for a Clean Community

Local governments pass guidelines to help people in a community stay healthy.

- Smoking is not allowed in public places. This helps keep you safe from breathing unhealthy air.
- Some laws require that waste water from buildings be cleaned before flowing into rivers, lakes, and streams.
- People who *litter*, or toss bits of rubbish on the ground, are given fines to pay.

Proper collection and storage of garbage is very important to a community's health.

INFOGRAPHIC

The Three R's—Reduce, Reuse, and Recycle

The places where garbage can be dumped are filling up fast. But the people in a community can help now by following the Three R's—reduce, reuse, and recycle.

REDUCE

You really can reduce, or make less garbage. Here are some ways to reduce garbage.

- Buy items packaged with less cardboard, plastic, and paper. The less packaging, the less you'll have to throw away.
- Use both sides of writing paper before you throw it out.
- Use cloth napkins and kitchen towels instead of ones made of paper. This will reduce the paper products you throw out.

REUSE

Don't just throw something away. Think about how you might reuse it, or use it again. Here are some good ideas about reusing.

- Store things in empty jars, bottles, boxes, and cans. For example, a jam jar can show off a seashell collection.
- Buy products in refillable containers.
- Bring your own shopping bag.
- Give your old clothes, toys, and books to younger children.

RECYCLE

To **recycle** means to do something to garbage so that it can be used. Aluminum cans, paper, and some glass and plastic products can be recycled. Here are some ideas than can help you recycle.

- Buy products that are made of recycled materials. These products will have a special symbol on the package.
- Find out about your community's recycling rules. Recycle as much as you can.

HEALTH ACTIVITY

"R" You Ready?

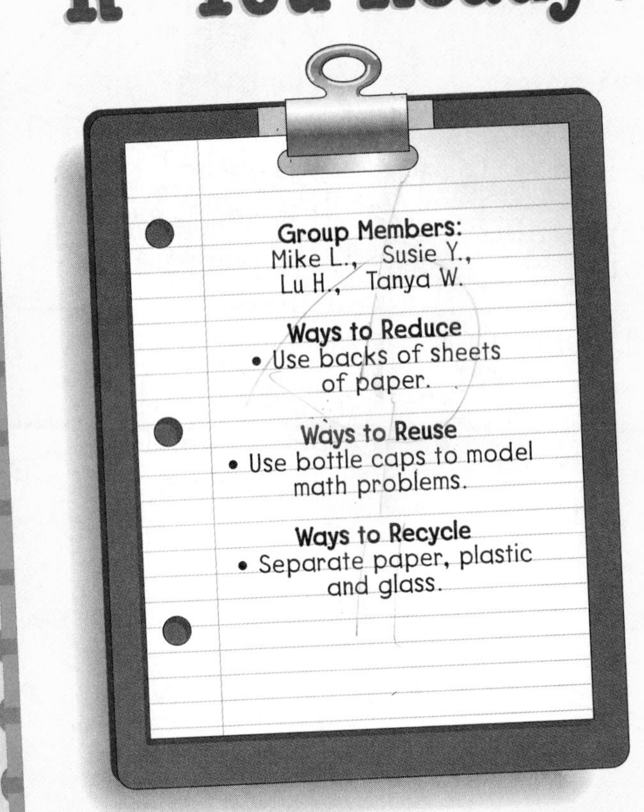

You will need: markers, poster board

1. Work with a group. Talk about ways to handle the amount of garbage your class makes.
2. Make a list of the best ideas. Combine your list with the lists from other groups.
3. Use the ideas to create a bulletin board about the Three R's. How could the ideas help improve the environment of your classroom?

Other Kinds of Community Clean-Up

Garbage and polluted water will be problems for communities for years to come. Solving those problems won't be easy. But here's what communities can do now to solve some of the problems.

A community can do something about polluted water. Often, the water supply for a community must be cleaned before people can use it. The water is cleaned in *water treatment plants*. Then it is stored, ready for the community to use. Water from *sewage*, or liquid waste, also can be cleaned and reused.

A community can do something about garbage, too. In some communities, garbage is burned. Burning gets rid of the garbage—but it makes smoke and ash that can be harmful.

Many communities have places where garbage is dumped. In other communities, the garbage is taken to a *landfill.* There it is packed down and covered with dirt. Later, buildings can be built on top of the landfill.

HEALTHWISE CONSUMER

Garbage That Won't Quit

Foam packaging and cups are permanent garbage. They are made of material that will never rot. This material is very harmful to the environment. If you have a choice between a product packaged in or made of foam or paper, choose the paper item. You will be helping the environment.

RESOLVE CONFLICTS

What Would You Do?

Two neighbors are arguing over a landfill that your town is planning. One person likes the idea. The other is against it. What can the neighbors do to help resolve the conflict?

LESSON WRAP UP

Show What You Know

1. How can workers and guidelines help keep a community healthy? Give an example of each.
2. Name one way to reduce the amount of garbage you use. Then name one way to reuse something in your home instead of throwing it out.
3. **THINK CRITICALLY** Why is managing a community's pollution problems so difficult?

Show What You Can Do

4. PORTFOLIO **APPLY HEALTH ACTIVITY** **Make Decisions** Design a comic strip about a character who doesn't know about the Three R's. He throws things away. In your comic, show how he decides to reduce, reuse, and recycle.
5. LIFE SKILL **PRACTICE LIFE SKILLS** **Practice Refusal Skills** A friend suggests that you both toss your lunch trash behind some bushes. Tell how you would refuse.

HANDBOOK LIFE SKILLS pp. 268–279

LESSON 3

PROTECTING PLANET EARTH

In this lesson, you will learn:

- how air, water, and land can become polluted.
- how pollution can hurt the environment and people's health.
- how you can help protect Earth's natural resources.

VOCABULARY

natural resource (nach′ər əl rē′sôrs′) anything that is part of Earth and that people need or find useful

contaminate (kən tam′ə nāt′) to spread something dirty into something clean

hazardous wastes (haz′ər dəs wāsts) wastes that can cause illness and must be thrown away very carefully

QUICK START You tell your little brother not to toss a candy wrapper onto the sidewalk. He asks, "Why not?" How can you explain that it is important not to litter?

Air, water, and land are parts of our planet, Earth. They are **natural resources**, the parts of Earth that people need and use. Natural resources include plants and animals, too.

Pollution can harm natural resources for the whole planet. It can harm people, too. In this lesson, you'll learn about some of the harm that pollution can do. You'll find out more about how you can fight pollution.

Clean natural resources make the outdoors a wonderful place.

Cars and factories are major sources of air pollution.

Air Pollution

To **contaminate** something clean means to make it dirty. Many things contaminate the air. The result is air pollution. Some causes are:

- *exhaust* (that is, burned fuel) from cars and trucks.
- ash and soot from factory smokestacks.
- smoke from burning fuels and garbage.
- cigarette smoke.

Air pollution can harm you in many ways. It can make your eyes itch, burn, and water. It can make your nose become stuffy. It can make your throat feel scratchy.

Air pollution also makes it harder to breathe. Small specks of pollution too small to see can get into your lungs. This can make people with lung or heart problems feel worse. Plants can be harmed by air pollution, too. They may grow poorly, or not at all.

HEALTH FACT

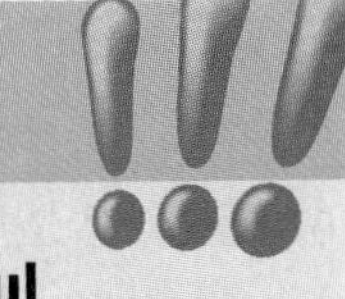

"Some harmful gases can't be seen or even smelled."

This is true. Carbon monoxide is a poisonous gas that cannot be seen or smelled. Carbon monoxide is made when certain materials are burned. Some people have carbon monoxide detectors in their homes. Like smoke detectors, they sound an alarm if the dangerous gas is present.

MAKE DECISIONS

What Would You Do?

Many people in a community take their cars to work. The business area has air pollution. What might you suggest to help reduce air pollution?

Water Pollution

Water pollution happens when wastes get into oceans, rivers, lakes, and streams. Factories may dump garbage and liquid waste into rivers and lakes. Ships carrying oil may leak and harm the wildlife. Soil may erode, or wear away, and wash into water supplies. And, remember—whatever you wash down the drain may enter nearby water supplies.

Drinking polluted water can make people sick. So can eating fish that have lived in polluted water. So can swimming in polluted water.

Land Pollution

Have you ever seen plastic bags or old tires along the side of the road? You were looking at land pollution. Land pollution is ugly—and unhealthy. Garbage that is left in the open will rot. It will attract pests that can spread disease.

Hazardous wastes are a special problem for land, water, and air. These wastes, such as pesticides, can cause illness. They must be thrown away very carefully. Otherwise, these chemicals can trickle down into the soil or nearby stream. Food grown in soil that has been poisoned by hazardous chemicals can make people sick.

HEALTHWISE CONSUMER

Handling Hazardous Wastes

Many household products that we use every day are considered hazardous wastes. Paint, glues, and batteries are just a few examples. These items can harm the environment if they are not thrown away properly. Save these wastes and their containers for a community hazardous waste pickup day. Or take them to special collection sites. Find out how your community handles household hazardous wastes.

Noise

Noise can pollute the environment, too. Loud noise comes from many sources—sirens, lawnmowers, power tools, airplanes, and car horns. It can also come from loud CD players, radios, or televisions.

Very loud noise can be harmful. It can damage a person's hearing. Loud noise can cause a headache. It also can make a person feel tense or stressed.

Protect yourself from loud noise. If you must be around loud noise, wear earplugs. If you listen to music through headphones, be sure that you could hear someone talking to you.

Protecting Earth

Protecting Earth is everyone's job. Governments from all nations have to work together. You and your community can do your share. You learned some ideas in Lesson 2. Here are some more.

- Be aware. Learn about pollution from news reports on TV and in newspapers.
- Help reduce noise in your environment. Don't play a radio or television too loudly. Try not to yell in the playground or on the street.
- Don't litter. Organize a pollution patrol. Your patrol can clean up a nearby park, pond, or sidewalk. Get adults to help. Be sure to wear gloves when touching litter.
- Obey community laws that reduce pollution. The environment—and you—will be healthier for it!

Cultural Perspectives

"Water flows over these hands. May I use them skillfully to preserve our precious planet."

Think about this short poem by Thich Nhat Hanh, a Vietnamese writer. What does this writer want to do? How might you help?

HEALTH ACTIVITY

Pollution Solutions

You will need: posterboard, markers

1. With your partner, choose one of four topics: air, water, land, or noise pollution
2. Make a poster. Show some causes of that pollution. Use arrows and labels to show how this pollution can affect the environment and people.
3. Set some goals that people can use to reduce this pollution and keep healthy. Add them to the poster.

LESSON WRAP UP

Show What You Know

1. Name one cause of air pollution, one cause of water pollution, and one cause of land pollution.
2. Name two ways you can help protect Earth.
3. **THINK CRITICALLY** How can something that pollutes land or water harm you?

Show What You Can Do

4. PORTFOLIO **APPLY HEALTH ACTIVITY** **Set Goals** Identify some pollution problems in your school. Think of ways that students might have helped cause this pollution. Set goals to solve the pollution problems.
5. LIFE SKILL **PRACTICE LIFE SKILLS** **Manage Stress** Think of a place in your home, school, or community where noise bothers you and causes stress. How might you handle that stress?

HANDBOOK LIFE SKILLS pp. 268–279

YOU CAN MAKE A DIFFERENCE

HEALTH HEROES

Bearable Times

Alexis Brown

Alexis Brown has spent a lot of time in the hospital. She was born with cerebral palsy. She also had a disease called lupus. She knows what it's like to be a sick child.

Alexis found that many children in the hospital were lonely, bored, or scared. She wanted to help them feel better.

Alexis started a newsletter for children in the hospital. She asked other children to write stories and poems and draw pictures. She published the newsletter in her own hospital. Soon it was going to 200 hospitals, and hundreds of children were reading it.

Since Alexis loves teddy bears, she called the newsletter "Bearable Times." Someday she hopes to publish her newsletter in hospitals around the world. With people like Alexis around, sick children don't have to feel alone and afraid.

SET GOALS

HELP HOSPITALIZED CHILDREN

Being in the hospital can be stressful. If you were in the hospital, what might make you feel better? What could you and your class do to cheer up children in the hospital? Set a goal to make a plan and then carry it out.

CHAPTER

10 REVIEW

VOCABULARY

Write the word from the list that best completes each sentence.

clinic
community
contaminate
environment
health care
natural resource
pollution
recycle

1. People can get many kinds of medical treatment at a __?__. (Lesson 1)
2. Anything that makes the environment dirty or impure is called __?__. (Lesson 2)
3. Glass and aluminum can be changed and made into new things if you __?__ them. (Lesson 2)
4. A factory that produces soot can __?__ the air. (Lesson 3)
5. The land is an important __?__. (Lesson 3)

REVIEW HEALTH IDEAS

Use your knowledge of community and environmental health from Chapter 10 to answer the following questions.

1. List four health care workers whom you might see in your community. (Lesson 1)
2. Describe the job of an emergency medical technician. (Lesson 1)
3. How can a person get emergency medical care? (Lesson 1)
4. Describe a guideline or law that can help keep a community healthy. (Lesson 2)
5. What is a landfill? (Lesson 2)
6. How do health care workers protect a community from pollution? (Lesson 2)
7. What are the Three R's that can help keep a community clean? (Lesson 2)
8. What are some causes of air pollution? (Lesson 3)
9. How can loud noise affect your health? (Lesson 3)
10. How can a pollution patrol help your community? (Lesson 3)

APPLY HEALTH IDEAS

1. Why are immunizations an important way to keep a community healthy? (Lesson 1)
2. How can reducing the amount of packaging help keep communities cleaner and healthier? (Lesson 2)
3. Why is it important for people to feel that they are a part of the environment? (Lesson 3)
4. PORTFOLIO **MAKE DECISIONS** Make a drawing of a healthier Earth. Show how people in different communities have made decisions to reduce pollution and save resources. (Lesson 3)
5. LIFE SKILL **SET GOALS** Natural resources are too valuable to waste. How is water wasted at home or school, or in the community? Set goals to reduce the waste. (Lesson 2)

Could you get your whole family involved in recycling? Find out what your community's rules are for preparing items to be recycled. Then have a family meeting. Talk about ways to recycle things in your home. Make a chart listing which items can be recycled and what to do.

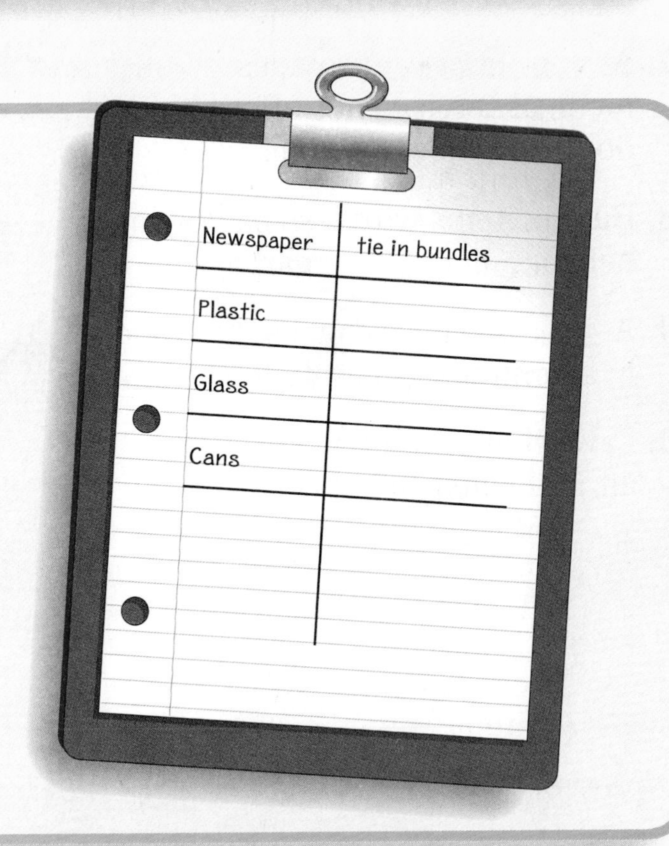

CHAPTER

10 TEST

Complete each sentence with the correct word or phrase.

1. Rotting garbage is a form of ___?___ pollution.
2. Workers from the ___?___ check that the water supply is safe to drink and use.
3. Special care is needed when throwing away ___?___.
4. Loud ___?___ from sirens and radios can pollute the environment.
5. A ___?___ is trained to fill doctor's prescriptions.
6. Itchy, burning, and watery eyes can result from ___?___.
7. A ___?___ provides medical services not offered in a doctor's office or clinic.
8. Buying items with less packaging helps ___?___ garbage.
9. A ___?___ checks that food in a community is safe to eat.
10. Laws that protect against dirty air and water help keep a ___?___ healthy.

Write a sentence or two to answer each question.

11. Describe places other than a hospital that offer health care.
12. Describe some effects of pollution on people's health.
13. How does a fine for littering help community health?
14. What is the job of a nurse?
15. How does a landfill get rid of waste?
16. Name one way land can become polluted.

17–19. Name ways to reduce, reuse, and/or recycle.

20. Name one thing you could do (or not do) to protect Earth.

Performance Assessment

Many community organizations need volunteer help. Write a radio ad. Talk about the need for help. Then ask people to give a few hours of their time to a community health or clean up project.

LIFE SKILLS HANDBOOK

LIFE SKILL 1: MAKE DECISIONS	268
LIFE SKILL 2: SET GOALS	270
LIFE SKILL 3: OBTAIN HELP	272
LIFE SKILL 4: MANAGE STRESS	274
LIFE SKILL 5: PRACTICE REFUSAL SKILLS	276
LIFE SKILL 6: RESOLVE CONFLICTS	278
NUTRITION	280
PHYSICAL ACTIVITY	284
SAFETY	288
FIRST AID	290
RESOURCES	292
GLOSSARY	294

Life Skill 1: Make Decisions

Part of growing up is making your own decisions. Some decisions, like what you wear, may only matter for a day. Other decisions, like not smoking, can affect your health, your whole life.

Thinking about the choices and possible results can help you make the best decision. Use this six-step plan.

Life Skill 1

MAKE DECISIONS

1. Name a decision you need to make.
2. List possible choices.
3. Think about the possible results of each choice. Which results are healthful? Are any results harmful to your health?
4. Think about your family's values. Which choices are in keeping with them?
5. Make a decision and take action.
6. Review your decision. Did your decision lead to the result you expected?

Practice Life Skills

Brad got very good grades this year. His parents offered him a choice of vacations. He could spend one week at a baseball camp. Or, the whole family would go on a four-day trip to a theme park!

Brad used the six decision-making steps. He made the following notes.

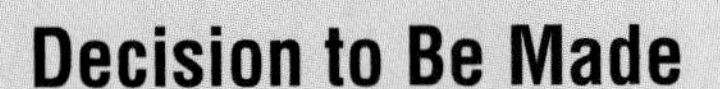

Decision to Be Made

Where will I go on vacation?

Choice 1
baseball camp

Choice 2
theme park

Possible Results

improve my baseball skills
meet baseball players
meet new friends
physical activity

Possible Results

go on rides
see interesting exhibits
visit a new state

Consider Values

I'll improve my self-esteem.
I'll keep fit.
I might get lonely.

Consider Values

I'll spend time with my family.
I might learn something new.
I'll have fun.

Decision

I really want a vacation that my whole family can enjoy. We can go to the theme park. I'll practice baseball with my friends.

MAKE DECISIONS

What Would You Do?

You want to earn some extra money. A neighbor offers to pay you $5 to help with yardwork on Saturday. Other neighbors offer to pay you $1 each weekday to walk their two dogs. Use the six steps to decide what you would do and why.

Life Skill 2: Set Goals

A goal is something you wish to achieve. You might set a goal to be a great baseball pitcher or a terrific singer. Each of these goals takes more than just wishing. Achieving a goal takes work.

This six-step action plan can help you meet your goals.

Life Skill 2

SET GOALS

1. Choose one specific goal and write it down. It can be a small goal or a larger, long-term goal.
2. Decide what steps you will do to reach the goal.
3. List who can help and support you.
4. Set a time limit to reach your goal.
5. Check how you are doing several times before the time limit is up.
6. Reward yourself when you have reached your goal.

Practice Life Skills

By studying a macramé book, Kendra has learned to make decorative items out of knotted cord. Kendra's mother's birthday is in one month. Kendra's goal is to make a macramé belt for her mother.

The belt is more complicated than any item Kendra has worked on so far. She uses the six steps to plan how she will reach her goal.

1. Goal
Make a belt for Mother's birthday.

2. Steps I Will Take
Follow the directions in the book carefully.

3. Who Can Help
My older sister Jeanelle has made macramé crafts. She can help me if I need it.

4. Time Limit
The belt has to be finished in 1 month (4 weeks).

5. Checkpoints
Week 1: Read directions, buy materials.
Week 2: Complete first half of belt.
Week 3: Complete second half of belt.
Week 4: Attach belt buckle, wrap present.

6. Rewards
When I finish, I'll make another belt for myself.

SET GOALS

What Would You Do?

Your drama club's goal is to put on a short play for a senior citizens' center. The club has two months to get ready. What steps does the club need to take to reach their goal?

Life Skill 3: Obtain Help

You can get help from many different people. Trusted adults, such as parents or teachers, can help with many health problems. Community workers, such as police or firefighters, can be called in emergencies.

Knowing how to ask for help plays a key part in good health. Use the five-step action plan below to obtain the help you need.

Life Skill 3

OBTAIN HELP

1. Know when help is needed.
2. Identify the kind of help you need. Is it an emergency or do you need advice or information?
3. Identify people who can give you help.
4. Create a clear message with details that explains the kind of help you need. Don't be afraid to ask questions.
5. Communicate the need for help.

Practice Life Skills

Marcia brushes and flosses her teeth. But her gums bleed when she brushes. Marcia wonders if there is something wrong with her teeth or gums, or if she is just brushing too hard.

Marcia used the five steps to think about her gum problem. She wrote her notes in the form of a flowchart.

1. Know when help is needed.

Bleeding gums may be a sign of a problem that needs treatment.

2. Identify the kind of help you need.

I need someone who can tell what is wrong by looking at my teeth and gums.

3. Identify people who can give you help.

parents, school nurse, dentist

4. Create a clear message about the help you need.

"My gums bleed whenever I brush. It seems to be getting worse. What is causing the bleeding? What can be done?"

5. Communicate the need for help.

I'll ask Mom to watch when I brush tonight. She'll help me get the help I need.

OBTAIN HELP

What Would You Do?

Your grandfather is in good health except for his poor eyesight. He has trouble reading books and newspapers. Sometimes he has problems reading the labels when he goes grocery shopping. What kinds of help could you get for your grandfather?

Life Skill 4: Manage Stress

Stress is the way your body and mind respond to the changes around you. Stress is a natural part of everyone's life. Stress can be caused by things, events, people, or places.

Sometimes, a little stress can give you the boost to do your best. But too much stress can be unhealthy. You might have trouble eating, sleeping, or doing schoolwork.

You cannot avoid all the stress in your life. However, there are healthful ways to deal with stress. Here's a four-step action plan to manage the stress in your daily life.

Life Skill 4

MANAGE STRESS

1. Be prepared. Plan your time. Don't leave important jobs for the last minute.
2. Get lots of rest, sleep, and physical activity.
3. In a stressful situation, try to relax. Take deep breaths.
4. Talk about the situation with a trusted adult or friend.

Practice Life Skills

Jon's group will present their safety project after lunch today. Everyone has worked very hard, but they are still nervous. What if something goes wrong? What if other students ask questions the group can't answer?

The group shared ideas on how to manage the stress they were feeling. Here's what they said:

Dealing with the STRESS of a REPORT

1. Be Prepared

Debbie said, "I wrote the key points of my report on index cards. Then I practiced in front of a mirror several times."

2. Get Sleep, Rest, and Physical Activity

"Let's play a quick game of catch during lunch," said Mike. "It will relax us and take our minds off the report."

3. Relax and Take Deep Breaths

"Every time I think about the report, my stomach hurts," said Midori. "Closing my eyes and taking deep breaths really helps."

4. Talk About It

"I think being nervous means we care about doing a good job," said Jon. "Right," said Lisa, "and we're all in this together."

MANAGE STRESS

What Would You Do?

You have a part in the school play. You're nervous about performing in front of a lot of people. What can you do to feel less nervous?

Life Skill 5: Practice Refusal Skills

Sometimes it is important to say "no." Refusal skills help you say "no" to something that isn't healthful or doesn't fit with your values or beliefs.

To decide when to say "no," ask yourself some questions. Is this good for my body? Is this dangerous or illegal? How will this make me feel about myself? Always think about what is right for you.

The five steps below can help you make people take "no" for an answer.

Life Skill 5

Practice Refusal Skills

1. Say "no" clearly to a dangerous situation or action or to a behavior you strongly believe is wrong.
2. Use a strong voice and a serious expression to show that you mean what you say.
3. Explain your reasons.
4. Suggest a possible alternative.
5. If necessary, walk away from the situation.

Practice Life Skills

Two of Gina's friends want to grab on to the back of a bus and ride for a few blocks. Gina doesn't think this is a good thing to do.

Here are some things Gina thought about to help her say "no."

1. Say No.
"A great big *NO* is what I want to say here. I don't want my friends to think I might change my mind."

2. Use a strong voice and a serious expression.
"I'm going to say *NO* and mean it. I want to look and sound like I know better."

3. Explain your reasons.
"This is dangerous and probably against the law. We could be hurt or killed, or just get into lots of trouble."

4. Suggest alternatives.
"I could suggest we go to the schoolyard and play some basketball instead."

5. If necessary, walk away.
"If I can't convince them this is crazy, I'm leaving. I don't want them to get hurt, but I can't help it if they don't listen."

LIFE SKILL

PRACTICE REFUSAL SKILLS

What Would You Do?

A friend wants you to sit close during a test and share your answers. You don't think this is right. Explain how and why you would refuse this request.

Life Skill 6: Resolve Conflicts

People do not always share the same opinions. Maybe you disagree with a friend about the people to invite to a party. Your feelings are so strong that you start to argue.

A strong disagreement is a conflict. Try to avoid conflicts. If a conflict is unavoidable, then you must find a way to resolve it peacefully. Use these five ways to help you deal with a conflict.

Life Skill 6

RESOLVE CONFLICTS

1. Be tolerant. Accept people as they are. Try to understand the other person's point of view.
2. Don't be prejudiced. It's never healthful to dislike people or ideas for their own sake. Avoid angry name calling and put-downs.
3. Communicate your thoughts and feelings clearly. Be respectful in what you say and how you listen to other people.
4. Try to reach a compromise without giving up safety, values, and basic rights.
5. If communication and compromise will not or cannot work, then try to delay the conflict or walk away.

Practice Life Skills

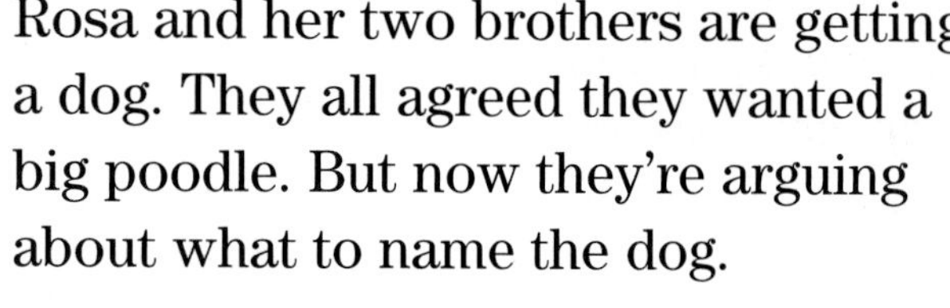

Rosa and her two brothers are getting a dog. They all agreed they wanted a big poodle. But now they're arguing about what to name the dog.

Rosa says they shouldn't fight, or they might not get the dog at all. She suggests some ideas based on the steps for resolving a conflict.

1. Be Tolerant
"All the names are good, but we can only pick one. The dog will still belong to all of us."

2. Avoid prejudices
"Let's not say any names are dumb or call each other stupid. We all think differently."

3. Communicate
"Maybe we should each give reasons for the name we chose. It may help us understand what we all want."

4. Compromise
"If we brainstorm some more, we may come up with a new name we all like."

5. Delay or Walk Away
"We're all tired now. Let's agree not to say any more about names until tomorrow. A good night's rest may give us some new ideas."

RESOLVE CONFLICTS

What Would You Do?

You and your brother are supposed to take turns walking the dog. You and he start to argue because you don't think he's doing his share of the walking. How can you resolve this conflict?

The Food Guide Pyramid

The Food Guide Pyramid can help you make healthful food choices. Use the tips below every day.

FATS, OILS, AND SWEETS
Use sparingly.
You should eat few foods made mostly of fats, oils, or refined (processed) sugar. These are foods with many calories but few nutrients. This category is not considered one of the five food groups. You can find these ingredients in foods from other groups.

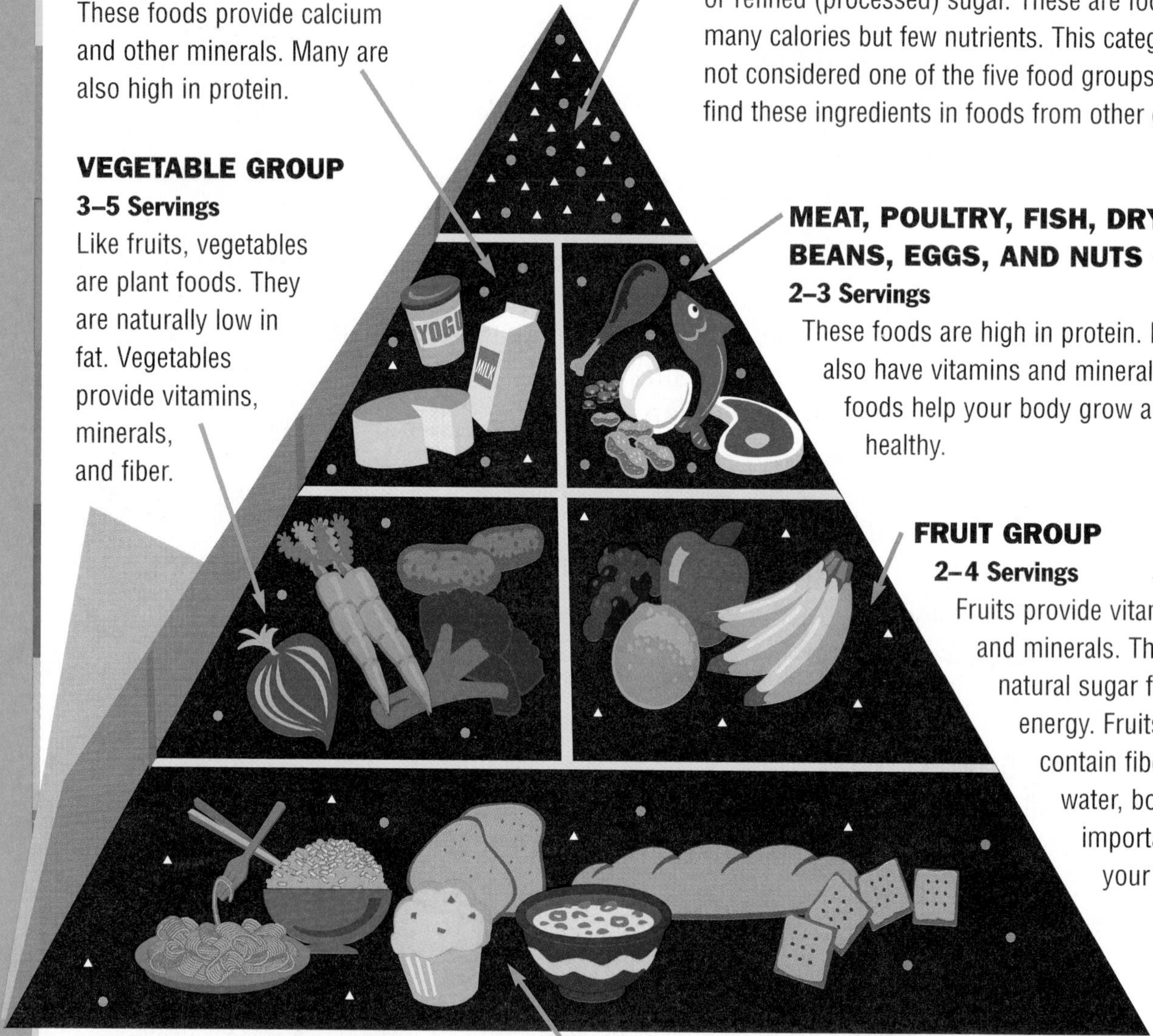

MILK, YOGURT, AND CHEESE GROUP
2–3 Servings
These foods provide calcium and other minerals. Many are also high in protein.

MEAT, POULTRY, FISH, DRY BEANS, EGGS, AND NUTS GROUP
2–3 Servings
These foods are high in protein. Most also have vitamins and minerals. These foods help your body grow and stay healthy.

VEGETABLE GROUP
3–5 Servings
Like fruits, vegetables are plant foods. They are naturally low in fat. Vegetables provide vitamins, minerals, and fiber.

FRUIT GROUP
2–4 Servings
Fruits provide vitamins and minerals. They have natural sugar for quick energy. Fruits also contain fiber and water, both important to your health.

BREAD, CEREAL, RICE, AND PASTA GROUP
6–11 Servings
Foods in this group are made from grains. Grains include wheat, corn, rice, and oats. Grains provide carbohydrates, protein, fiber, vitamins, and minerals.

KEY
- Fat (naturally occurring and added)
- Sugars (added)

These symbols show fats, oils, and added sugars in foods.

What Is a Serving?

The Food Guide Pyramid recommends a range of servings for each food group. For example, the Food Guide Pyramid shows that you should eat between 6–11 servings of food from the Bread, Cereal, Rice, and Pasta group. But how do you know whether to eat 6 servings or 11 servings or something in between? And how much food is one serving anyway?

- The number of servings depends largely on your age. The label "6–11 servings" includes all ages from age 5 to adults. Servings for young people ages 9 to 12 are from the lower number to a mid-range. See the chart below.
- Very active people may need more servings per day.
- Daily servings come from a combination of daily meals plus snacks.
- Remember that a single serving size is often smaller than what people may be served at a meal. Check food packages to find out how many servings are actually in the package. Study the chart below.

Food Group	One Serving Equals	Recommended Daily Servings for Ages 9–12
Bread, Cereal, Rice, and Pasta	1 slice bread; 1 ounce dry cereal; 1/2 cup cooked cereal, cooked rice, or pasta; 1/2 bagel	6 to 9 servings
Vegetables	1/2 cup chopped raw or cooked vegetables; 1 cup raw leafy vegetables; 1 medium potato; 3/4 cup vegetable juice	3 to 4 servings
Fruits	1 medium-sized apple, banana, or orange; 1/2 cup canned or cooked fruit; 1/2 grapefruit; 3/4 cup fruit juice	2 to 3 servings
Milk, Yogurt, and Cheese	1 cup milk or yogurt; 1 1/2 ounces natural cheese; 2 ounces processed cheese	2 to 3 servings
Meat, Poultry, Fish, Dry Beans, Eggs, and Nuts	2 1/2 to 3 ounces cooked lean meat, poultry, or fish; 2 tablespoons peanut butter; 1 egg or 1/2 cup cooked dry beans count as 1 ounce of meat	2 to 3 servings

Healthful Snacks

Everyone enjoys the right snack when hunger strikes. It's okay to snack. The goal is to choose foods that have a lot of nutrients and fiber but are low in calories and salt. Here are some suggestions for healthful snacking.

FRUITS

Apples, pears, nectarines, peaches
Fresh cherries, grapes, plums
Dried fruit, such as raisins or prunes
Baked apples and pears
Frozen bananas or grapes
Grapefruit or orange sections
Pineapple, apple, or melon spears
Chopped fruit mixed with nonfat yogurt

GRAINS, NUTS, AND BEANS

Shredded wheat, nuts, and raisins
Wheat germ and yogurt mixed with fruit
Whole wheat pretzels covered with sesame seeds
Unsalted, dry roasted peanuts
Unsalted almonds, pecans, or other nuts mixed with raisins
Air-popped popcorn (no salt, butter, or margarine)
Roasted pumpkin or sunflower seeds
Natural peanut butter or sesame butter (no salt or sugar) on crackers
Salt-free taco chips with chopped tomatoes, onions, and green pepper

UNCOOKED VEGETABLES

Carrot or celery sticks
Broccoli or cauliflower
Radishes
Zucchini strips or slices
Green or red pepper strips
Cherry tomatoes

THIRST QUENCHERS

Unsweetened fruit juices
Sparkling water or seltzer mixed with unsweetened grape juice
Vegetable juice (low salt)
Orange juice ice cubes
Lowfat or skim milk

PROTEIN POWER

Hummus (mashed chick peas mixed with lemon juice and chopped garlic) on pita bread

1/2 cup water-packed canned tuna mixed with 2 tablespoons yogurt, dash of lemon juice, onion, celery, mustard and pepper on crackers or whole grain bread

Peanut butter and jelly on whole grain bread

Cottage cheese, seasoned cucumber slices, lettuce, and tomato in a pita pocket

Tips for a Healthy You

1. **Start each day with a healthful breakfast.**
   Try cold cereal with fruit and lowfat or skim milk.
   Breakfast gives you energy to start your day right.

2. **Balance your food choices.**
   Use the Food Pyramid on page 280 as your guide.
   You don't need to give up all your favorite foods as long as you have a balanced diet.

3. **Eat healthful snacks.**
   See the suggestions on page 282.

4. **Get physical!**
   Do 30 minutes of physical activity a day.
   Try brisk walks; climb stairs instead of using escalators; go for a jog or a bicycle ride.

5. **Work up a sweat 3 to 5 times a week.**
   Try exercise routines that are about 20 minutes long.
   Include 5 minutes of warm-up and cool-down stretching and gentle movement.

6. **Get your family and friends to join in the fun.**
   Eat meals with your family when you're at home.
   Work out with friends.
   Join sports teams at school.
   Try new sports, games, and other activities—and sample new foods, too!

Warm-Up and Cool-Down Stretches

A safe workout includes warm-up and cool-down activities. Always begin and end your workout with stretches; they keep you from having muscle and joint injuries. Choose stretches from these pages to warm up, cool down, and improve your flexibility.

Stretching Tips

- Spend about 5 minutes warming up and cooling down.
- Relax and breathe easily while stretching; don't bounce or jerk.
- Do each stretch until you feel a gradual pull in the muscles.
- Hold each stretch for 5–10 seconds. Work up to holding for 20 seconds.
- Do a stretch 3 to 5 times. Over time, increase to 10 times.

1. Reach for Your Toes
(Thigh–calf and lower-back stretch)
- Sit with legs straight out, heels about 5 inches apart.
- Slowly reach fingertips forward as far as you can.

2. Crouch and Stretch
(Back-thigh stretch)
- Crouch on the floor with your hands flat under your shoulders.
- Stretch your left leg straight back, leaning forward gently.
- Repeat with your right leg stretched back.

3. Wide Knee

(Inner-thigh stretch)

- Sit with the soles of your feet together.
- Grasp your ankles and press your elbows gently against your knees.

4. Elbows Over the Head

(Upper back–shoulder stretch)

- Put your arms over your head.
- Hold the elbow of one arm with the hand of the other.
- Stretch the other hand down your back.

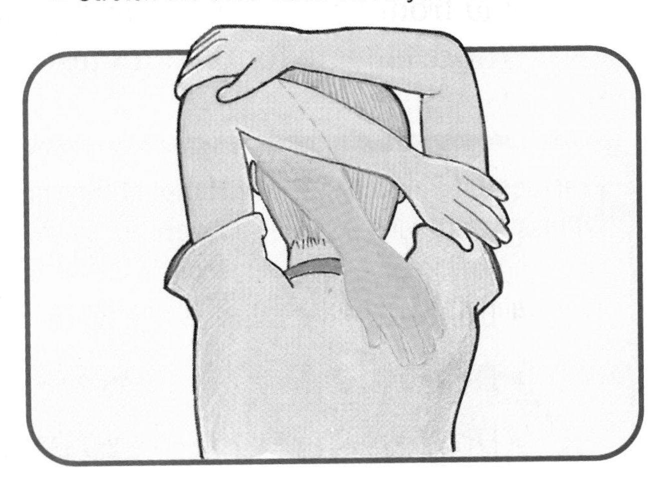

5. Shake Hands in Back

(Shoulder–chest stretch)

- Clasp your fingers together behind your back.
- Straighten your arms and stretch them downward.

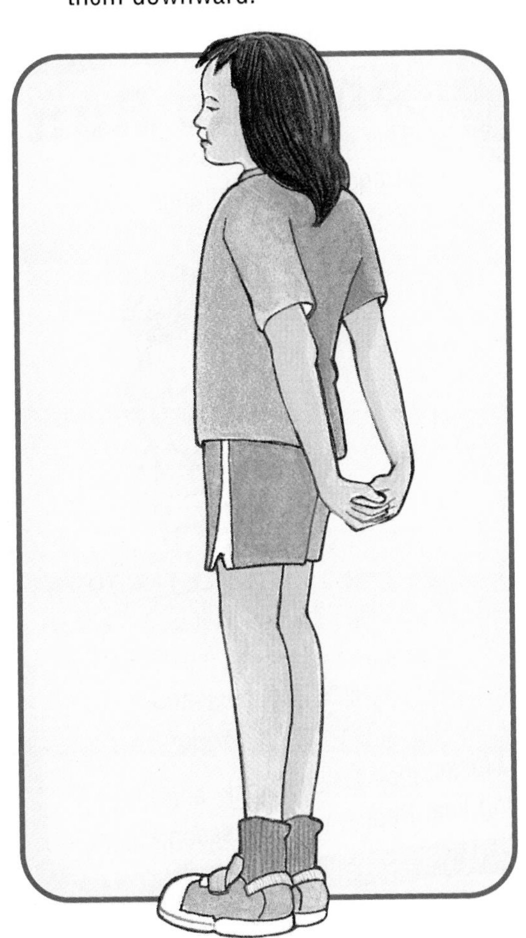

6. Wall Stretch

(Calf–heel stretch)

- Bend your left leg forward and lean against a wall.
- Stretch your right leg back.
- Keeping the right heel on the floor, bend the right knee slightly and lean forward.
- Repeat with your left leg back.

The President's Challenge

The Presidential Physical Fitness Award is a physical fitness challenge program for students from 6 to 17 years of age. Students who participate are eligible for one of these three awards:

Presidential Physical Fitness Award for students who score in the top 15 percent of their group.

National Physical Fitness Award for students who score in the top 50 percent of their group.

Participant Award for students who participate but do not score in the top 50 percent of their group.

1 Curl-ups or Sit-ups

This exercise measures your abdominal muscle strength.

Have a partner hold your feet down as you lift your upper body off the floor. Lower your upper body until it just touches the floor and start again.

2 Shuttle Run

This exercise measures leg strength and endurance.

Run to the blocks, pick up one block, and bring it to the starting line. Repeat with the second block.

3 One Mile Run / Walk

This exercise measures the strength of your leg muscles and your heart and lung endurance.

Complete the mile as fast as you can. You can walk if you get tired.

4 Pull-ups

This exercise measures the strength and endurance of your arm and shoulder muscles.

Hang by your hands from a bar. Pull your chin up until it is over the bar. Lower your body without touching the floor and start again.

5 V-sit Reach

This exercise measures the flexibility of your legs and back.

Sit on the floor with your feet behind the line. Reach forward as far as you can.

Indoor Safety

ELECTRICAL SAFETY

Do not overload outlets.

Do not use appliances with frayed cords.

CHEMICAL SAFETY

Keep cleaners in a safe place.
Make sure cleaners have labels.

FIREARM SAFETY

Never touch or play with a gun or rifle.
If you find one, tell an adult or call 911.

FIRE SAFETY

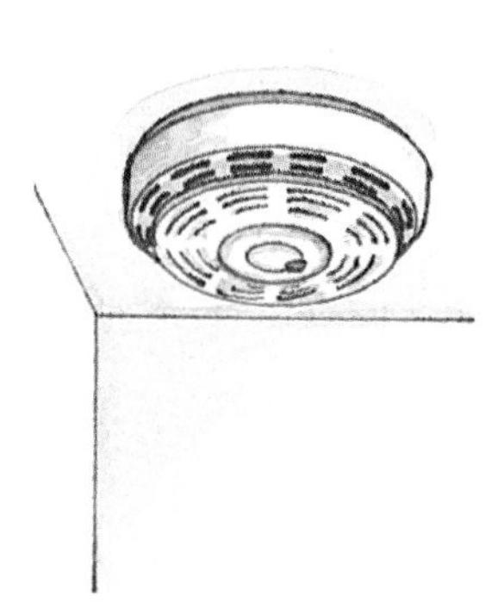

Put fresh batteries in your smoke detector.

Never play with matches.

IN CASE OF FIRE

Get out fast if you can.

Stay low. Smoke rises.

Do not open a warm or hot door.

Line doors to keep smoke out.

Open a window and call for help.

Outdoor Safety

CAR AND PEDESTRIAN SAFETY

WHEN IN A CAR:

- Always wear a safety belt.
- Don't distract the driver.
- Don't stick your head or hands out of the vehicle.

WHEN WALKING:

- Cross at crosswalks or intersections. Obey the crossing guard if one is present.
- Cross with the light.
- Look left, right, and left again before crossing.
- Avoid walking in deserted alleys or streets.
- Don't walk alone, if possible.

BICYCLE SAFETY

- Ride with a buddy whenever possible.
- Always wear a helmet.
- Obey all traffic signs.
- Ride in the same direction as traffic.
- Watch for cars pulling out.
- Use hand signals.
- Don't let a passenger share your bike.
- Don't ride barefoot.
- Don't ride at night without lights and reflectors.
- Don't try stunts like riding without holding on.

PLAYGROUND SAFETY

- Always play with a buddy.
- Follow all playground rules.
- Play inside the fenced area.
- Don't play on broken equipment.
- Don't play near a construction site or in an abandoned building.

First Aid

HOW TO TREAT . . .

INSECT STINGS

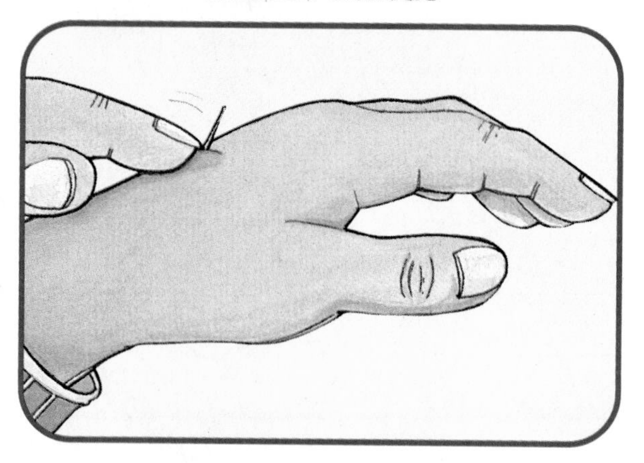

- Remove the stinger with a fingernail.
- Wash the injury with soap and water.
- Apply a cold cloth and some first aid cream.
- In case of serious swelling or trouble breathing, get emergency help.

POISONOUS PLANT RASHES

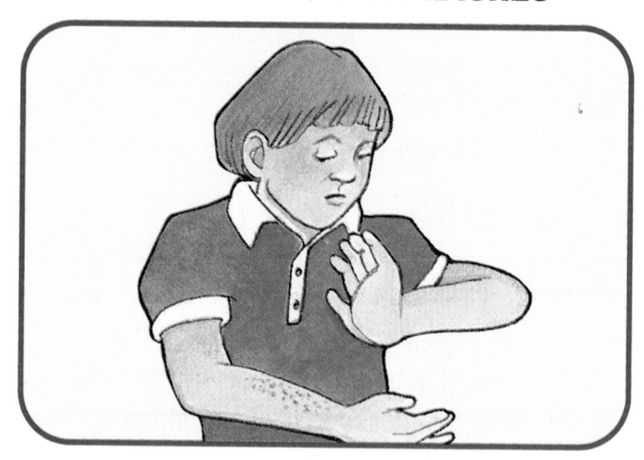

- Wash your skin with soap and water. This will remove the sap.
- Do not scratch bumps or break blisters.

A NOSEBLEED

- Sit and lean forward in a chair.
- Pinch both nostrils shut with your thumb and index finger.

BURNS AND BLISTERS

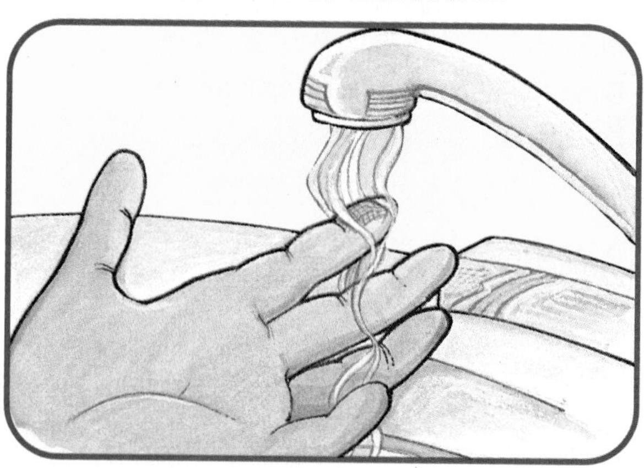

- Run cold water over a burn.
- Do not break a blister.
- If a blister breaks on its own, wash it with soap and water. Pat it dry with a clean cloth.
- Put on a bandage.

First Aid for Choking

IF SOMEONE ELSE IS CHOKING

Wrap your arms around the person from behind. Make a fist with one hand and grasp it with the other.

Pull the thumb side of your fist into the person's stomach. Use quick, hard, upward pulls to press your fist into the person's stomach.

IF YOU ARE ALONE AND CHOKING

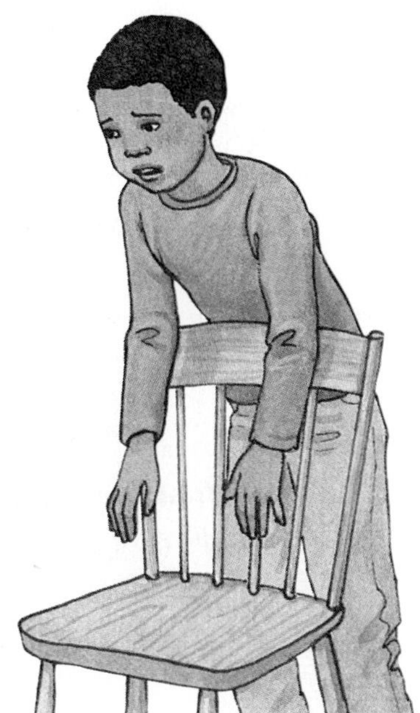

Lean with your stomach against the back of a chair.

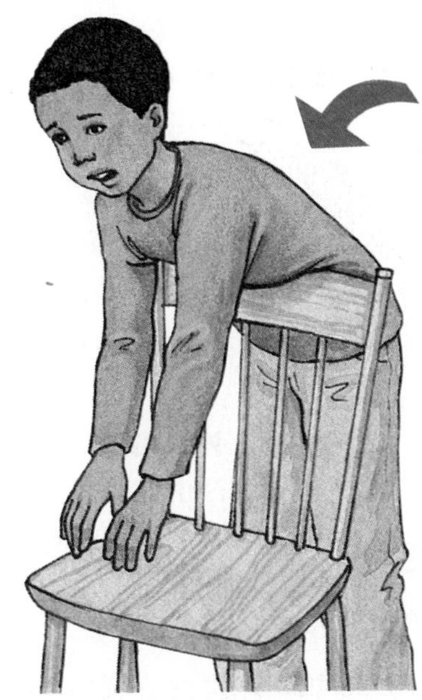

Press against the chair with a quick, hard push. Be sure not to press so hard that you break or injure a rib.

Field Trips and Class Visitors

These places can be field trips or a visitor from any of them may be invited to your school to speak to the students.

A DENTIST'S OFFICE

Dentists can tell you the best ways to care for teeth.

SET GOALS

Follow-Up Activity

A Visit to the Dentist Create a booklet for younger children. Explain what to expect when they visit the dentist.

QUESTIONS TO ASK

- How often should I brush and floss my teeth?
- What type of toothbrush should I use?
- How often should I get my teeth checked?

Bring a question or two of your own.

QUESTIONS TO ASK

- What skills do doctors need?
- How can a doctor help you stay healthy?
- When should people go to a doctor?

Bring a question or two of your own.

A DOCTOR'S OFFICE

Doctors can help you when you are sick. They also can help you to stay healthy.

OBTAIN HELP

Follow-Up Activity

Doctor! Doctor! Make a drawing showing one way a doctor can help a person stay healthy. Write a caption to explain how the doctor can help.

A FIRE HOUSE

Firefighters put out fires and save lives. They can also help you avoid fires and stay safe.

MAKE DECISIONS

Follow-Up Activity

Fire Safety First Create a cartoon strip showing how to avoid fire hazards.

QUESTIONS TO ASK

- What skills do firefighters need?
- How can people avoid fire hazards?
- What's the best way to stay safe in a real fire?

Bring a question or two of your own.

Books About Health Topics

PHYSICAL, EMOTIONAL AND INTELLECTUAL, AND SOCIAL HEALTH

Dinosaurs Alive and Well! A Guide to Good Health
by Laurie Kransny Brown and Marc Brown
Little, Brown and Company, 1990

A family of dinosaurs show how to take care of your physical, emotional and intellectual, and social health.

Follow-Up Activity

Pick a health tip from the book showing how to improve each of the three parts of health. Include your tip in a "Good Health" pamphlet. Illustrate the tips with characters of your own design.

NUTRITION

The Kids' Around-the-World Cookbook
by Deri Robins
Kingfisher, 1997

Here are lots of delicious, nutritious, and easy-to-make recipes from all corners of the globe.

Follow-Up Activity

Try one of the recipes and share the results with some classmates. Compare and discuss your responses to the food you prepared.

PERSONAL HEALTH/PHYSICAL FITNESS

Fit for Life
by Alexandra Parsons
Franklin Watts, 1996

What we eat and drink and how much we exercise are the keys to our health.

Follow-Up Activity

Draw a cartoon to show how you would refuse alcohol, tobacco, or drugs. Use some of the ideas from this book.

GLOSSARY

This Glossary gives the pronunciation and meanings of the vocabulary and other important terms in this book. It also tells where these items can be found.

A

adolescence (ad′ə les′əns) the period of time between childhood and adulthood when a person begins to look more like an adult (p. 31)

adulthood (ə dult′hůd′) after adolescence beginning around the age of 18 and lasting through old age (p. 31)

aerobic exercise (â rō′bik ek′sər sīz′) any nonstop activity that makes you breathe deeply and speeds up your heart rate (p. 141)

agility (ə jil′i tē) being able to change direction quickly (p. 135)

AIDS (Acquired Immune Deficiency Syndrome) (ādz) a very serious disease in which the immune system is extremely weak (p. 170)

alcohol (al′kə hôl′) a drug in beer, wine, and liquor and in some medicines (p. 196)

antibodies (an′ti bod′ēz) a chemical made by the immune system to fight a particular disease (p. 167)

apologize (ə pol′ə jīz′) to admit that you were wrong; to be sorry (p. 72)

appreciation (ə prē′shē ā′shən) feeling that everyone is special and important (p. 67)

artery (är′tə rē) a blood vessel that carries blood away from the heart (p. 43)

attitude (at′i tüd′) a way of feeling that affects the way you behave (p. 90)

B

bacteria (bak tîr′ē ə) a kind of one-celled living thing (p. 157)

balance (bal′əns) being able to keep the body in a steady, upright position (p. 135)

balanced diet (bal′ənst dī′it) meals and snacks made up of foods from all five food groups in healthy amounts (p. 115)

blood vessel (blud ves′əl) a tube that carries blood (p. 43)

body systems (bod′ē sis′təmz) a group of organs that work together to perform a particular job for the body (p. 33)

brain (brān) the main organ of the nervous system; the command center of your thoughts and actions (p. 52)

C

caffeine (ka fēn′) a drug that speeds up the body activities (p. 203)

carbohydrates (kär′bō hī′drāts) nutrients used by the body as its main source of energy (p. 104)

cavity (kav′i tē) a hole in a tooth caused by decay (p. 11)

cell (sel) the smallest living part of the body (p. 32)

childhood (chīld′hůd′) from the end of infancy to about the ages of 11 or 12 (p. 31)

circulatory system (sûr′kyə lə tôr′ ē sis′təm) body system made up of the heart, blood, and blood vessels (p. 43)

clinic (klin′ik) a local place where people can get many kinds of medical treatment (p. 249)

cocaine (kō kān′) an illegal drug made from the coca plant; can have lasting, dangerous effects on the body (p. 204)

communicable disease (kə mū′ni kə bəl di zēz′) disease caused by germs, that can spread to a person from another person, an animal, or an object (p. 160)

competition (kom′pi tish′ən) contest between people or teams (p. 144)

compromise (kom′prə mīz′) to settle an argument or reach an agreement by give and take (p. 72)

conflict (kon′flikt) a struggle or disagreement between people or ideas (pp. 71, 220)

consideration (kən sid′ə rā′shən) thinking about other people and their feelings (p. 67)

contaminate (kən tam′ə nāt′) to spread something dirty into something clean (p. 259)

cool-down (kül′doun) gentle body movements like stretching done after physical activity to relax the body (p. 141)

cooperation (kō op′ə rā′shən) working together for the same purpose or goal (pp. 68, 86)

coordination (kō ôr′də nā′shən) using more than one part of the body at the same time (p. 135)

crack (krak) a very harmful form of cocaine that can be smoked (p. 204)

D

dandruff (dan′drəf) white specks of dead skin that fall from the scalp (p. 23)

dependence (di pen′dəns) a strong need for something (p. 192)

dermis (dûr′mis) the layer of skin just below the epidermis (p. 21)

diet (dī′it) everything you eat and drink every day (p. 115)

digestion (di jes′chən) the process that breaks down food into a form that the body can use (p. 48)

digestive system (di jes′tiv sis′təm) the body parts and organs that work together to help your body use food (p. 48)

disease (di zēz′) an illness; condition that keeps the body from feeling or working well (p. 155)

dosage (dō′sij) amount of medicine a patient should take (p. 187)

drug (drug) a substance other than food, that causes changes in the body (p. 185)

drug misuse (drug mis ūs′) using any medicine improperly (p. 188)

E

eardrum (îr′drum′) a thin layer of skin inside the ear that passes sound waves to the hearing nerves (p. 18)

emergency (i mûr′jən sē) a serious situation in which help is needed right away (p. 235)

emotion (i mō′shən) strong feeling that affects the things you do (p. 63)

emotional and intellectual health (i mō′shə nəl ənd in′tə lek′chü əl helth) health of the mind, having to do with feelings and thinking (p. 3)

enamel (i nam′əl) the hard, shiny outer covering of a tooth (p. 11)

endurance (en dủr′əns) being able to continue an activity for a while without tiring (p. 131)

environment (en vī′rən mənt) everything around you, including the air, water, and land (pp. 34, 252)

epidermis (ep′i dủr′mis) the outer layer of skin (p. 21)

exercise (ek′sər sīz′) an activity that works on a skill or a part of fitness (p. 140)

F

fallacy (fal′ə sē) a false or mistaken belief

fats (fats) nutrients that give the body long-lasting energy (p. 104)

fever (fē′vər) when body temperature is higher than normal (p. 155)

pronunciation key

a **at**; ā **ape**; ä **far**; âr **care**; e **end**; ē **me**; i **it**; ī **ice**; îr **pierce**; o **hot**; ō **old**; ô **fork**; oi **oil**; ou **out**; u **up**; ū **use**; ü **rule**; ủ **pull**; ûr **turn**; hw **white**; ng **song**; th **thin**; th **this**; zh **measure**; ə **about**, **taken**, **pencil**, **lemon**, **circus**

fiber (fī′bər) material that helps move waste through the digestive system (p. 106)

first aid (fûrst′ ād′) immediate care given to a person who is injured or ill (p. 238)

flexibility (flek sə bil′ə tē) the ability to bend and move your body easily (p. 131)

fluoride (flůr′īd) makes tooth enamel strong and protects against cavities (p. 12)

food group (füd grüp) a group of foods that contain similar nutrients (p. 109)

Food Guide Pyramid (füd gīd pir′ə mid′) a diagram of the food groups that helps you plan your food choices (p. 110)

friend (frend) someone who is close to you; someone whom you care about and who cares about you (p. 93)

frostbite (frôst′bīt′) injury caused when uncovered skin freezes from very cold weather (p. 232)

fume (fūm) a gas that is harmful; inhaling this gas can make a person dizzy or sick (p. 213)

G

germ (jûrm) a tiny particle or living thing too small to see that can cause disease (pp. 7, 156)

glands (glandz) parts of the body that makes substances needed by the body, such as oil and sweat (p. 21)

good sport (gůd spôrt) a person who plays in a way that lets everyone have a good time (p. 147)

grooming (grü′ming) keeping neat and clean (p. 7)

guidance (gī′dəns) advice (or other help) (p. 89)

H

hazard (haz′ərd) something that creates a dangerous situation or risk of harm (p. 213)

hazardous wastes (haz′ər dəs wāsts) wastes that can cause illness and must be thrown away carefully (p. 260)

head lice (hed līs) small insects that can live on people's scalps (p. 23)

health (helth) being free from illness (p. 3)

health care (helth kâr) services that keep people healthy; includes preventing and treating problems (p. 248)

health care product (helth kâr prod′əkt) something you can buy to help you stay healthy (p. 8)

health department (helth di pärt′mənt) part of the government that works to prevent the spread of disease (p. 250)

heredity (hə red′i tē) passing of traits from parents to children (p. 34)

HIV (Human Immunodeficiency Virus) (āch ī vē) the virus that attacks the immune system and leads to AIDS (p. 171)

hospital (hos′pi təl) provides special care and equipment that people cannot get at a doctor's office or clinic, including delivering babies, performing surgery, and giving special medical tests (p. 249)

I

immune system (i mūn′ sis′təm) all the body parts and activities that fight disease (p. 164)

immunity (i mū′ni tē) the body's ability to protect itself or fight diseases caused by germs (p. 167)

immunizations (im′ yə nə zā′shənz) vaccines that protect people from diseases (p. 249)

infancy (in′fən sē) the first year after birth (p. 31)

ingredient (in grē′dē ənt) any one of the parts that are mixed together to make food (p. 119)

injury (in′jə rē) any kind of physical damage or harm to a person (p. 213)

J

joint (joint) a place where two bones meet (p. 40)

junk food (jungk füd) food that has few useful nutrients (p. 111)

L

landfill (land′fil) place where garbage is packed down and covered with dirt (p. 257)

large intestine (lärj in tes′tin) the organ that removes water from unused food (p. 50)

litter (lit′ər) rubbish on the ground (p. 253)

M

marijuana (mar′ə wä′nə) an illegal drug made from the hemp plant; it affects thoughts and actions and speeds up the heart (p. 203)

medicine (med′ə sin) any drug used to prevent, treat, or cure an illness or injury (p. 185)

minerals (min′ər əlz) nutrient used by the body for muscles and nerves to work properly (p. 104)

minor injury (mī′nər in′jə rē) physical harm to a person that can be treated easily (p. 235)

mold (mōld) a type of living thing that grows on food and other moist materials (p. 122)

muscular system (mus′kyə lər sis′təm) a body system made up of all the muscles in your body (p. 37)

N

natural resource (nach′ər əl rē′sôrs′) anything that is part of the Earth and that people need or find useful, includes plants and animals (p. 258)

nerve cell (nûrv sel) cell that carries messages to and from all parts of the body (p. 53)

nervous system (nûr′vəs sis′təm) a body organ system made up of the brain, the spinal cord, and the nerves (p. 53)

nicotine (nik′ə tēn′) a harmful drug found in all tobacco products (p. 191)

nutrient (nü′trē ənt) a substance in food that the body needs for energy and growth (p. 104)

O

oil glands (oil glandz) in the dermis; these glands make oil to keep your skin soft and waterproof (p. 21)

organ (ôr′gən) a kind of tissue that does special jobs; the heart, brain, lungs, eyes, and ears are examples of an organ (p. 33)

over-the-counter medicine (ō′vər t͟hə koun′tər med′ə sin) medicine that can be bought without a prescription (p. 186)

oxygen (ok′sə jən) a gas in the air that cells need to stay alive (p. 43)

P

passive smoke (pas′iv smōk) breathing in smoke from other people's cigarettes (p. 193)

pedestrian (pə des′trē ən) a person who travels by walking (p. 215)

peer pressure (pîr presh′ər) a kind of stress in which people your age try to make you do what they want (p. 95)

peers (pîrz) people your own age (p. 95)

personal flotation device (PFD) (pûr′sə nəl flō tā′shən di vīs′) life preserver; device that helps a person float in water (p. 229)

personality (pûr′sə nal′i tē) everything that makes you a special person, such as things you do, think, and feel (p. 63)

pharmacist (fär′mə sist) a person trained to prepare medicines (p. 186)

physical fitness (fiz′i kəl fit′nəs) the condition in which your body works at its best (p. 131)

pronunciation key

a **at**; ā **ape**; ä **far**; âr **care**; e **end**; ē **me**; i **it**; ī **ice**; îr **pierce**; o **hot**; ō **old**; ô **fork**; oi **oil**; ou **out**; u **up**; ū **use**; ü **rule**; u̇ **pull**; ûr **turn**; hw **white**; ng **song**; th **thin**; t͟h **this**; zh **measure**; ə **about**, **taken**, **pencil**, **lemon**, **circus**

physical health (fiz′i kəl helth) health of the body; being able to work and play well (p. 3)

plaque (plak) a sticky film of food particles and germs that can weaken tooth enamel (p. 11)

poison (poi′zən) a drug or substance that harms or kills (p. 213)

pollution (pə lü′shən) something that makes the air, water, or land dirty or impure (p. 252)

posture (pos′chər) the way you hold your body (p. 40)

power (pou′ər) a combination of strength and speed (p. 136)

prescription (pri skrip′shən) a doctor's order to prepare medicine (p. 186)

proteins (prō′tēnz) nutrients that the body uses for growth and the repair of cells (p. 104)

R

reaction time (rē ak′shən tīm) time it takes to notice and respond to something (p. 136)

recycle (rē sī′kəl) to do something to garbage so that it can be used (p. 255)

resolve (ri zolv′) to settle a problem or conflict (p. 72)

respect (ri spekt′) a feeling that someone is valuable (p. 86)

respiratory system (res′pər ə tôr′ē sis′təm) a body organ system that helps you breathe and use the air you take in (p. 45)

responsibility (ri spon′sə bil′i tē) something you are expected to do; a job (p. 86)

root (rüt) the part of the tooth that is attached to the jawbone (p. 11)

S

safety equipment (sāf′tē i kwip′mənt) protective gear used to reduce the risk of injury (p. 146)

saliva (sə lī′və) liquid in your mouth that helps soften and break down food (p. 49)

sanitarians (san′i ter′ē ənz) special health department workers that check that the food in a community is clean and safe to eat (p. 250)

scalp (skalp) the skin on the top of your head (p. 23)

school personnel (skül pûr′sə nel′) adults who work at your school; want to help you learn (p. 89)

self-concept (self′kon′sept) the picture that comes to mind when you think about yourself (p. 63)

self-esteem (self′e stēm′) how good you feel about who you are (p. 64)

sense organs (sens ôr′gənz) the eyes, ears, nose, skin, and tongue which receive messages from the outside world and send messages to the brain (p. 53)

sensory nerve cell (sen′sə rē nûrv sel) a nerve cell that carries messages from your sense organs to your spinal cord or brain (p. 53)

serious injury (sîr′ē əs in′jə rē) physical harm to a person that requires special emergency help (p. 235)

sewage (sü′ij) liquid waste (p. 256)

side effects (sīd′ i fekts′) unwanted changes caused by medicines (p. 188)

skeletal system (skel′i təl sis′təm) a body system that supports your body (p. 37)

skeleton (skel′i tən) the framework of bones that supports the body (p. 37)

small intestine (smôl in tes′tin) tubelike organ where most digestion happens and is completed (p. 50)

smoke detector (smōk di tek′tər) a fire safety device that sounds an alarm when there is smoke (p. 223)

smokeless tobacco (smōk′lis tə bak′ō) chewing tobacco or snuff which users can hold inside their mouth (p. 193)

social health (sō′shəl helth) health having to do with relationships with other people (p. 3)

speed (spēd) being able to move quickly (p. 136)

spinal cord (spī′nəl kôrd) a long bundle of nerves that travels inside your spine to your brain (p. 53)

spoiled (spoild) no longer safe to eat or drink (p. 122)

stomach (stum′ək) an organ whose walls are made of strong muscles that squeeze and mash food (p. 49)

strength (strengkth) something you do well; the ability to lift, push, and pull objects (pp. 63, 131)

stress (stres) the way the body and mind responds to changes around you (p. 75)

stressor (stre′sər) things, events, people, or places that cause stress (p. 75)

sweat glands (swet glandz) in the dermis; when your body gets hot these glands make sweat; as air dries the sweat on your skin, you feel cooler (p. 21)

symptom (simp′təm) a sign of a disease (p. 155)

T

tar (tär) sticky brown liquid made when tobacco burns (p. 191)

teamwork (tēm′wûrk′) working with other people in a group or on a team to reach a common goal (p. 146)

tissue (tish′ü) a group of cells, usually of the same type, that work together to do a certain job (p. 33)

tobacco (tə bak′ō) a plant; its leaves are dried and made into cigarettes, cigars, or smokeless tobacco (p. 191)

V

vaccine (vak sēn′) a medicine that causes the body to form antibodies against a certain disease (p. 168)

vein (vān) a blood vessel that carries blood from the body back to the heart (p. 43)

violence (vī′ə ləns) use of strong physical force to harm someone (p. 219)

virus (vī′rəs) a tiny particle smaller than a bacterium that can multiply only inside a living cell (p. 158)

vision (vizh′ən) seeing; your sense of sight (p. 17)

vitamins (vī′tə minz) nutrients used by the body for growth and energy; some vitamins prevent diseases (p. 104)

W

warm-up (wôrm′up) gentle body movements, such as stretching, that prepare the body for physical activity (p. 141)

water treatment plants (wô′tər trēt′mənt plants) place where water supply for a community must be cleaned before people can use it (p. 256)

weakness (wēk′nis) something you do not do well (p. 17)

weapon (wep′ən) something that can be used to attack someone, such as a knife or a gun (p. 220)

white blood cells (hwīt blud selz) cells in the blood that fight bacteria, viruses, and other germs (p. 166)

pronunciation key

a **at**; ā **ape**; ä **far**; âr **care**; e **end**; ē **me**; i **it**; ī **ice**; îr **pierce**; o **hot**; ō **old**; ô **fork**; oi **oil**; ou **out**; u **up**; ū **use**; ü **rule**; ů **pull**; ûr **turn**; hw **white**; ng **song**; th **thin**; t͟h **this**; zh **measure**; ə **about**, **taken**, **pencil**, **lemon**, **circus**

INDEX

This Index lists many topics that appear in the book, along with the pages on which they are found.

A

adolescence, 30, 31, 294
adrenaline, 75
ads, 120, 192
adulthood, 31, 294
aerobic exercise, 138, 141, 294
agility, 134–136, 294
AIDS (Acquired Immune Deficiency Syndrome), 170–173, 294
- and diet, 172
- related illnesses, 172
- treatment, 172

air pollution, 259
alcohol, 196–200, 294
- and driving, 199–200
- and health problems, 197
- and pregnancy, 199
- and the law, 200
- dependence, 197
- effects on behavior, 199
- effects on the body, 197–198
- refusing, 200

anger, 218–219
antibacterial, 22
antibody, 164, 167, 294
apologize, 70, 72, 294
appreciation, 66, 67, 294
artery, 42, 43, 294
attitude, 88, 90, 294

B

bacteria, 22, 154, 157, 294
- types of, 156–157

balance, 134–136, 294
balanced diet, 114, 115, 177, 294
bandages, 239
bicycle safety, 230, 289
blizzard safety, 232
blood, 43
blood vessel(s), 42, 43, 132, 294
body fat, 132
body systems, 33, 59, 294
bones, 36–42
- number of, 37

booster (vaccine), 168
brain, 42, 52, 294

C

caffeine, 105, 202, 203, 294
caffeine-free, 203
calcium, 34, 104
carbohydrates, 102, 104, 294
carbon dioxide, 45
carbon monoxide, 259
careers, in health-related fields, 57, 97, 149
car safety, 216, 289
cavity, 10, 11, 294
cell(s), 30, 32, 294
- blood cell, 32
- bone cell, 32
- muscle cell, 32
- skin cell, 32

Chapter Opener, 1, 29, 61, 83, 101, 129, 153, 183, 211, 247
Chapter Review, 26–27, 58–59, 80–81, 98–99, 126–127, 150–151, 180–181, 208–209, 244–245, 264–265
Chapter Test, 28, 60, 82, 100, 128, 152, 182, 210, 246, 266
checkup, 27, 177
chemical safety, 213, 288
childhood, 31, 294
cigarettes. See *tobacco*.
circulatory system, 43, 44, 294
- caring for, 44

classrooms, 88–90
- around the world, 89
- communication in, 90
- cooperation in, 90
- personnel, 89
- respect for, 90
- responsibilities and rules of, 90

cleanliness
- and self esteem, 7
- in preparing and handling food, 123

clinic, 248, 249, 294
clothing, and weather, 232
cocaine, 202, 204, 294
cold weather safety, 232
communicable disease(s), 160–162, 173, 294
- preventing spread of, 162
- protecting against, 165–168
- spread of, 161

communication, 90
community clean-up, 252–257
community health care, 248–250
- facilities, 249
- health departments, 250
- workers, 249

competition, 67, 144, 147, 294
compromise, 70, 72, 294
conflict, 70–72, 218, 220, 295
- resolving, 220

consumer, 14
consideration, 66, 67, 81, 295
contaminate, 231, 258, 259, 295
cool-down (exercises), 138, 141–142, 284–285, 295
cooperation, 66, 68, 84, 86, 90, 135, 295

coordination, 134–136, 295
crack, 202, 204, 295
Cultural Perspectives, 7, 34, 63, 89, 112, 115, 136, 161, 185, 219, 261
culture, 7

D

dandruff, 23, 295
decaffeinated, 203
decay (tooth), 11
deficient, 170
dentist, 14
dependence, 190, 192, 197, 295
dermis, 20, 21, 295
diet, 114, 115, 295
digestion, 48–50, 295
  helping, 50
digestive system, 48, 49, 50, 106, 295
  caring for, 50
disease(s), 154–158, 295
  and vaccines, 168
  causes of, 156–158
  communicable, 160–161, 294
  preventing spread of, 162
  protecting against, 165–168
  spread of, 161
  symptoms of, 155
  who to tell if you are sick, 155
dispel, 63
dosage, 187, 295
drug, 184, 185, 202–205, 295
  dependence, 204
  illegal, 203–205
  medicines, 184–188, 297
  misuse, 188, 295
  refusal, 205
drug store, 250

E

ear
  care for, 16, 18–19
  eardrops, 18
  eardrum, 16, 18, 295
  problems, 18
Earth, protecting, 261
eating
  and emotions, 115
  habits, 111–112, 115
  snacks, 116
electrical safety, 214, 288
emergency, 234–236, 295
  getting help, 236
emergency medical technicians (EMT), 236
emotion(s), 62, 63, 70–71, 115, 295
emotional and intellectual health, 2, 3, 295
enamel, 10, 11, 295
endurance, 130, 131, 139, 140, 295
energy, 48, 75, 103
environment, 30, 34–35, 252–257, 295
epidermis, 20, 21, 295
exercise(s), 140, 295
  aerobic, 141, 294
  cool-down, 141, 284–285, 295
  warm-up, 141, 284–285, 299
exhaust, 259
expiration date, 187
eye(s)
  care for, 16–17
  common problems of, 17

F

fairness, 144–147
falls, 214
family(ies), 84–86
  cooperation of, 86
  health of, 86
  respect for, 84, 86
  responsibilities and rules in, 86
  types of, 85
fat, 102, 104, 132, 120, 295
feelings. See *emotion.*
fever, 155, 295
fiber, 102, 106, 296
field trips, 292
firearm safety, 220, 288
fire extinguisher, 223
fire safety, 223–224, 288
  equipment, 223
  fire escape plan, 224
  staying safe in a fire, 224, 288
  stop, drop, and roll, 224
first aid, 238–241, 290, 296
  and emergencies, 235–236
  for choking, 291
  for insect bites and stings, 241, 290
  for minor burns and sunburn, 240, 290
  for minor cuts and scrapes, 240
  for nosebleeds, 240, 290
  for reactions to poisonous plants, 241, 290
  kits, contents of, 239
fitness. See *physical fitness.*
flexibility, 130, 131, 139, 140, 296
fluoride, 12, 296
follicle, 21
food, 102–123, 280–282
  ads, 120
  and balanced diet, 115
  and fiber, 106
  and health, 103, 112, 283
  and stress, 115
  choices, 112, 116
  groups, 108, 109–110, 296
  junk food, 105, 111, 296
  labels, 119, 123
  nutrients in, 104
  safety, 122–123
  servings, 112, 281
  spoilage, 122–123
Food Guide Pyramid, 108, 110, 112, 115, 280, 296
friend, 92–94, 296
  being a friend, 93
  finding a friend, 93, 94
  keeping a friend, 94

friendship, 92–94
frostbite, 228, 232, 296
fume, 213, 296

G

games, 67, 135
garbage, 253, 257
germ(s), 7, 154, 156, 164–168, 181
  killing, 165–168
  preventing spread of, 162, 181
  spread of, 161
glands, 20, 21, 296
  oil, 21
  sweat, 21
good sport, 147, 296
grooming, 6, 7, 296
growth, 30–35
  and environment, 34–35
  and heredity, 34
  and physical change, 31
  helpers, 39
growth and development, 30–55
guidance, 88, 89, 296
gums, 11

H

hair care, 23
hazard(s), 212, 213, 296
  electrical, 214
  falls, 214
  heat, 214
  household products, 213
hazardous wastes, 258, 260, 296
head lice, 20, 23, 296
health, 2–4, 296
  and environment, 252–261
  departments, 250
  emotional and intellectual, 2, 3, 295
  physical, 2, 3, 132, 300
  resources, 292–293
  social, 2, 3, 298
  tips for, 177, 283
Health Activity, 5, 9, 15, 19, 24, 32, 41, 47, 51, 56, 69, 73, 78, 87, 91, 96, 106, 113, 117, 121, 124, 132, 137, 143, 148, 159, 163, 169, 175, 178, 189, 195, 201, 206, 217, 221, 226, 233, 237, 242, 251, 256, 262
health care, 248–249, 296
health care product(s), 6, 8, 14, 23, 239
health care workers
  dentists, 14, 249
  emergency medical technicians (EMT), 236, 249
  family doctors, 249
  nurses, 249
  pharmacists, 186, 249
  sanitarians, 250
  specialists, 249
health department, 248, 250, 253, 296
Health Fact, 11, 44, 54, 75, 86, 106, 162, 167, 172, 177, 188, 191, 199, 216, 239, 259
Health Fallacy, 4, 37, 71, 120, 132, 142, 158, 229
Health Heroes, 25, 207, 263
HealthWise Consumer, 14, 18, 22, 39, 50, 67, 93, 116, 123, 135, 147, 192, 203, 223, 236, 250, 257, 260
heart, 42–44, 132, 191, 192, 198, 203
heartbeat, 44
heredity, 30, 34, 296
HIV (Human Immunodeficiency Virus), 170–174, 296
  and AIDS, 170–172
  spread of, 173–174
  symptoms of, 171
home alone safety, 225–226
hospital, 249, 296
hot weather safety, 232
hurricane safety, 232

I

illegal drugs, 203–205
  cocaine, 202, 204, 294
  crack, 202, 204, 295
  marijuana, 202, 203, 297
immune deficiency, 170
immune system, 164, 166, 176–177, 296
  strengthening, 177
immunity, 164, 167, 296
immunizations, 168, 248, 249, 296
infancy, 31, 296
Infographic
  alcohol, effects of, 198
  classroom, 90
  cleaning teeth and gums, 12–13
  fighting germs, 165
  Food Guide Pyramid, 110
  hazards, 214
  nervous system, 55
  physical fitness routine, 141
  stress, 76–77
  Three R's—reduce, reuse, and recycle, 254–255
ingredient, 118, 119, 296
injury, 212, 213, 234, 238, 296
  minor, 234–235, 238
  serious, 234–235
insect bites and stings, 241

J

joint(s), 36, 40, 296
junk food, 105, 108, 111, 296

L

labels, 119, 127, 187, 209
landfill, 257, 297
land pollution, 260
large intestine, 48, 50, 297
Latex gloves, 239
life cycle, 31
Life Skills
  Make Decisions, 9, 19, 22, 27, 49, 54, 56, 59, 64, 69,

85, 112, 113, 116, 120, 124, 127, 132, 133, 136, 139, 143, 151, 159, 163, 178, 181, 189, 199, 213, 231, 236, 242, 256, 257, 260, 265, 268–269, 292
Manage Stress, 18, 35, 51, 75, 78, 96, 121, 127, 131, 133, 148, 162, 168, 175, 221, 239, 262, 274–275
Obtain Help, 5, 19, 24, 35, 47, 65, 71, 87, 89, 91, 117, 137, 143, 155, 173, 178, 186, 189, 195, 201, 206, 217, 219, 227, 233, 237, 242, 245, 250, 251, 272–273, 292
Practice Refusal Skills, 4, 14, 47, 73, 78, 94, 96, 99, 105, 107, 121, 145, 169, 175, 181, 195, 201, 203, 209, 226, 227, 257, 276–277
Resolve Conflicts, 7, 15, 27, 37, 44, 67, 73, 81, 87, 123, 148, 151, 221, 245, 257, 278–279
Set Goals, 5, 9, 15, 24, 32, 35, 41, 56, 59, 65, 69, 81, 91, 99, 113, 117, 124, 137, 163, 177, 206, 209, 217, 224, 233, 237, 251, 262, 265, 270–271, 292

litter, 253, 297

liver, 198

lungs, 42, 45, 132, 191, 192

M

Make Decisions, 9, 19, 22, 27, 49, 54, 56, 59, 64, 69, 85, 112, 113, 116, 120, 124, 127, 132, 133, 136, 139, 143, 151, 159, 163, 178, 181, 189, 199, 213, 231, 236, 242, 256, 257, 260, 265, 268–269

Manage Stress, 18, 35, 51, 75, 78, 96, 121, 127, 131, 133, 148, 162, 168, 175, 221, 239, 262, 274–275

marijuana, 202, 203, 297

medical identification tags, 236

medicine, 158, 184–188, 297
labels, 187
misuse (drug), 188
over-the-counter, 186–187
prescription, 186–187
safety, 188
side effects, 188, 298

minerals, 104, 297

minor injury, 234, 235, 297

mold, 122, 297

mucus, 165

muscle, 36–43

muscular system, 37, 38, 297

N

natural resource, 258, 297

nerve cell, 52, 53, 297

nerves, 53

nervous system, 52–55, 297
caring for, 54

nicotine, 190, 191, 297

noise pollution, 261

nosebleeds, 240

nutrient(s), 104, 297

nutrition, 102–123, 280–283
and nutrients, 104
balanced diet, 115
food groups, 109–110
Food Guide Pyramid, 110, 280, 296
making food choices, 105, 111–112, 116, 120
serving, 112, 281

O

Obtain Help, 5, 19, 24, 35, 47, 65, 71, 87, 89, 91, 117, 137, 143, 155, 173, 178, 186, 189, 195, 201, 206, 217, 219, 227, 233, 237, 242, 245, 250, 251, 272–273, 292

oil glands, 21, 297

ointment, 239

oral health, 10–14
caring for teeth and gums, 12–13
parts of teeth and gums, 11
visiting the dentist, 14

organ(s), 22, 33, 42, 297

organism, 157

outdoor safety, 228–232

over-the-counter medicine, 186–187, 297
expiration dates of, 187
labels of, 187

oxygen, 42, 43, 297

P

passenger safety, 216

passive smoke, 190, 193, 297

pasteurization, 162

patient, 186

pedestrian safety, 212, 215, 289, 297

peer pressure, 92, 95, 297

peers, 95, 297

Performance Assessment, 28, 60, 82, 100, 128, 152, 182, 210, 246, 266

personal flotation device (PFD), 228, 229, 297

personal health, 1–24
caring for, 6–8
eye and ear care, 16–18
skin and hair, 20–23
teeth and gums, 10–14

personality, 62, 63, 297

pharmacist, 186, 297

physical activities, 130, 145, 284–285
and fitness, 130–142
and safety, 145–146

physical fitness, 129–133, 134–136, 138–142, 297
activities that build, 139
and emotional and intellectual health, 133
and physical health, 132
and social health, 133

guidelines for, 142
parts of, 131
President's Challenge, 140, 286–287
program/routine, 140–141
skills, 134–136
physical health, 2, 3, 298
and fitness, 133
playground safety, 231, 289
plaque, 10, 11, 298
poison, 157, 212, 213, 298
poisonous plants, 241
pollution, 252, 258–260, 298
air, 259
and health, 259–261
land, 260
noise, 261
water, 260
Portfolio Assessment, 5, 9, 15, 19, 24, 27, 35, 41, 47, 51, 56, 59, 65, 69, 73, 78, 81, 87, 91, 96, 99, 107, 113, 117, 121, 124, 127, 133, 137, 143, 148, 151, 159, 163, 169, 175, 178, 181, 189, 195, 201, 206, 209, 217, 221, 227, 233, 237, 242, 245, 251, 257, 262, 265
posture, 40, 298
power, 134, 136, 298
Practice Refusal Skills, 4, 14, 47, 73, 78, 94, 96, 99, 105, 107, 121, 145, 169, 175, 181, 195, 201, 203, 209, 226, 227, 257, 276–277
prescription, 184, 186, 298
President's Challenge, 140, 286–287
proteins, 102, 104, 298

Q

Quick Start, 2, 6, 10, 16, 20, 30, 36, 42, 48, 52, 62, 66, 70, 74, 84, 88, 92, 102, 108, 114, 118, 122, 130, 134, 138, 144, 154, 160, 164, 170, 176, 184, 190, 196, 202, 212, 218, 222, 228, 234, 238, 248, 252, 258

R

rain forest, 185
reaction time, 134, 136, 298
recycle, 252, 255, 265, 298
reduce, 254
relationships, 84–86, 88–90, 92–95
relatives. See *family*.
resolve, 70, 72, 298
Resolve Conflicts, 7, 15, 27, 37, 44, 67, 73, 81, 87, 123, 148, 151, 221, 245, 257, 278–279
resources, health
books, 293
respect, 84, 86, 90, 298
respiratory system, 45, 46, 298
caring for, 46
responsibility, 84, 86, 90, 298
in classrooms, 90
in families, 86
reuse, 255
root, 10, 11, 298

S

safety, 122–123, 144–147, 188, 213–216, 222–230, 232, 245, 288–289
belts, 216
bicycle, 147, 230, 289
boating, 229
chemical, 288
electrical, 288
equipment, 142, 144, 146, 223, 298
fire, 223–224, 288
fishing, 229
food, 122–123
home-alone, 225–226
indoor, 213–214, 222–227, 288
medicine, 188
outdoor, 215, 228–232, 289
passenger, 216, 289
pedestrian, 215, 289, 297
playground, 231, 289
skating/skateboarding, 146, 231
soccer, 146
softball, 146
swimming, 146, 228, 229
violence prevention, 218–221
weather, 232
safety equipment
sports, types of, 146
saliva, 49, 165, 298
sanitarians, 250, 298
scalp, 20, 23, 298
school personnel, 88, 89, 298
Science Connection, 41, 51, 106, 107, 159, 169
self–concept, 62, 63, 298
self–esteem, 62, 64, 298
senses, 16, 52
hearing, 16, 52
seeing, 16, 52
smell, 52
taste, 52
touch, 52
sense organs, 16–18, 53, 298
sensory nerve cell, 53, 298
serious injury, 234, 235, 298
Set Goals, 5, 9, 15, 24, 32, 35, 41, 56, 59, 65, 69, 81, 91, 99, 113, 117, 124, 137, 163, 177, 206, 209, 217, 224, 233, 237, 251, 262, 265, 270–271, 292
sewage, 256, 298
treatment plants, 256
Show What You Can Do / Show What You Know, 5, 9, 15, 19, 24, 35, 41, 47, 51, 56, 65, 69, 73, 78, 87, 91, 96, 107, 113, 117, 121, 124, 133, 137, 143, 148, 159, 163, 169, 175, 178, 189, 195, 201, 206, 217, 221, 227, 233, 237, 242, 251, 257, 262
side effects, 188, 298

skateboard safety, 231
skating safety, 231
skeletal system, 37, 38, 298
skeleton, 36, 37, 298
skin, 20–22
  care for, 22
  parts of, 21
sleep, 4, 177
small intestine, 48, 50, 298
smoke detector, 222, 223, 298
smokeless tobacco, 193, 298
smoking. See *tobacco*.
snacks, 116
social health, 2, 3, 298
soot, 253
speed, 134, 136, 299
spinal cord, 52, 53, 299
spoiled, 122, 301
stomach, 48, 49, 198, 299
stop, drop, and roll, 224
strangers, 225–226
strength, 63, 130, 131, 139, 301
stress, 74–77, 176, 177, 299
  signs of, 76
  managing, 77
stressor, 74, 75, 299
stretching, 284
sun protection factor (SPF), 22
sunscreen, 22
sweat glands, 21, 299
swimming safety, 229
symptom, 154, 155, 171, 299
syndrome, 170

T

tar, 191, 299
teamwork, 144, 147, 299
technology, 79, 125, 179, 243
teeth, 10–15
  and gums, 13
  caring for, 12–13
  parts of, 11
temper, 71
thunderstorm safety, 232
tissue(s), 33, 299
tobacco, 190–194, 299
  ads, 192
  dangers to nonsmokers, 193
  dependence, 192
  effects on the body, 191
  health problems related to, 192
  laws regulating smoking, 194
  nicotine, 190, 191, 297
  passive smoke, 190, 193, 297
  quitting use of, 192
  refusing, 194
  smoke, 191
  smokeless, 193, 300
  Surgeon General and, 194
  tar, 191, 299
tornado safety, 232
touches, 227
trait, 34
tweezers, 239

V

vaccine(s), 164, 168, 299
values, 95
vein, 42, 43, 299
violence, 218–220, 299
  prevention, 218–220
  weapons and, 220
virus, 154, 158, 299
vision, 16, 17, 299
vitamins, 104, 299

W

warm-up (exercises), 138, 141–142, 284–285, 299
water, 50, 107, 142, 260
  and digestion, 50, 107
  and physical fitness, 142
water pollution, 260
water safety, 229
water treatment plants, 256, 299
weakness, 17, 63, 299
weapon, 218, 220, 299
weather safety, 232
What Would You Do? 4, 7, 14, 18, 22, 35, 37, 44, 49, 54, 64, 67, 71, 75, 85, 89, 94, 105, 112, 116, 120, 123, 131, 136, 139, 145, 155, 162, 168, 173, 177, 186, 194, 199, 203, 213, 219, 224, 231, 236, 239, 250, 260
white blood cells, 166, 299
windpipe, 45

X

X–ray, 14, 37

Y

You Can Make a Difference, 25, 57, 79, 97, 128, 149, 179, 207, 243, 263
Your Health at Home, 27, 59, 81, 99, 127, 151, 181, 209, 245, 265

CREDITS

ILLUSTRATIONS: Johnee Bee/Liz Sanders Agency: pp. v, 67, 71, 75, 110, 120, 163, 165, 192, 193, 199, 231, 232, 280; Olivia Cole-Hauptfleisch: pp. 12, 13; Gwen Connelly: p. 214; Barbara Cousins/Bookmakers, Ltd.: pp. 11, 21, 38, 43, 45, 49, 53, 198; Larry Daste/Evelyne Johnson Associates: pp. 76, 77; Rob Dunlavey: pp. 18, 79, 185, 194, 261; Janice Edelman-Lee: pp. iii, 5, 9, 15, 24, 27, 32, 47, 65, 69, 81, 91, 99, 106, 113, 124, 127, 132, 137, 143, 151, 175, 178, 189, 206, 209, 245, 256, 262; Patrick Girouard/Publishers Graphics, Inc.: pp. 94, 174; Patti Goodnow: pp. 31, 131, 224, 230; Ann Iosa/Carol Bancroft & Friends: pp. 90, 140; N. Jo, Inc.: p. 139; John Jones/Cornell & McCarthy: pp. iv, 85, 254, 255; David Kelley: pp. 33 t., 39, 40, 55, 158, 241; Aaron Koster: pp. 104, 115; Rita Lascaro: p. 179; Karen Loccisano: pp. 288, 289 c. and b., 291; Miles Parnell: p. 95; L.S. Pierce Illustration: pp. 289 t., 290; Jeff Shelly: pp. 8, 50, 213, 239, 260; Ronnie Shipman: p. 141; Tom Sperling: pp. 284, 285, 286, 287; Karen Viola: pp. 269, 271, 273, 275, 277, 279; Nadeem Zaidi/ Mecca Studios: pp. vi, 33 b., 64, 119, 146, 172, 187, 235, 249

PHOTOGRAPHY CREDITS: cover: All photos by the McGraw-Hill School Division; iii: © Chip Henderson/Tony Stone Images; iv: David S. Waitz for McGraw-Hill School Division; v: David S. Waitz for McGraw-Hill School Division; vi: David S. Waitz for McGraw-Hill School Division; xi: David S. Waitz for McGraw-Hill School Division; **Chapter 1** iii: © Chip Henderson/Tony Stone Images; iv: David S. Waitz for McGraw-Hill School Division; v: David S. Waitz for McGraw-Hill School Division; vi: David S. Waitz for McGraw-Hill School Division; xi: David S. Waitz for McGraw-Hill School Division; **Chapter 2** 29: © Tom & Dee Ann McCarthy/The Stock Market; 30: © Bachmann/Photo Researchers, Inc.; 34: t.l. © Walter Hodges/Tony Stone Images; t.r. © Mark Lewis/Tony Stone Images; 35: © Art Gingert/Comstock, Inc.; 36: © Tony Freeman/PhotoEdit; 37: © Scott Camazine/Photo Researchers, Inc.; 41: David S. Waitz for McGraw-Hill School Division; 42: © Roy Morsch/The Stock Market; 44: © Uniphoto; 46: © Blair Seitz/Photo Researchers, Inc.; 48: © Lawrence Migdale/Tony Stone Images; 51: © PhotoDisc; 52: © Ted Horowitz/The Stock Market; 54: © Franklin Viola/Comstock, Inc.; 57: t.l. David S. Waitz for McGraw-Hill School Division; c.l. Courtesy of Jackie West; **Chapter 3** 29: © Tom & Dee Ann McCarthy/The Stock Market; 30: © Bachmann/Photo Researchers, Inc.; 34: t.l. © Walter Hodges/Tony Stone Images; t.r. © Mark Lewis/ Tony Stone Images; 35: © Art Gingert/Comstock, Inc.; 36: © Tony Freeman/PhotoEdit; 37: © Scott Camazine/Photo Researchers, Inc.; 41: David S. Waitz for McGraw-Hill School Division; 42: © Roy Morsch/The Stock Market; 44: © Uniphoto; 46: © Blair Seitz/Photo Researchers, Inc.; 48: © Lawrence Migdale/Tony Stone Images; 51: © PhotoDisc; 52: © Ted Horowitz/The Stock Market; 54: © Franklin Viola/Comstock, Inc.; 57: t.l. David S. Waitz for McGraw-Hill School Division; c.l. Courtesy of Jackie West; **Chapter 4** 29: © Tom & Dee Ann McCarthy/The Stock Market; 30: © Bachmann/Photo Researchers, Inc.; 34: t.l. © Walter Hodges/Tony Stone Images; t.r. © Mark Lewis/Tony Stone Images; 35: © Art Gingert/Comstock, Inc.; 36: © Tony Freeman/PhotoEdit; 37: © Scott Camazine/Photo Researchers, Inc.; 41: David S. Waitz for McGraw-Hill School Division; 42: © Roy Morsch/ The Stock Market; 44: © Uniphoto; 46: © Blair Seitz/Photo Researchers, Inc.; 48: © Lawrence Migdale/Tony Stone Images; 51: © PhotoDisc; 52: © Ted Horowitz/The Stock Market; 54: © Franklin Viola/Comstock, Inc.; 57: t.l. David S. Waitz for McGraw-Hill School Division; c.l. Courtesy of Jackie West; **Chapter 5** 101: © Comstock, Inc.; 102: © Robert E. Daemmrich/Tony Stone Images; 103: © Lawrence Migdale/ Tony Stone Images; 106: © PhotoDisc; 107: © M.R. Vert/Photo Researchers, Inc.; 108: © Lawrence Migdale/Tony Stone Images; 109: © Comstock, Inc; 110: © Superstock, Inc.; 111: © James Lemass/The Picture Cube; 112: David S. Waitz for McGraw-Hill School Division; 114: © Roy Morsch/The Stock Market; 116: © Spencer Grant/The Picture Cube; 117: David S. Waitz for McGraw-Hill School Division; 118: © Philip & Karen Smith/ Tony Stone Worldwide, Ltd.; 121: © PhotoDisc; 122: David S. Waitz for McGraw-Hill School Division; 123: © Myrleen Cate; 125: t.l. David S. Waitz for McGraw-Hill School Division; c.l. Gamma Liaison; **Chapter 6** 129: © Don B. Stevenson/The Picture Cube; 130: © Tony Freeman/PhotoEdit; 133: © Chuck Savage/The Stock Market; 134: © Dana White/Photo Edit; 135: © Jon Feingersh/The Stock Market; 136: © David Young-Wolff/PhotoEdit; 138: © Richard Hutchings/PhotoEdit; 142: David S. Waitz for McGraw-Hill School Division; 144: © David Young-Wolff/PhotoEdit; 145: © David Young-Wolff/PhotoEdit; 146: © Al Bello/Tony Stone Images; 147: © David Stoecklein/ The Stock Market; 148: t.l. David S. Waitz for McGraw-Hill School Division; t.r. © PhotoDisc; 149: t.l. David S. Waitz for McGraw-Hill School Division; c.l. Courtesy of Robert S. Leathers & Associates; **Chapter 7** 153: © Jeff Greenberg/The Picture Cube; 154: © John Fortunato/Tony Stone Images; 155: © Charles Gupton/Uniphoto; 156: © David M. Phillips/Visuals Unlimited; 156: © M. Abbey/Visuals Unlimited; 157: © David M. Phillips/Visuals Unlimited; 160: © John Watney/Science Source/ Photo Researchers, Inc.; 161: © Uniphoto; 162: © Tony Stone Images; 166: © Comstock, Inc.; 167: © Science/Visuals Unlimited; 168: © Tom McCarthy/The Picture Cube; 169: David S. Waitz for McGraw-Hill School Division; 170: © Myrleen Cate; 171: © Evan Agostini/Gamma Liaison; 173: © Myrleen Cate/ Cate Photography; 176: © Julie Houck/Uniphoto: 179: David S. Waitz for McGraw-Hill School Division; **Chapter 8** 183: © M.K. Denny/PhotoEdit; 184: © David Young-Wolff/PhotoEdit; 186: © Chuck Savage/Uniphoto; 188: © Michael Newman/PhotoEdit; 190: © PhotoDisc; 191: © Jeffry W. Myers/Uniphoto; 195: © PhotoDisc; 196: © Pictor/Uniphoto; 200: © Bob Daemmrich/ Uniphoto; 201: David S. Waitz for McGraw-Hill School Division; 202: David S. Waitz for McGraw-Hill School Division; 203: © Myrleen Cate; 204: © Myrleen Cate; 205: m.r. © Comstock, Inc.; b.l. © Picture Cube; 207: t.l. David S. Waitz for McGraw-Hill School Division; c.l. Loren Santow/Impact Visuals; **Chapter 9** 211: © Bob Daemmrich/Uniphoto; 212: © Tom McCarthy/The Picture Cube; 215: © David Witbeck/The Picture Cube; 216: Richard Hutchings/Photo Edit.; 217: David S. Waitz for McGraw-Hill School Division; 218: David S. Waitz for McGraw-Hill School Division; 219: David S. Waitz for McGraw-Hill School Division; 220: David S. Waitz for McGraw-Hill School Division; 221: David S. Waitz for McGraw-Hill School Division; 222: David S. Waitz for McGraw-Hill School Division; 223: Myrleen Cate; 225: David S. Waitz for McGraw-Hill School Division; 226: David S. Waitz for McGraw-Hill School Division; 227: © Robert Finken/The Picture Cube; 228: © Myrleen Cate; 229: © Bob Kramer/The Picture Cube; 234: © Henley & Savage/Uniphoto; 235: © Jeff Greenberg/The Picture Cube; 236: David S. Waitz for McGraw-Hill School Division; 237: David S. Waitz for McGraw-Hill School Division; 238: © Stephen McBrady/PhotoEdit; 239: © Myrleen Cate; 240: David S. Waitz for McGraw-Hill School Division; 242: David S. Waitz for McGraw-Hill School Division; 243: David S. Waitz for McGraw-Hill School Division; **Chapter 10** 247: © David Young-Wolff/PhotoEdit; 248: © David Young-Wolff/PhotoEdit; 249: © Joseph Nettis/Tony Stone Images; 250: © Charles Gupton/ The Stock Market; 251: David S. Waitz for McGraw-Hill School Division; 252: © Tony Freeman/PhotoEdit; 253:© Robert Brenner/PhotoEdit; 258: © Nancy Sheehan/PhotoEdit; 259: © Phil Borden/PhotoEdit; 263: t.l. David S. Waitz for McGraw-Hill School Division; c.l. Paula Lerner/Woodfin Camp & Associates; 268: David S. Waitz for McGraw-Hill School Division; 270: David S. Waitz for McGraw-Hill School Division; 272: David S. Waitz for McGraw-Hill School Division; 274: David S. Waitz for McGraw-Hill School Division; 276: David S. Waitz for McGraw-Hill School Division; 278: David S. Waitz for McGraw-Hill School Division; 281: David S. Waitz for McGraw-Hill School Division